BLITHFIELD

A PARISH IN TIME

and

OTHER HISTORIES

To

my parents,

Eric and Lucy,

who loved
this place.

BLITHFIELD
A PARISH IN TIME
and
OTHER HISTORIES

Terence Cooper

TeeCee Publications

First published by

TeeCee Publications
The Cottage
Drointon
Stafford
ST18 0LX
01889 500611
teeceepublications@btinternet.com

2018

ISBN 978-1-5272-3210-5

Printed by
The Benhill Press Ltd
Brook Square
Rugeley
Staffs
WS15 2DU

PICTURE CREDITS

Page	
Front cover	Andrew Mason
Title page	Andrew Mason
xiii	Andrew Mason
1,2	Reproduced courtesy Domesday Alecto Historical Editions
44	Richard and Mary Bagot - Reproduced courtesy of Staffordshire County Council
53	Elizabeth I - unknown artist c.1592
	Robert Deveraux, 2nd Earl of Essex- studio of Gheeraets 17th c.
	Tomb -The William Salt Library SVII. 55b
97	Staffordshire Record Office D1386/2/2
99	The William Salt Library SVII. 47
	The William Salt Library SVII. 51
106	The Staffordshire Record Office D3259/Add/1/1
113	William Yates Map courtesy Staffordshire Record Society
152	The William Salt Library SVII. 72b
188	© The Imperial War Museum HU 129637
190	©The Imperial War Museum Q 1997
209	©The Imperial War Museum CH 018411
228	Andrew Mason
245	(Top) Reproduced courtesy Mr S Shipley
257	Reproduced courtesy Harold Martin
267	(Top) Andrew Mason
278	The William Salt Library CB/Blithfield/1
292	Detail of painting by John James Chalon (left)
	Painting by Sir William Quiller Orchardson (right)
300	©The Imperial War Museum Q005574
312	Reproduced courtesy South Staffs Water Plc

Images of the Bagot family reproduced courtesy of
Mr and Mrs C. Bagot-Jewitt and the Estate of Nancy, Lady Bagot
Illustrations on pages 8,10,14,24,98 - the author
Images on pages 221,223,224,227, 312 reproduced
courtesy South Staffs Water plc.

ACKNOWLEDGEMENTS

In September 2016, the 930th anniversary event to celebrate the existence of a church in the parish, and held in St Leonard's Church Blithfield, was possible through the support of the Rector, Churchwardens and Parochial Church Council.

The material on display was such that many visitors were of the view that its inclusion in a book would be worthwhile. In the first instance I must thank all these people for their passive encouragement which has led to this publication.

Two books have been previously published concerning the history of the parish. The first, very nearly 200 years ago in 1824, entitled Memorials of the Bagot Family, by William, Second Lord Bagot. The other, almost exactly 100 years later, in 1919, entitled Notes on the Early History of Blithfield, by D.S.Murray. Both these books have been an inspiration and great help in my attempt to bring the history of the parish up to date another 100 years hence.

I extend most grateful thanks to Mrs Ruth Glew who spent much time in correcting my many mistakes in the text of this book.

Likewise, Mr Andrew Mason gave much of his time to produce some of the excellent photographs included in these pages, as did Mr Graham Knight.

My grateful thanks must go to Mr and Mrs Charles Bagot-Jewitt for allowing me access to Blithfield Hall in pursuit of my own photographic endeavours.

I thank Mr Ernest Barnes for his time and help with research and loan of research material. Mr Chris Pattison of South Staffs Water plc was generous in allowing me access to the historical archive of that company for my enquiries into the history of Blithfield Reservoir.

I must extend thanks to all those listed in the bibliography who have allowed me to include information in my book from their publications thereby enabling this book to benefit from their hard work.

I thank Mr and Mrs Charles Bagot-Jewitt, Mr and Mrs Charles Simpson and Mr Stuart Shipley who have allowed me to include certain photographs.

I would like to thank the staff of The Staffordshire Record Office and William Salt Library in Stafford, and Mr Peter Griffiths and his staff at The Lichfield Heritage Centre in Lichfield for allowing me closer access to items in their custody belonging to St Leonard's Church.

I am grateful to Mr John Walton of The Beamhurst Museum, Uttoxeter for information concerning Civil Defence during the Second World War in the Uttoxeter area and to Mr Philip Charles for his contributions.

I also thank Mr Greg Slater of The Benhill Press, Rugeley for his assistance.

Last, but by no mean least, I thank my brother, Neville, for his valuable help and quiet encouragement during my writing of this book.

While every effort has been made to verify historical information included in these pages, I have no doubt that errors may have crept in.

I take full responsibility for these, excepting those where lack of information has led me to make certain assumptions, although where these occur, I have, hopefully, drawn the readers attention to them.

INTRODUCTION

For the vast majority of villages and hamlets in England, the parish church has stood resolutely rooted in the landscape for hundreds of years, in some instances since Saxon times, and they stand as a testament to people from their parishes, past and present. In most cases, the church represents the oldest building in the parish and provide an ideal portal through which to explore parish history, containing as they do parish records going back in some cases, as far as 1538. They are each highly individual in their architecture and contain gravestones, memorials and monuments to those long gone, which once investigated, can tell fascinating stories. Consequently the parish church can be immensely rewarding for any visitor who chances to pass over its threshold. In most cases however, it is only possible to glean faint idea of this history by a casual visit and it requires some perseverance to uncover the stories which lie behind the stone.

It must not be forgotten however, that principally, they are places of worship and have served the spiritual needs of parishioners for many centuries, and still do. Consequently they manage to maintain a sanctified and hallowed atmosphere, which to many is a welcome relief and antidote to the fraught and frazzled pace of every-day life.

St Leonard's Church in the parish of Blithfield, which is situated in the heart of rural Staffordshire, is just one representative of thousands throughout the country. It is not necessarily outstanding for its architecture or its very famous people or families contained therein. It is sufficiently important however, in that it was made a Grade One listed building in 1966 for ' its architectural or historic interest '.

It has nonetheless made its mark on the locality, and the parish has been home to people who, down the ages have contributed in some way to the history, not only of the parish, but that of the county, country and the world.

The Bagot family, who are still resident at the Hall, have been part of the Blithfield story for nearly 700 years and have been involved in some of the most famous events in English history. Early on, they were among the most powerful families in England and although their influence gradually declined, their resilience has proved remarkable amid the twists and turns of history.

This book endeavours to give a brief insight into their lives, and while it will be of local interest, some effort has been made to connect the exploits of past local inhabitants of the parish to the wider context of historical events, as it weaves their stories into some interesting snippets of history.

Consequently, it is hoped this will give the book a broader appeal.

This is the story of one church and one small parish, but could equally be similar to that of stories to be found in any church in the country.

The basis of this book has been drawn from an exhibition which was held in St Leonard's Church in September 2016 which celebrated the 930th anniversary of Christian worship here.

Our starting point is Domesday Book, compiled in 1086 by William the Conqueror and said to be one of the most important and valuable records in existence in any country in the world. It is in this book that many of today's villages and towns are first mentioned in official records, and its contents give a unique record of the structure of society in 11th century England. The lack of historical evidence prevents too much detail concerning this, but by including the brief detail given to Blithfield and adding information from our Anglo-Saxon past, it is hoped the reader will be able to have a small insight into life in England 1,000 years ago.

The centuries are then followed one by one detailing the exploits, achievements and sacrifice of those from the parish as they contribute to history down the ages.

This year of 2018, will see the centenary of the end of the First World War, and as with many parishes in the land, Blithfield sent men off to fight for King and Country, some never to return.

In the final part, the book includes brief details of these men, again giving them a context into their place in time, and the battles in which they fought which resulted in their making the ultimate sacrifice.

It concludes by taking the story of the parish into the 21st century.

It has been said that no man is an island, and the same can be said for an English country parish. The history of people and places inevitably spills over into that of other people and other places and their woven together stories can make interesting reading.

Terence Cooper

October, 2018

FORWARD

BLITHFIELD
A PARISH IN TIME
and
OTHER HISTORIES

Time has been kind to the parish of Blithfield.
It has remained relatively unchanged since the first recorded details appeared in The Domesday Book in 1086. The River Blithe still meanders its merry way through the peaceful meadows of the parish, its flow only impeded since 1953 by Blithfield Reservoir, and then from there, finding its way into the River Trent near Kings Bromley. Even the reservoir has arguably enhanced the parish rather than detracted from it, encouraging as it does the fisherman, bird watcher and sailor pursuing their relaxing pastimes far away from the stresses of everyday life at the beginning of the 21st century.

A church existed in 1086, and it does now, (although not the same one), and farming remains the principle economic activity in the parish. It contains neither shop or public house, and never has, although a school and a post office existed in the village of Admaston up until 1944 and the late 1990's respectively. No new roads have been driven through the parish since the early 19th century, and aside from new houses built to replace old stock and some redundant farm barns and stables being converted into desirable dwellings, the last new house to be built in the parish was in the early 20th century.

The parish of Blithfield covers an area of 3158 acres in the middle of rural Staffordshire and has a population of 225 in 96 households (2001 census). It consists of two villages, Newton and Admaston and the number of households has remained relatively stable since 1830.

In character with many other rural villages, the population of farm working families whose surnames sometimes appear for centuries in parish records have now largely disappeared. Their homes are now occupied with those who have retired from city occupations, and young professionals who are keen to escape urban living for the quietness of rural surroundings.

In the middle of the second decade of the 21st century, rampant progress, which is effecting the sensibilities of those residents in other rural areas of Staffordshire, - and the country, - will miss Blithfield by a whisker. A proposed High Speed railway line (HS2) is due to by–pass the parish only

200 yards from it's southern boundary cutting through the Staffordshire countryside as it travels from Birmingham to Crewe and beyond. It proposes to whisk passengers along at over 120 miles per hour.
However, time will only tell if this project will bring pressure to increase amenities in rural Staffordshire (and Blithfield) for the expanding population of England.
Nonetheless, the parish is home to new technology which is playing its part in helping to reduce the country's dependence on fossil fuels by generating clean energy from the wind and sun.

Nearly one thousand years ago water was used to power corn mills in the parish and along with other aspects of life past, events today seem to indicate that we are returning to where we've been!

Please turn the pages of the centuries to reveal Blithfield's story...

BLITHFIELD 2018

Front Cover	St Leonard's Church, Blithfield.
Title Page	The Churchyard Cross, St Leonard's Church.
Opposite	A Staffordshire Folio Page - The Domesday Book.

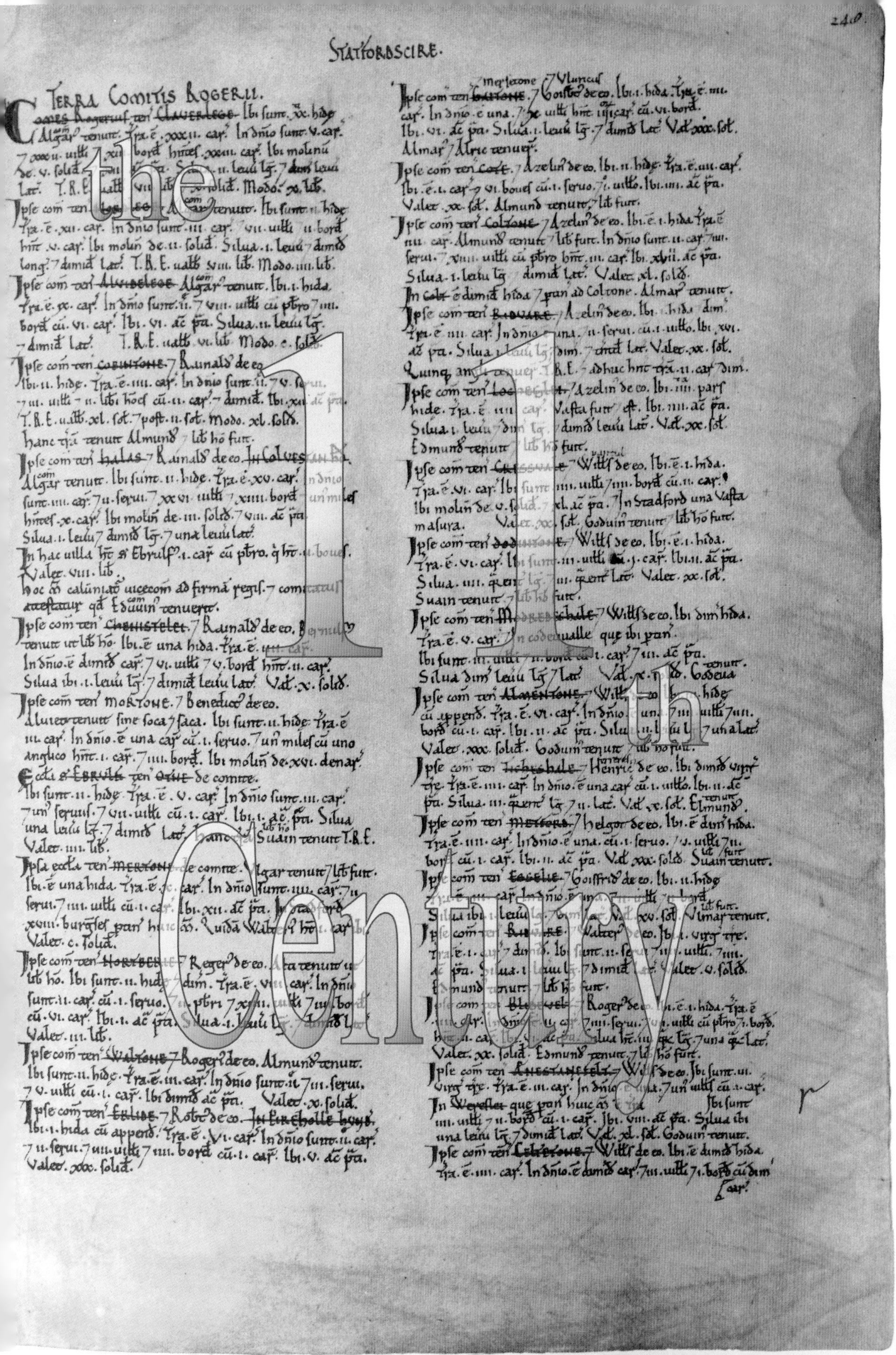
the
11th
Century
STATFORDSCIRE.
TERRA COMITIS ROGERII.
240

BLITHFIELD AT THE TIME OF THE DOMESDAY BOOK

In the beginning: -

For the year 1085, 19 years after the Norman Conquest of England, the writer of the Anglo-Saxon Chronicle wrote:

Then at Christmas the king was at Gloucester with his council and held his court for five days... After this the king had much thought and very deep discussion with his council about this country- how it was occupied and with what sort of people. Then he sent his men over all England into every shire and had them find out how many hundred hides there were in the shire or what land and cattle the king had himself in the country, or what dues he ought to have in twelve months from the shire...what or how everybody had who was occupying the land in England, in land and cattle and how much it was worth. So very narrowly did he have it investigated that there was no single hide nor virgate of land, nor indeed... one ox nor one cow nor one pig which was there left out, and not put down in his record............

And so, the following year, William the Conqueror's men went out and the famous 'Domesday Book' was compiled.
In the Staffordshire folio of the book, we read King William's men came to Blithfield and found a priest, therefore implying the existence of a church here.

The entry for Blithfield in the Domesday Book, translated from Latin, reads as follows under the heading 'Land held by Earl Roger' -

The earl himself holds BLITHFIELD, and Roger [holds] of him.
There is one hide. There is land for 4 ploughs. In desmense are 2 ploughs,
and 4 slaves; and 7 villans with a priest and 1 bordar have 2 ploughs.
There are 6 acres of meadow. The woodland is 3 furlongs long and
1 furlong broad. It is worth 20s. Edmund held it and he was a free man.

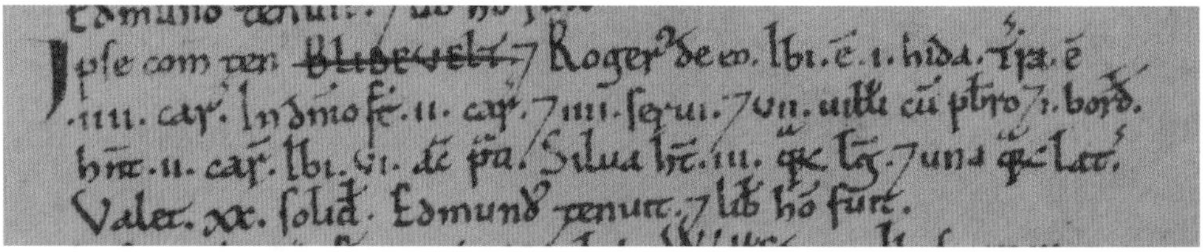

The entry for Blithfield in the Staffordshire folio of the Domesday Book

The earl – was Roger de Montgomery, Earl of Arundel and Shrewsbury who was granted Blithfield by William the Conqueror at the time of the Conquest along with many other manors. The manor was the basic economic, political and judicial unit of administration and they varied greatly in size.
Blidevelt – Blithfield, derives from *Blithe,* (the river)[1] meaning gentle or merry and *Field,* meaning open space.

Blithfield[2] as a village no longer exists. It is thought to have been sited in the grounds of, or nearby the existing Blithfield Hall, the original building being built with a moat, by Sir John Bagot in 1394.
There is no mention of the village after 1334 and so it could have been cleared away to make way for the hall or at some later time. Certainly in the 17th and 18th centuries villages were swept away to improve the outlook from many grand houses of that period.
The village is now classed as a "Deserted Medieval Village".
Blithfield only exists now as the Hall and it's grounds, the church and the Old Rectory which was devastated by fire in 1961 and re-built in the 1980's into apartments.

Roger – was Roger de Lacy who was tenant of Blithfield under Earl Roger.
In return for these privileges, both men were obliged to offer military service to the king by way of trained knights or in lieu cash payments.

From the entry in Domesday we can read that Blithfield was populated by 13 men (4 plus 7 plus 1 and the priest) - it is unlikely women or children would have been included – and so we can translate that, by including their families, into a population of Blithfield in 1086 as being between 50 to 60 souls. [3]
There is some doubt however, as to the accuracy of the entries and therefore this can only be taken as a rough estimate.
These people were the peasantry who could be free or unfree and who, depending on their status, rented land from their lord and paid him rent by way of cash, labour or produce from the land. The lord also could move unfree peasants between his manors and had the power to approve or prevent marriages.

Slaves – are assumed have been under the thrall of the land-holder, the earl, or his tenant Roger. They were at the bottom of the social order, had no property rights and could be bought and sold by the lord. They consisted of

1 This spelling varies. Officially it is spelt 'Blithe', it can be spelt 'Blythe'
2 Pronounced 'Bliffield'
3 It is thought that the total population of England at the time of Domesday was between one and one and a half million.

perhaps around 10 per cent of the country's population.

Villans- made up around 40 per cent of the population and were the wealthiest of the unfree peasants. Although they could own between 30 and 40 acres of farm land and could work for themselves, they had to work for the lord for a few days a week.

A *Bordar*- is thought to have been a cottager who lived away from the main settlement and occupied a small holding of a few acres. They were the class of peasant whose debt of service to the lord was the greatest.

A Priest – would at the time of Domesday have been regarded in most cases as little more than the average peasant and would have worked alongside them to earn his living. However, there are a few exceptions to this as some held land and property in their own right and were therefore relativel wealthy.
There are 30 priests mentioned for Staffordshire in the Domesday Book, although it is thought some may have been omitted.

A *Hide*- is thought to have been around 120 acres.

Ploughs- refer to plough teams of eight oxen. They would have drawn the plough itself, which would have been a wooden beam equipped with iron tipped coulters, which penetrated and cut the soil. This was then turned by wooden mouldboards. Each plough team was driven by two men.

Meadow- is thought to refer to land which was susceptible to flooding. This could have been the case here as the River Blithe flowed through the manor. It would also have been used for grazing livestock.

A *Furlong*- is one eighth of a mile.

An *Acre*- is thought be around the same area as it is today although it was based on the square perch- the perch being equivalent to anything from 14 ft to 18ft depending on the locality. (There was no defined standard on measurements in the 11th century).
Property was handed down from father to son although, if there were no heirs, the land was repossessed by the lord.

Demesne - (pronounced dim-ayn) is the land attached to a landed property and occupied by the owner not the tenant.

Edmund- was the holder of the vill or feudal township of Blithfield at the time of King Edward (the Confessor), before the Norman Conquest.
20s- 20 shillings. The shilling (*s- Latin solidus*) made up of 12 pennies, was not minted as a separate coin, neither was the pound (*£ - Latin libra*) made up of 20 shillings. The only coin struck in England in the period was the silver penny (*d- Latin denarius*) There were 240 pennies in the pound [1]
There was a mint at Stafford and Tamworth.
The values of other local townships mentioned in the Domesday Book are as follows:-

Newton- 40s,
Abbots Bromley- 20s
Colton- 40s,
Great and Little Haywood- 40s 40d
Rugeley- 30s
Cannock- 20s
Lichfield- £15

The values relate to the tax revenue which would have been payable to the king.

The economy of England at the time of Domesday was entirely dependent on agriculture and the values detailed were wholly due to the level of agricultural productivity. This was governed largely by the quality of the land under cultivation, although, because of King William's efforts to subdue rebellion of the English, particularly in some of the northern counties, large areas of land were taken out of use, or laid waste to deny sustenance to the rebels and their followers.
Those areas were valued at nothing in Domesday and those that included cultivated land were reduced in value from that before the Norman Conquest.

The manor of Newton listed above was gradually absorbed into the parish of Blithfield as its lands were added to the Blithfield estate of the Bagot family. Its entry in the Domesday Book, reads as follows :

The same Reginald (de Bailleul) holds NEWTON. Godwine held it, and he was a free man. There is half a hide. There is land for four ploughs. In demesne half a plough; and 8 villans and 5 bordars with 3 ploughs. There is 1 slave, and a mill rendering 4s., and 2 acres of meadow,(and) woodland 1 furlong long and 1 broad. It is worth 40s

---

1 These denominations of coinage continued until 1971 when decimalisation was introduced. The £ was then divided into 100 new pence, the shilling being made equal to 5 new pence, 4 shillings 20 new pence and 10 shillings 50 new pence.

The mill is thought to have been situated in the natural hollow in the ground just outside the village where the present road travels towards Abbots Bromley. The water course which fed it is now piped to an outlet opposite Manor Cottage and would have been originally dammed to form a mill pond.

During this time there were another three local townships, Hampton, Booth and Steenwood. Over time, the first two were absorbed into Newton and Steenwood in to Admaston.

There is evidence from records of the 16th century to suggest both Newton and Admaston possessed their own chapels. Indeed a field, opposite the turning in Newton to The Lea, is still locally called the chapel field.

In ancient records, Booth is referred to as 'Bold' or 'Bould' meaning dwelling place, the present name having thought to have evolved from the local pronunciation of this last word during the 19th century. There is strong evidence to suggest that a village did indeed exist here as there are distinct depressions in the ground outlining ancient dwelling foundations and also those of an oratory.[1]

In the records, mention is made of a resident of Bold, 'Hereman de la Bold' who appears to have been a very wealthy man, for he is fined 65s 8d and his chattels forfeited to the Crown after failing the ' water ordeal '.[2]

The name Domesday dates from 1170 when a certain Richard fitzNigel wrote: '*This book is called by the English Domesday...not because it passes judgement...but because it is not permissible to contradict its decisions, any more than those of the Last Judgement.*

The original spelling still used from the Anglo-Saxon *Domesdaeg,* serves to retain this distinction.

The Domesday Book was last consulted for legal precedent in 1982, 896 years after it was written by the scribe of William the Conqueror.

---

1 See Other Histories – Deserted Medieval Villages. p.266

2 The water ordeal was one form of medieval trial under which the accused was subjected, where their arm was submerged in boiling water, bandaged and after three days, examined. If it had begun to heal the accused was declared innocent, if not, the guilty verdict was given. It was seen as being the direct judgement of God.

BLITHFIELD'S 'FIRST' CHURCH AND ANGLO SAXON CHURCHES AT THE TIME OF THE NORMAN CONQUEST

There is little doubt that a church existed in Blithfield in 1086, for the mention of a priest in the Domesday Book would imply this. What form the church took is not known for there is no physical evidence of it, although evidence does exist for a Norman church, which the present church replaced during the middle of the 13th century. It is probable, but unlikely, that it was the Norman church which stood on the site of the present church, or nearby, at the time of Domesday. The influence of Norman architecture and building techniques would have been known in England, even before the 1066 conquest, but the practical application of these would conceivably have been the privilege of very wealthy individuals and not common-place throughout Anglo-Saxon England.

On their arrival in the country as the new ruling class, the Normans soon began to stamp their authority on the conquered Anglo-Saxons by building castles, cathedrals and churches in their trade mark material, stone.

Hitherto, the favoured building material of the Anglo-Saxons was timber, with stone buildings being reserved for those who could afford them.

So, if the church at Blithfield in 1086 was a Norman building, it was a very early and unusual example. It is known from the Domesday Book that Staffordshire was not a wealthy county and that it was also heavily wooded, and so with these two facts alone, it can be concluded that in 1086 a church built of timber existed with a thatched roof and of Anglo-Saxon origin.

However, it could not have been much later when the Norman church replaced it, for the oldest feature of the present church is a pillar piscina which has been dated to the first half of the 12th century. Indeed, it has been estimated that stone churches were being built in Staffordshire in large numbers during the 12th century, so the stone, Norman church at Blithfield could well have been one of them.

The Anglo-Saxon church could well have been a manorial church attached to the manor house of Edmund, the Saxon nobleman at Blithfield in 1066. Churches of this period were viewed as being status symbols.

Many early settlements, together with their churches, were built near to rivers (the River Blithe flowed only half a mile away, now submerged by the reservoir) where early baptisms could well have taken place.

Not many Saxon churches survive in England in their original form and those that do are built of stone. Many have been altered down the centuries, and in most cases include some of the features of the original

Saxon building.
No timber built churches have survived with the exception of that at Greensted in Essex.

Before the 11th century there was no concept of the 'parish church' and Saxon churches were largely private chapels and built at the expense of the lord or theign. The late 11th century was a time when many manorial churches were being built, for a Domesday Book entry for a manor in Worcestershire, reads... *'there are oxen for one plough, but they are hauling stone to the church'.* Many of these early buildings were the forerunners of medieval churches such as St Leonard's at Blithfield.

Blithfield's first church?

The timber Saxon church at Greensted, Essex. The tower and chancel are later additions.
Shown on the right are the original timber walls of the Saxon nave.

THE VILL, OR VILLAGE OF BLITHFIELD IN 1086

With the vast majority of Anglo-Saxon buildings being constructed of wood very little evidence remains of them as they have long since dissolved into the soil. The same is true of the vill or village of Blithfield. It is highly likely that any evidence which does remain, will be beneath the existing Blithfield Hall.

Archaeological evidence from sites that have been excavated suggest Anglo- Saxon villages consisted of a group of houses and ancillary buildings built of wood with thatched roofs which varied in size from 3m x 3.5m to the larger 10m x 5m 'hall'. Evidence also indicates these building only had one room and that each building was used for different purposes. The hall would have been the focal point of the settlement and used as a meeting place for eating, drinking and story telling- in modern day parlance, the 'pub'. The smaller buildings were variably used for sleeping and eating, storage and for workshops, in which the necessities of life by way of clothing and perhaps basic domestic items were produced. It is also thought that the vill was home to extended family groups of perhaps three or four. Food was cooked on an open fire in the middle of the floor and smoke escaped through the thatch or a hole in the roof

The village layout did not yet conform to the pattern with which we are now so familiar, with houses built along street frontages in a planned fashion. They were built randomly, usually within a palisaded fence, to keep out wolves and wild boar, which then freely roamed the country.

There is no doubt however that villages would have been sited, and houses been built, to take advantage of the prevailing weather conditions and evidence suggests that planned village layouts began to appear very soon after the Norman Conquest in the late 11th century.

Very few buildings were constructed of stone but this was soon to change with the arrival of the Normans. Their prowess with the material made its mark quickly in England, when castles, churches and cathedrals began to spring up- the Tower of London and Durham Cathedral being two famous examples.

The Anglo-Saxons kept cows, which provided milk, and sheep provided wool for clothes, which were rarely changed. Oxen were used to draw wooden ploughs; pigs were kept for pork, and hens, ducks and geese provided eggs. Fish would have been caught in the nearby River Blithe.

For most peasants, bread, stewed vegetables, wild fruit and occasionally cheese and fish were the main components of their diet. The wealthier peasants, priest and noble or head man would enjoy a richer diet of red meat. The land would have been ploughed using the 'strip' system where narrow strips of land would have been ploughed, cultivated, planted and alternately left fallow on an annual basis.

Life would have been precarious and the weather a critical factor in enabling enough food to be produced in order to avoid famine. [1]
Beer was the main beverage and was brewed in large quantities although mead, made from honey, was a luxury for special occasions.
Disease would have been ever present and life expectancy around 35 to 40 years of age, the dead being buried in cemeteries outside the village boundary.

By 1086 the church was becoming a familiar feature of Anglo-Saxon villages and by then the church at Blithfield could well have been surrounded by a fence within an existing cemetery area.

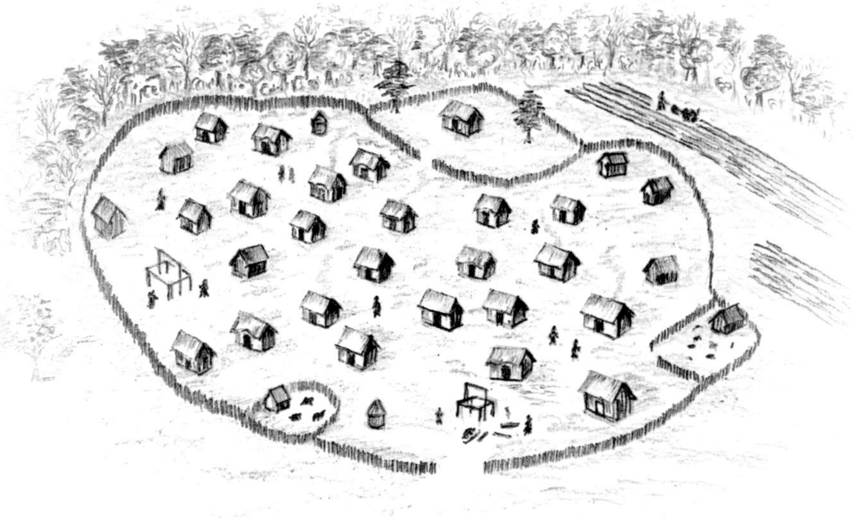

An artists impression of the vill of Blithfield as it could have looked in 1086. In all probability, it existed where the present Blithfield Hall now stands, and the Saxon church on the site of the present church.

1 During the 11th century, on average, England experienced one famine every 14 years.

the 12th Century

THE EARLY LORDS OF BLITHFIELD.
The family de Blithfield and the first Bagot of Blithfield.

At the time of the Norman Conquest and as detailed in Domesday Book, Blithfield was in the possession of Edmund, a Saxon Thane. It is thought he gave his name to Admaston, which from the earliest times was frequently written as Ædmundeston and was along with Newton, a neighbouring township of Blithfield.

After the Conquest, Edmund was dispossessed and William the Conqueror granted Blithfield, along with other lands to Roger de Montgomery, Earl of Arundel and Shrewsbury, but his connection with Blithfield was short lived. Roger de Lacy (Roger in the Domesday entry) held under Roger de Montgomery, and as well as Blithfield held Norbury and Walton (in Gnosall)

Richard de Blithfield

Rector at Blithfield c.1185

However, the actual resident landowners, certainly sometime before 1136, were the de Blithfield's. They occupied it for the next nine generations before dying out towards the end of the 14th century, when they merged with the Bagot family of Bagot's Bromley. A certain Heremann appears in the Blithfield records at the beginning of the 12th century and his grandson, Sir John, assumed the name de Blithfield from an old and extinct family.

The first Rector of Blithfield whose name is known was Richard de Blithfield who was installed c.1185. It is thought that it is his carved head at the junction of the hood moulding on the north arcade of the Church, and that it is his badly eroded tomb[1] which is to be found outside of the south wall of the chancel of the Church. Originally it would have been brightly painted. Evidence of this can still be seen in the form of geometrical patterns under the arch.

---

1 This supposition does not relate to the inscription on a small plaque above the tomb. This states- in Latin- that it is the tomb of 'Alfred Priest of Hulcrombe son of William and brother of Almeric and John de Blithfield '. It appears there could have been some confusion when this defaced inscription was translated from the original in the 17th century due to it deteriorating. In any case, Hulcrombe is in Worcestershire and begs the question, why would a priest from his church and county be brought to Blithfield for burial, assuming of course, he did not die while visiting Blithfield. It is known that Richard de Blithfield was a brother of those named above.

The tomb of Richard de Blithfield in the
outside south wall of the chancel showing
faint evidence of the geometrical decoration

Indeed, much of the interior of the Church would have been painted as was the custom in this period before the Reformation when Roman Catholicism was the doctrine of the English church. The vast majority of this decoration was removed from churches during the reformation to the Protestant church in the reign of Henry VIII.

Further descriptions of the carved stone heads in St Leonard's Church will be given in later pages.

It was during the time of another Richard de Blithfield (c.1248-1293) that the present church replaced that of the old Norman building.
There is no documentary evidence of this church being built but the architectural style strongly indicates this period.

It was probably a sign of the relatively lawless times that found the de Blithfield family embroiled in disputes and arguments with others.
In 1250, a dispute arose when Robert de Edmundeston accused James de Blithfield and his son John, of pulling down of a hedge in Colton which necessitated a visit from the sheriff. [1] In another (return match) in 1269

1 It is thought that the lane leading to Colton from the B5031 at Lea Lane- Sherracop Lane- commemorates this event.

the argument was with Robert de Edmundeston when he was sued by Richard de Blithfield over five acres of common pasture, also in Colton.

More seriously, in the year 1303, there is an account of Thomas de Blithfield being tried for murder!

The account reads as follows:

"Thomas son of Richard de Blythefeld, taken and detained for the death of Thomas son of William de Lutteleye, put himself on the country; and Robert de Pype and the other jurors say that on the day of Circumcision of the Lord, 30 Ed. I a dispute arose at Blythe between Thomas son of William de Lutteleye and Thomas son of Richard de Blythefeld, and Thomas son of William de Lutteleye drew his bow with an arrow in it, meaning to shoot Thomas son of Richard, and Thomas son of Richard perceiving his malice, drew his dagger, and Thomas son of William de Lutteleye tried to kill him, and Thomas son of Richard then ran away as far as the cemetery close of the vill and attempted to climb over the fence in order to escape from the other, and he could not climb over the fence owing to its height and he fell to the ground, and the said Thomas son of William was pursuing him all the time with his knife drawn, meaning to kill him as he lay on the ground, and Thomas son of Richard perceiving he could escape death no other way, struck Thomas son of William with his knife in the stomach, as he was lying on him, so that he died, and they say positively that the said Thomas son of Richard de Blythefeld killed Thomas son of William de Lutteleye in self-defence and not feloniously or by malice aforethought. He is therefore remitted to gaol to await the King's pardon."

Nearly three years later, at the Gaol Delivery of the County of Stafford December 1305, he was indicted afresh for this very matter, but was able to produce the King's pardon from Lent, 10th April 1303.

On Michaelmas day 1312 he himself met with a violent death at Penkridge

when *" John de Kneclet feloniously killed Thomas de Blythefeld at Pencrich on the Thursday the feast of St Michael, 5 Ed II..."*
Thomas de Blithfield's father, Richard, is listed as being MP for Staffordshire in 1328-9

It is yet another Richard de Blithfield (c.1327-1361), grandson of the 'church builder ', who is considered to be the last Lord of that family [1]. It was in the year c.1357 that his daughter and only child and heiress of Blithfield, Elizabeth, married Ralph Bagot of Bagot's Bromley, the neighbouring manor to Blithfield. He then became the first Bagot, Lord of Blithfield, after Richard's death in c.1361.

In the words of Nancy, Lady Bagot - (died 2014), " he married the girl next door".

1 It is probable that the last de Blithfield's were carried away by the return of the Great Pestilence (Black Death) of August 1361- May 1362

THE ORIGINS OF THE BAGOT FAMILY

The Bagot family have been synonymous with Blithfield for nearly 700 years and are one of the very few who can trace their lineage back to the time of the Norman Conquest and claim an authentic Norman ancestor. Bagot [1] is suspected to be a Breton family from Brittany and Breton's were known to be looked down on by the Normans in the 11th century.

A certain 'Bagod' (Bagot) is named in the Domesday Book as holding land in Bramshall [2] (near Uttoxeter) under his feudal lord, Robert de Stafford and was one of his retinue at the time of the Conquest. It is worth noting that the manor of Bromley (adjoining the manor of Blithfield), later known as Bagot's Bromley because of that family's association with it, is not directly mentioned in the Domesday Book. However, an entry in Domesday is listed as 'Bradelie' and held by Robert de Stafford, (as was the manor of Bramshall), but it is noted by scholars as being 'of unknown or uncertain identification'. It is thought by them, for various reasons, that it is a clerical error by the scribe and a misspelling of 'Bramelie' (Bromley), although this entry does not list a Bagot. (see note [2]) The notion that a Bagot existed in the area before the conquest could hold true in that there is no reason to suppose all Normans came to England in 1066.

The next 'Bagod' appears as a witness to a deed in 1122 and it is thought he could be the son of the Domesday Bagod and if so, the two would be the first links in the chain of that family line which still exists at Blithfield- and beyond, to this day.

Hervey fitzBagot (fitz- son of) occurs in 1130 when the date of his succession seems to be 1129- c.1130.

A branch of the Bagot family were known as the Bagot's of the Hyde (Hyde Lea, near Stafford). Hervey Bagot, thought to be from this side of the family, married Millicent de Stafford and took her name. During the reign of Richard I their descendants became Earls of Stafford and subsequently the ill-fated Dukes of Buckingham. By 1339, the Bagot's of the Hyde had died out and their lands inherited by the Earls of Stafford. Scholars have not found it easy to trace the Bagot lineage, so much so that one wrote:-

The Bagot's were such a prolific race, and founded so many branches at this

---

1 The name Bagot is thought to derive from ' Waggo ' the old Norman word for warrior or fighter. There are around 1700 Bagot's in France at the present time. In other parts of the world, notably the USA, the name has morphed to Baggot and Baggett.

2 There is confusion here among historians. Some argue the entry in the Domesday Book refers to Bromley not Bramshall.

period, that it is very difficult to distinguish the various members of the family.

The Bagot's of Bagot's Bromley held lands of their ancestors, the Baron's of Stafford, during the reign of Henry II, and are recorded as: William, succeeded 1166; Simon[1] 1198-1203; Hugh 1203-1242; Richard 1256-c.1270; William 1272-1290; John 1290-1334; Sir John 1335-1349 and Ralph 1355-1376.

The stained glass window dating from the 14th century in the chancel of Blithfield Church depicting the Arms of the Bagot and de Blithfield families, left and right respectively

Sir John Bagot probably fought at the Battle of Crecy with Edward III. He almost certainly fought in the king's army against the Scots at the Battle of Halidon Hill in 1333, when they were ousted from the English border town of Berwick and the English re-gained control of Scotland. He represented Staffordshire in the Parliament of 1348 along with Simon de Ruggelye, and is thought to have been a victim of the Great Pestilence (Black Death) of 1348- 49 at the age of 35.

Ralph Bagot who succeeded Sir John became the first Bagot of Blithfield when he married Blithfield heiress Elizabeth de Blithfield in 1360. The Bagot home at Bagot's Bromley [2] was abandoned and the Bagot family made their permanent home at Blithfield Hall. The original building was built by Ralph Bagot's successor another Sir John Bagot, with a moat about the year 1394 and the family have been in residence there ever since.

---

1 The first Bagot of Bromley

2 In 1820, William 2nd Lord Bagot records that- *In 1811, Lord Bagot pulled down the old farm house within the Moat, at Bagot's Bromley (where had been the ancient residence of the Bagot's) where he discovered considerable remains of the old mansion and with foundation stones, (of what appeared to have been the Hall and upon which rested many oak, carved pillars). He built a monument with a small marble slab...* The inscription on it, in Latin, records the event. This can still be seen where the building originally stood in the field opposite the junction of the Abbots Bromley to Newton road.

the
13
th
Century

BLITHFIELD'S 'NEW ' CHURCH

Henry III 's carved head in St Leonard's Church

St Leonard's Church was built during the reign of Henry III [1] and it is thought that it is his carved head in the nave at the junction of the hood moulding of the pillar. of the north arcade. Henry III married Eleanor of Provence [2] in December 1236.

It seems that the Church was built over an extended period of time beginning in the early 13th century and that the nave and tower were constructed first and may even have been built onto the then existing Norman chancel. Evidence of this can be seen in the form of stones with the distinct and typical Norman chevron pattern carving, which were found in the churchyard in the 19th century and are thought to have been part of this Norman chancel arch. They are now incorporated into the internal stonework in the corner of the west wall of the tower. This building would seem therefore to have replaced a Norman church which in turn would have replaced the original Saxon building of 1086. It is not known when either of these were built or what form they took. Indeed, there are no records of this church being built.

Chancel arch stones with Norman chevron decoration

Henry was only nine years old when he was crowned in 1216. His carved features in the Church seem to suggest the nave arcades at least, were completed sometime around the year 1240. The nail-head ornamentation around the south pillar of the north arcade is typical of the late 12th or early 13th century. It seems that the aisles and the tower were completed after this, although the existing window openings of the aisles are thought to have been inserted up to 100 years later as the aisle roofs show evidence of being raised.

---

1 See Other Histories – Henry III p.268

2 See Other Histories – Eleanor of Provence p.270

The original aisle windows are thought to have been the size of the small two light window in the west wall of the south aisle.

The new chancel was added in the 14th century as the glass in the chancel is thought to have been installed by Sir Ralph Bagot c.1360.

The clerestory [1] of the Church was added in the late 15th or early 16th century by Sir Lewis Bagot, and the outline of the old nave roof can still be seen on the east wall of the nave and also on the west wall. However this is now obscured by the organ which was installed in 1965. Other significant features such as the porch and the vestry were added in Victorian times.

Another relic thought to have been part of the Norman church is the pillar piscina which has been converted into an alms box. It has been dated to the first half of the 12th century and was reputedly found in a garden in Admaston and returned to the Church circa 1850 by the then Rector, Hervey Bagot who also converted it. It now stands by the pillar opposite to the south door and is supposed to be the only example in the county.

The Norman pillar piscina alms box in Blithfield Church.

The 13th century was a period when many churches and cathedrals were being built or rebuilt in the British Isles, and Europe and has been referred to as the Golden Age of church building. New trends and fashions in architecture, increasing wealth in England- particularly from the trade in wool for which England was famous throughout Europe -as well as the expanding population and power and influence of the church, all provided the impetus for this.

As can be seen, the Church has a north and south aisle which served the purpose of accommodating the expanding population of the period. Earlier Saxon buildings, be they built in wood or stone, consisted only a nave and sometimes a chancel or sanctuary.

Some of the cathedrals which were under construction, being constructed re-built or completed during the 13th century were: Gloucester, Hereford Wells, Lincoln, Canterbury, St Paul's (The old

[1] Clerestory - an upper row of windows above the level of the aisle roofs.

cathedral), Lichfield, Exeter, Salisbury, Westminster Abbey, Glasgow, and Peterborough [1].

The same story is true in Europe where many of the well known cathedrals were being built, among them were Chartres Cathedral, La Sainte -Chapelle and Notre Dame in Paris.

There are some curious features to be seen in and around Blithfield Church. The step down into the chancel from the nave is unusual but is probably due to the natural fall of the ground from west to east.

Outside, in the west wall of the north aisle is a recess which is thought to be an aumbry or small cupboard, but why this should be outside the Church is strange. There is the possibility however that there was once an anchorite's cell built as a lean-to in this position.[2] The superior condition of the stonework up to the level of the small window in the north wall of the tower seems to suggest this wall was at some time protected by some such structure. However, any idea that the recess in the outside wall was used as a window or squint in order that the anchorite could view the proceedings of church services, can be discounted as the recess extends into the north wall of the nave.

The Churchyard Cross

Alternatively, this room could have served as a Sacristy where the church vestments and sacred vessels were kept.

Although it appears ancient, the doorway, or porch built into the wall which provides an entrance to the church yard from Blithfield Hall was, according to William 2nd Lord Bagot in 1823, 'modern'. Built into the early 18th century boundary wall to the right of this doorway, is a circular opening which begs the question as to its use. The most likely explanation is that it was used by the rector who would send an altar boy to watch for the approach to Church of Lord and Lady Bagot, in order to enable him to be ready to welcome them as they approached the chancel doorway into church.

Intriguingly however, this feature has all

1 See Other Histories – The Architect p.272

2 There is an anchorage in this aspect at the parish church of St Michaels and All Angels, Hartlip in Kent. There is also clear evidence of a structure once being in the same position on the old Chancel Church in Rugeley. See Other Histories- The Anchorites.

the appearances as having been once an anchorites cell window. Has this stone been reclaimed from the demolished anchorite's cell which is thought to have existed, and re-used for the purpose as indicated above?

The Churchyard Cross has steps and a base to the shaft which are original to the 14th century. In 1904, a Cross which had been not been correctly suited or adapted to the base and had become ruinous, was replaced by the one seen now, which was thought to be similar to that which originally existed. This Cross is typical of the period when they were used as stations for outdoor processions, particularly on Palm Sunday, and they were also intended to provide a communal memorial to all the dead of the parish. On the west side it has The Crucified Christ accompanied by the Virgin Mary and St John, on the east side is The Angel of Judgement and the on the north and south sides are St. Chad and St Leonard, Patron Saints of the Diocese and the Parish. The custom of building these crosses faded away after the Reformation. The cross at St. Leonard's was Grade II listed in 1985 by Historic England.

SAINT·LEONARD
St. Leonard as depicted in stained glass at Blithfield

St Leonard, to whom the Church is dedicated, was a Frankish noble in the court of King Clovis I and converted to Christianity along with the king in the year 496. Leonard asked the king to grant him the personal right to release prisoners he thought worthy, and at any time of his choosing.

He secured the release of a number prisoners and has since become their patron saint. Declining an offer of a bishopric from the king, he chose to enter a monastery near Orleans and then, according to legend, he became a hermit in a forest near Limousin where he gathered a number of followers. Prisoners, who sought St Leonard's intercessions and claimed to have seen their chains break before their eyes, joined him and he gave them parts of his vast forest to clear for cultivation, thereby giving them the means to lead honest lives.

He has also become known as the patron saint of women in labour.

Through Leonard's prayers it is said that

the queen of the Franks was safely delivered of a male child resulting in him being granted royal lands at Noblac around which a village grew, Saint Leonard-de-Noblat. He died in the year 559.

In the 11th century, his cult spread throughout Europe with many villages and churches being named after him as, to the medieval mind, he would have been the ' pop star' of the day.

It can only be guessed why Blithfield Church was named in his honour, although there are 176 other churches in the UK named after him. Maybe the priest of the time at Blithfield, Roger de Verney,[1] being of French extraction, had ancestors from the region of France where St Leonard lived. That area had been under the English Crown at the beginning of the reign of King John in 1199.

An artists impression of how St. Leonard's Church Blithfield may have looked after its completion sometime in the early 14th century. The most striking addition to the Church was made in the early 16th century by Sir Lewis Bagot when he added the clerestory.

[1] It is thought to be his carved stone head in the nave of Blithfield Church and depicted on the opening page to this chapter.

the 14th Century

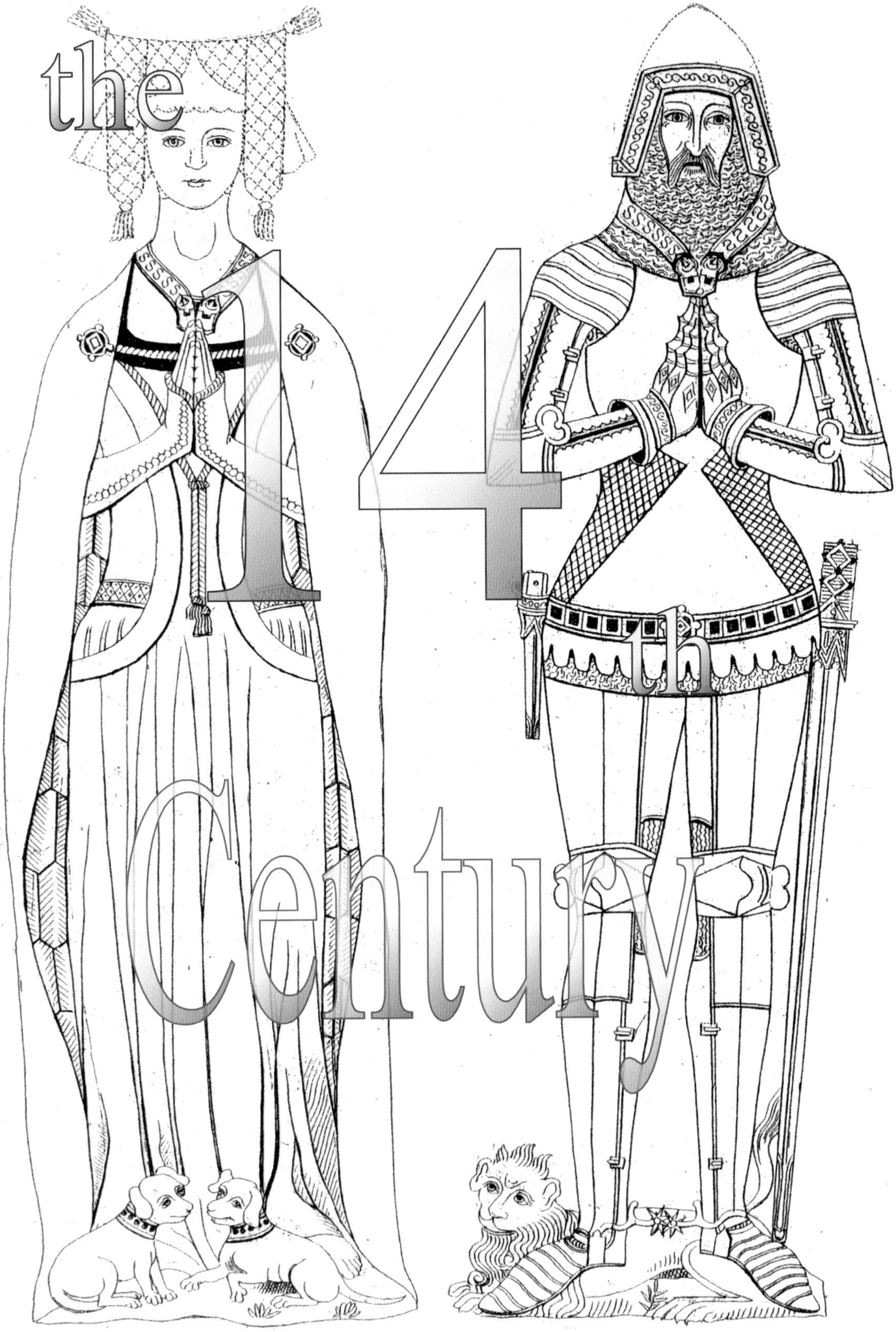

SIR WILLIAM BAGOT c.1354-1407

Sir William Bagot was not directly connected with the parish of Blithfield although it is thought he could have been the brother, or half brother, of Sir John Bagot, whose story follows. Consequently there is no reason to suppose that he was not born in Blithfield. He was not an heir to the family estates and although he held land in Staffordshire, which was not of great value, he established considerable land holdings in Warwickshire and Cheshire and made his home at Baginton in Warwickshire.

He merits inclusion here due to his political acumen and astuteness which ensured his survival in a period when 'backing the wrong horse' in the corridors of power could mean certain death.

He trod the tight rope of survival by being closely allied to King Richard II, and also being well associated with John of Gaunt, duke of Lancaster, uncle of Richard, and his son Henry Bolingbroke. However, fault lines soon began to appear between the king and his two relations, while Sir William at times, managed to antagonise both parties.

Richard was crowned at aged 10 and John of Gaunt virtually ruled the country during his minority, but as time progressed, parliament and leading nobles (the 'appellant lords') grew distrustful of Richard's retainers. At the 'merciless parliament' of 1388 five of them were condemned to death and executed.

On his coming of age in 1389, Richard struck against the 'appellant lords' and, ignoring parliament, proclaimed that he had taken the government of the realm '*upon his own person'*. In 1397 he took revenge on those who had humiliated him by forcing the execution of his court officials, and in turn had them executed.

By 1398, his rule was becoming ever more despotic and he enraged Henry Bolingbroke and the Duke of Norfolk, accusing them of treasonable language against him. They were summarily exiled and their lands forfeit.

Sir William Bagot was, with Sir John Bussy and Sir Henry Green, one of King Richard's 'continual counsellors' during the last years of Richard's reign. They were so closely involved with him that Bagot went to great lengths to allay any fears Henry Bolingbroke may have had of his having any disloyalty towards him. It was a shrewd and timely move.

In 1399, King Richard was confident enough in his position that he appointed Bagot, Bussy and Green to administer his affairs- in effect they were ruling the country- when he left for Ireland in order to reinforce his position there.

Henry Bolingbroke, who by now had become duke of Lancaster on the death of his father, seized the opportunity to return to England, where he raised an army. Richard, on his return from Ireland, finding his support had melted away, surrendered to Bolingbroke after being offered terms by which he would remain king, although he was almost immediately arrested and imprisoned. It is thought he was held briefly in the castle at Lichfield [1] from where he tried to escape.

For their part, Bussy and Green sought refuge in Bristol castle while Bagot elected to flee to Ireland. Bussy and Green were captured and immediately executed. It was not long before Bagot surrendered himself to face trial by Bolingbroke who had been crowned Henry IV on 13th October.

Through intercessions by retainers of the new king and his father, John of Gaunt, and helped by his previous connections with the king, Bagot was able to wriggle free of the ultimate penalty for treasonous behaviour. He was even granted £100 per year by the king for his sustenance. He was however imprisoned in the Tower of London for twelve months, released in November 1400 and afterwards enjoyed other privileges from Henry.

King Richard II died in mysterious circumstances in Pontefract Castle in February 1400.

There are two accounts of his demise. In one, he is said to have resisted an attack on him whilst dining, with such vigour that he killed four of his assailants with an axe. The other, and more likely, supposes he was left to fall victim to starvation and cold in the damp conditions of his cell.

Sir William Bagot died peacefully at his home in Warwickshire on 6th September 1407, although this is not the end of the story.

Some 200 years later, Sir William finds himself entering into the fertile mind of one William Shakespeare. In his play Richard II, Shakespeare recounts the drama of that king's reign and features Sir William as one of the characters along with Bussy and Green. In it, Henry IV has the lines -

'*But we must win your grace to go with us to Bristol castle, which they say is held by Bushy, Bagot and their complices, The caterpillars of the commonwealth, which I have sworn to weed and pluck away* '.

Shakespeare also refers to Bagot as '*a creature of the King*' and has him beheaded!

Perhaps King Richard himself, when confined in Pontefract Castle, had cause to think along the same lines as Shakespeare when, in the same play, he wrote these words on behalf of the king:-

...For God's sake, let us sit upon the ground
And tell sad stories of the death of Kings:
How some have been depos'd; some slain in war;

---

1 Lichfield castle no longer exists.

Some haunted by the ghosts they have depos'd; [1]
Some poisn'd by their wives; some sleeping kill'd.
All murder'd - for within the hollow crown
That rounds the mortal temples of a king
Keeps death his court; and there the antic sits,
Scoffing his state, and grinning at his pomp;
Allowing him a breath, a little scene
To monarchize, be fear'd, and kill with looks;
Infusing him with self and vain conceit
As if this flesh, which walls about our life
Were brass impregnable; and, humour'd thus,
Comes at the last, and with a little pin
Bores through his castle wall, and- farewell King!...

King Richard II spent his Christmas of 1397 at Lichfield, it is said in the very castle he was to be kept prisoner two years later. During the 12 days of festivities, he and his followers are said to have consumed 200 tuns[2] of wine and 2,000 oxen. He also paid visits to Lichfield on official business in 1386 and 1398.

Around this time, popular legend has it that Richard II visited Blithfield when he is supposed to have presented Sir John Bagot with the famous Bagot goats in appreciation of the good hunting he had enjoyed in Bagot's Park.[3]

There is some element of doubt concerning this story, for although the king was at Lichfield and it is highly probable he did visit Blithfield due to his close connections with the Bagot family, another more likely origin for the goats has been proposed. Until relatively recent times the Bagot goats were said to be from Switzerland and had been brought to England by the returning Crusaders. DNA tests carried out in 1997 have however proved their origin to be the French Pyrenees, which would fit well with the possibility that the goats arrived in England with Sir John Bagot, when he accompanied John of Gaunt to Castile when he went to claim the throne of that country in 1386. It was the custom at that time that any long expedition of a large group of people would have been accompanied by animals, to provide fresh milk and meat for the journey. It is certain that Sir John was the first to utilise the goat in the Bagot family coat of arms.

---

1 Some historians suspect the early (peaceful) demise of Henry IV was aided by the guilt of his usurping the crown.

2 Tun – a liquid measure of wine amounting to 216 gallons although in the Middle Ages this varied.

3 See Other Histories - Bagot's Park and the Bagot Goats. p.276

Brass to Sir William Bagot and his wife, Margaret, in Baginton Church, Warwickshire. Near to the church are the excavated ruins of Bagot's tower house which he built c.1390 and where Richard II is said to have visited in 1398

the 15th Century

SIR JOHN BAGOT c.1358 – c.1437

Sir John was the son and heir of Sir Ralph Bagot, the first Bagot of Blithfield, and was probably knighted at the coronation of Richard II in 1377. He was one of the most distinguished Shire knights to represent Staffordshire in the House of Commons from 1391 to 1421 in no fewer than nine parliaments. This was no doubt helped by the fact that his family had consolidated it's position in the country by loyal service to the Crown and through lucrative marriages. He was appointed sheriff of the county of Stafford in 1413.

He inherited substantial estates through his father and mother and by 1402 enjoyed a landed income of about £93 per year and he continued to acquire property throughout his life greatly increasing his wealth.

As a result of problems with his inheritance and his lack of success in obtaining redress after he came of age around 1379, he obtained a compulsion for litigation and was a plaintiff on at least 11 occasions in lawsuits against his neighbours and servants, in charges including debt, trespass, abduction, negligence and theft.

Sir John Bagot was involved in an argument with local woman, the apparently formidable Joan de Mauveisin, and had travelled to meet her in order to try to reconcile their differences in a property dispute. Sir John was also in a violent disagreement with one Hugh de Erdeswyk[1] who had heard of their meeting and was intent on murdering his adversary, records stating that:

...Hugh de Erdeswyk, with many other malefactors, to the number of 300, arrayed in manner of war with coats of mail, brigandines [2] and all kinds of armour, had come to Rydeware-Mauveisin on the Thursday before the Feast of John the Baptist 8 H.IV. (1407) with a view of killing John Bagot, knight, and from thence because they could not find him, had ridden with horns and clarions to a vill belonging to him called Blythbury, and from thence from place to place, seeking to kill him and not finding him had thrown sheaves of his corn into the River Blythe and driving his cattle so that many perished, to the value of 20 marks. ' [3]

However, by 1421 it seems the two men had reconciled themselves for Sir John had been chosen as an arbitrator between Erdeswyk and another

---

1 The Erdeswyks were a powerful Cheshire family

2 A form of body armour, usually sleeveless and made of heavy cloth, canvas or leather and lined with small overlapping steel plates.

3 The mark was not a unit of English currency but one of accountancy. Originally a weight of metal, it was valued at 128 silver pennies.

adversary, Lord Ferrers of Chartley and that year the two men both represented Staffordshire in the House of Commons.

It seems clear that Sir John was closely connected with his kinsman, Sir William Bagot, so much so, that some historians maintain a role reversal between the two men. They were certainly both in Parliament and could have shared a political interest and like Sir William, Sir John was able to navigate the perilous political waters throughout Richard II's reign to find favour with his successor, Henry IV.

Sir John Bagot 's career as a crown official began in earnest during the reign of Henry IV [1] when he sat on numerous commissions. Consequently it is possible he fought at the Battle of Shrewsbury on 21st July 1403 when the king's position was secured with victory over Henry Percy's (Hotspur) challenge to his crown.

Sir John's military and administrative experience made him a welcome member of Henry V's first expedition to France in 1415 when he fought with a retinue of three men-at-arms and nine archers.

These men would have accompanied Sir John as part of his commitment to the king in providing him with fighting men in return for the privileges Sir John had received. It could well be some of these could have been Sir John's own retainers from Blithfield.

Men-at-arms were the elite fighting force of a medieval army and were drawn from varied social classes, from Royal Dukes to lesser landowners. They were highly trained from an early age in the use weapons and horsemanship and were highly paid for their services. Archers were drawn from those of lower social status, the higher ranks of peasantry and servants of noble families.

Of lower rank they may have been, and not as well paid, but it was at this time that the English archer became the scourge of any enemy, as was to be proved at the Battle of Agincourt when they decimated a French army of much superior number and nobility. These men too, were well trained, and archery practice on Sundays was compulsory with games such as football banned.

It is said that the English archer was so feared by his enemy that any prisoners taken during battle had their two bow string fingers cut off.

This prompted archers to raise these two fingers up in defiance of their enemy before any battle commenced.

Archers it seems, achieved some social status through their military service as they were referred to as 'yeomen' in the muster rolls

There is an element of doubt as to whether Sir John fought at the Battle of Agincourt on 27th October 1415, for, although being a knight in the king's household who would have been bound to follow the king, he is listed as

1 The king was to come face to face with another Bagot from Blithfield over 400 years later!

one of the knights left to garrison Harfleur after it fell to Henry's five week siege a month earlier [1]
This was the last time he bore arms but his advancing years saw him continuing in the service of his country and county.

Henry V's campaign against the French was an effort to secure the French crown for himself, which initially he had tried to do through diplomatic channels while at the same time preparing for war.
His army was transported across the English Channel aboard 1500 vessels and his intention, after capturing the large port of Harfleur, was to march on Paris in order to secure his aim. The port fell only after a five week siege and dysentery reduced Henry's army by one third, thus preventing his march on Paris.
Deciding to march on to English-held Calais, his army crossed the River Somme[2] only to find their way barred at Agincourt, near Arras, by a French force of 20,000. This contained the cream of French nobility, while Henry's army numbered only 5,500 men.
Henry's army, mainly foot soldiers, stood their ground as the French mounted knights attacked out of necessity on a narrow front due to woodland and over soaking wet ground. The ensuing rain of arrows from the longbows of Henry's Welsh and English archers wreaked havoc on the French, whose horses with their heavily armoured riders were unable to manoeuvre. A subsequent French attack also fell victim to the carnage leading the French to withdraw the battlefield leaving over 6000 dead, while the English toll numbered fewer than 500. Henry returned to England and a hero's welcome on 23rd November 1415

Henry V was not to achieve his aim of becoming king of France. He died of

---

1 Of Harfleur -

Once more unto the breach, dear friends, once more;
or close the wall up with our English dead.
In peace there's nothing so becomes a man
As modest stillness and humility:
But when the blast of war blows in our ears,
Then imitate the action of the tiger;
Stiffen the sinews, summon up the blood
Disguise fair nature with hard favour'd rage;
...I see you stand like greyhounds in the slips,
Straining upon the start. The game's afoot:
Follow your spirit, and upon this charge
Cry 'God for Harry, England, and Saint George'.

HENRY V, Act 3 Scene 1 William Shakespeare.

2 Another Bagot was destined to do battle here 500 years later.

dysentery in 1422 while campaigning in France at the age of 34 leaving his son, Henry VI to be crowned king of France in 1431 at the age of only 11.

It was Sir John Bagot who acquired the manor of Field, in the parish of Leigh, adding to the growing Bagot family estate.

Sir John died circa 1437 and is said to have been buried at the Augustinian priory in Stafford, which no longer exists.

He was succeeded by his only son, Richard born c.1388 and died c.1475. He was succeeded by his son, also Richard, who was to take part in another of English history's most famous battles.

ANTIQUUM
OBTINENS

The Bagot Coat of Arms with the Bagot goats as depicted in the east window of Blithfield Church. First adopted by Sir John Bagot towards the end of the 14th century, the family motto -Antiquum Obtinens - is "Possessing Antiquity"

RICHARD BAGOT
and
THE BLITHFIELD SALLET

One of the treasures of Blithfield Church is the Blithfield Sallet, a battle helmet dating from the late 15th century. The sallet, mounted on the chancel wall to the left of and above the altar is a replica. The original sallet is on loan to the Lichfield Heritage Centre in Lichfield and can be seen on display there.

It is thought to have belonged to Richard Bagot, born c.1419, who fought alongside Henry Tudor at the battle of Bosworth on 22nd August 1485 when Henry triumphed against Richard III, took his crown to become Henry VII and the first monarch of the Tudor royal house.

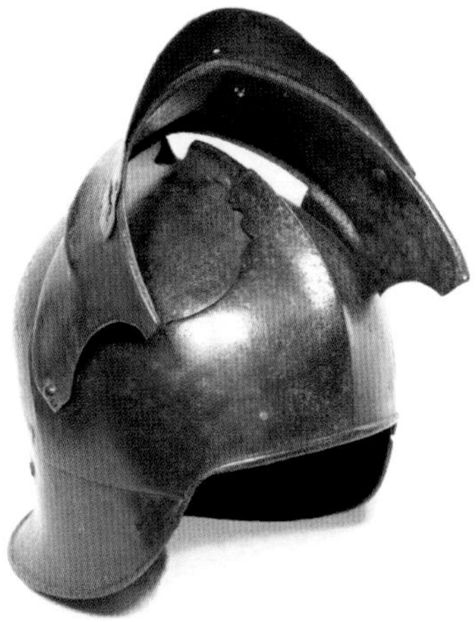

The Blithfield Sallet c .1480 shown with the visor open and one of a group of only four known to exist.

It is on display at the Lichfield Heritage Centre,

The wooden goat's head is not an original part of the helmet, but an addition fitted as a funerary crest in the 16th century, for the funeral of Richard Bagot, great great grandson of the owner in 1596.

Examples of medieval armour, preserved in English churches, comprise the majority of armour from the Middle Ages and have been important in our understanding of armour from this period.

The Blithfield sallet belongs to a group of only three more known to exist. The others are in the Historiches Museum Basle, Switzerland; The Royal Armouries Museum (the Witton-le-Wear sallet) and the Herbert Art Gallery and Museum Coventry (the Coventry sallet)

Although not identical, the Blithfield sallet shares the feature of having a half visor with the Basle and Royal Armoury examples which, unlike non-visored helmets, were popular in England and France.

There was a flourishing export trade in armour during the 15th century

and it is thought the Blithfield sallet was made in Italy to suit the English market c.1470-80, although it could have originated in Bruges where Milanese armourers also had their workshops.
It is not known if the helmet was being worn by Richard Bagot at Bosworth.

The Battle of Bosworth Field received world-wide publicity in 2015 when the remains of King Richard III were finally reburied in Leicester Cathedral 530 years after his death in the battle, at the age of 32.
After being killed, his body disappeared and it's whereabouts had been speculated over ever since. It is known it was unceremoniously slung across the back of a horse after the battle, taken to Leicester, paraded through the city and was thought, by some, to have been thrown in the river there.

In 2012, after what can only be described as a series of inspired hunches, devotees of King Richard found his remains at their first attempt, under a town centre car park which covered the site of a medieval monastery where the frightened monks had hastily buried him. Subsequent painstaking scientific detective work confirmed his identity and Richard III's remains were given a ceremonial funeral on 26th March 2015.

In a bid to take the English crown from Richard [1], (who usurped the throne by confining his nephews, Edward V aged 12 and his brother in the Tower of London and supposedly having them murdered), Henry Tudor landed in England from France and arrived at Stafford in August 1485.
Along the way he had gathered enthusiastic support and arrived in the town with an army of 5,000 men for the Lancastrian cause, and then made his way to Lichfield, where his army camped on 15th August.
It would not be too fanciful to suggest Henry's army marched through Blithfield, where Richard Bagot and his retainers could have joined Henry and their date with destiny at Bosworth on 22nd August.
Interestingly, it is said Lord Stanley and his army camped near Lichfield on 13th August, but retired on the approach of Henry. It was Lord Stanley who crucially, and at at the last minute during the battle, threw his lot in with Henry Tudor and abandoned Richard III and the Yorkist cause to their fate in the final battle of the Wars of the Roses which began in 1460.
Richard III was the last Plantagenet king, and the new Tudor dynasty was to last 117 years.

Richard Bagot died of wounds received in the battle.
Where Richard Bagot was eventually buried is not known. His wife, Isabella, is buried in Blithfield Church under a slab of alabaster in the floor of the chancel. It is her name and date of death only that appears on the brass plate, placed there in 1819 by the second Lord Bagot in order preserve the original inscriptions which by that time had worn away.

1 Richard III was born in 1452 at Fotheringhay Castle, Northamptonshire.

Richard Bagot was succeeded by his son John, thought to have been born c.1440, who was only able to survive his father by five years, dying on 24th June 1490. He is buried between his two wives beneath an alabaster slab in the chancel of Blithfield Church, with a brass plate affixed also by the second Lord Bagot. He was succeeded by his son Lewis.

The Blithfield Sallet with the visor down. The hole in the top of the skull and the plate riveted to the base of the visor were added c.1597 when it was modified into a funerary piece for the funeral of Richard Bagot, great grandson of the owner.
It weighs 6¼ lb and is 8¾" high

the 16th Century

Richard Bagot Esq.

SIR LEWIS BAGOT c.1460 – 1534

Sir Lewis Bagot was the grandson of Richard Bagot who was killed at the Battle of Bosworth in 1485.
He was married five times, his first bride taken when he was only 14 years old in 1475. His child bride was known as 'Mistress Lucy' and it seems she died young for, in around 1480, Sir Lewis married Emma, who is thought to have been Lucy's sister, and she bore him eleven children. Dame Emma died before 1503, for by then Sir Lewis is married to wife number three, Dame Anne, with whom he has eight children. The eldest, Thomas, succeeded his father on the latter's death. Dame Anne died in September 1514.
By 1530 Sir Lewis is married to his fourth wife, Mary Vernon, who must have died very soon after, because, before his death in 1534, he had time to marry wife number five although no children came forth from these last marriages.

Sir Lewis Bagot was Esquire of the Body [1] to King Henry VII and Sheriff of Staffordshire in 1507.
King Henry VIII succeeded to the throne in 1509 and soon after, it appears, Sir Lewis was approached by the king by way of a letter in which the king styles him....

'Our trustie, and well beloved Knight, Sir Lewis Bagot.'
By THE King
H.R.
Trustie and well beloved, we grete you well...for preparing of a competent nombre of hable men, horsed and harnessed, to do unto us service, when the caas shall require...
The king goes on to explain in his letter the manner in which Sir Lewis, and others to whom the king has written, is expected to recruit and retain these *' talle and hable men...whiche of thair good free wills wolbe aggreable to do unto us service, in your company, and at your lendinge'.*

In September 1513, Sir Lewis accompanied the king to do battle with the French of Louis XII. The French were defeated at the 'Battle of the Spurs', so called for the hasty retreat of the French cavalry from the battlefield.

By 1520, an initiative was made to reconcile the English and French and a meeting was arranged near Calais, then an English possession, between Henry and the new French king, François I.

---

1 A formal position in the Royal Household which gave the bearer frequent access to the monarch. Consequently, it was a title of great honour.

The courtiers and nobles with their ladies and retinue, accompanied their respective monarchs and numbered a total of 10,000 people. Sir Lewis Bagot was one of eight knights from Staffordshire, including Sir John Giffard from Chillington, in attendance at the meeting which became known to history as The Field of the Cloth of Gold.

The meeting, in June, lasted six weeks and no expense was spared by either monarch when a field was levelled and an elaborate temporary palace was erected of wood and canvas on brick foundations and made to imitate the real thing. Glass, then an expensive commodity, was used for the many windows and the temporary pavilions, tents, and chapels were adorned with cloth of gold- a fabric sewn with silk and gold thread.[1]

The entourage of both monarchs were dressed in cloth of gold with pearls and precious stones. They wore different and more expensive finery for each day and priceless gifts were exchanged.

Every day, vast banquets consumed huge quantities of food, with cygnets, heron, pike, venison, wren, sturgeon, peacock, egrets and stork included on a lavish menu, all washed down with the best wines France could produce. Temporary gilded fountains poured forth wine for the less distinguished guests and in the tilt yard, the English and French kings jousted against one another.

Despite all the extravagance, no significant improvement in relations was achieved and within three years both countries were again at war.

The following year, Edward Stafford, 3rd Duke of Buckingham – a Bagot ancestor- who played a leading role at the 1520 extravaganza, was executed at the Tower of London for allegedly plotting against Henry VIII.

Sir Lewis was again Sheriff of Staffordshire in 1521.

He died on 31st May 1534 and is buried under the alabaster altar tomb in the chancel at Blithfield and shown between two of his wives, with Mistress Lucy peeping over the shoulder of her husband and with his nineteen children engraved at their parents' feet. It is thought Sir Lewis's altar tomb was carved before his death as their seems to be room left for the additional children expected from Sir Lewis's last two marriages.

It has to be wondered if Henry VIII was rather envious of Sir Lewis's reproductive achievements!

At his death his estate is listed as amounting to: *100 messauges* [2]*, 2000 acres of land, 200 acres of meadow, 1000 acres of pasture, 1000 acres of woodland, 100 acres of furze and heath together with £20 rent in Blythefeyld, Feld, Bromley Baggott, Colton, Neweton, Admaston, Ley, Blythere, Bromley Abbots, Stafford, Heywood and Dunstall.*

1 Gold is beaten and worked into thin strips or into wire and then wound around silk thread. It produces a cloth which is very heavy-and expensive.

2 Messuage-a dwelling house with out-buildings and land assigned to its use.

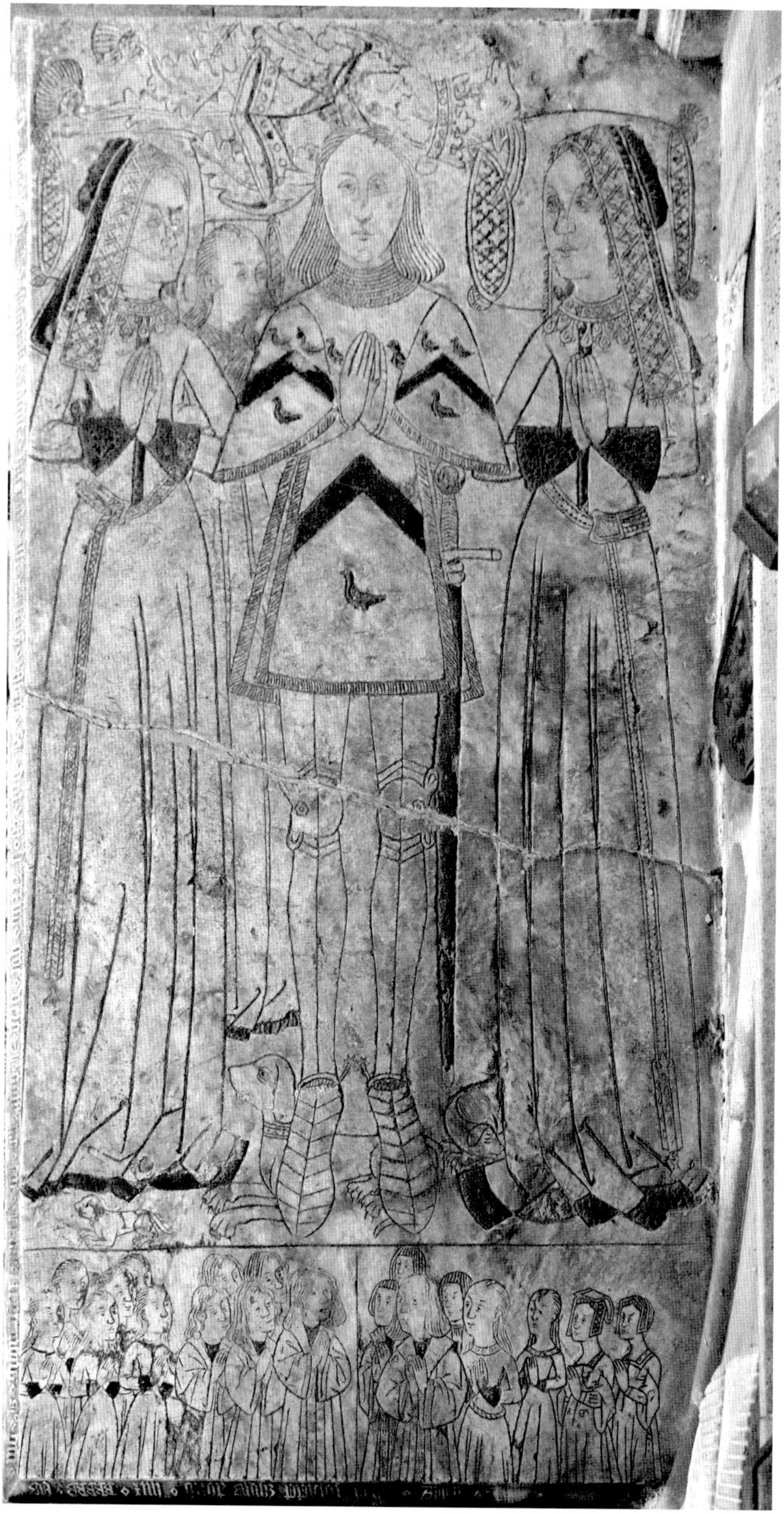

Sir Lewis was succeeded by Thomas, the eldest son of his second wife, of whom very little is known. It is recorded that his brother Edward was implicated in a murder in a dispute over one of Thomas's tenants and, although both men were ordered before council, nothing more is known of the case. Thomas died in 1541 and was succeeded by his son Richard.

The table top altar tomb of Thomas Bagot in Blithfield Church
and
PREVIOUS PAGE
The table top altar tomb of Sir Lewis Bagot in the chancel of Blithfield Church showing Sir Lewis, three of his wives and nineteen children.

RICHARD BAGOT c.1530 – 1597

1584
Richard Bagot Efq.

Richard Bagot and his wife Mary

Richard Bagot lived during the period of English history when the country was in the process of great change and religious turmoil. He was Deputy Lieutenant and Sheriff for the County of Stafford in 1570 and 1578.
He gained the respect and trust of Queen Elizabeth I and was steward of her manors and Woodward [1] in Staffordshire, including that of Lord Paget of Beaudesert [2], near Rugeley, who had his forfeit by the Crown in 1582 due to his alleged plot against the Queen and his Roman Catholic faith.

Earlier in the century, King Henry VIII had divorced his wife and England from the Europe of the Pope and their Roman Catholic view of the Christian religion, in favour of Henry's preferred Protestant view, and he had made himself head of the new Church of England.
England, however, was by no means secure in her new position as the religious faith of the monarch was crucial in determining the country's eventual fate.

---

1 Woodward-Forest keeper

2 Thomas, 3rd Baron Paget. His lands were restored to his son William by James I.

Edward VI had succeeded his father and carried forward his reforms only to die early in his reign. He was succeeded by Mary Tudor who, being a staunch catholic, reversed Edward's reforms with vigour and cruelty.
On dying childless, Mary's half sister Elizabeth ascended the throne in 1559 and again re-introduced her father, Henry VIII's protestant view of the Christian faith. But what to do with Mary Queen of Scots, her cousin, who was a staunch Catholic and had a legitimate claim to the English throne?
Suspicious that Mary was plotting against her, Elizabeth had her imprisoned and Mary is confined and moved to various locations until her treachery is confirmed.
It is here where we pick up Richard Bagot's story.

For over 35 years, he was privy to events in this period of English history which has fascinated historians, and those with only a passing interest in it, for it's drama, intrigue and ultimate tragedy. Some time previously, the Bagot family had nailed their colours of religious allegiance to the mast of Protestantism, and consequently Richard Bagot became very useful to Queen Elizabeth and her counsellors in their quest to further the Protestant cause in England.

Along with many other famous men of the period, Richard Bagot was on very friendly terms with Robert Devereux, second Earl of Essex who, in turn was an intimate at the court of Queen Elizabeth and known as 'the favourite', a position that would eventually lead to the Earl's downfall.
Many letters went to and fro between the Earl and Richard Bagot. The earl's seat in Staffordshire was at Chartley Hall, [1] only a few miles away from Blithfield, and in November 1585 the Queen and her ministers determined to move Mary Queen of Scots from Tubury Castle to Chartley.
The Earl of Essex did not approve of this proposal, as we can read in his letter to Richard Bagot.

(This, and other letters included in this chapter, are transcribed in their original form, which by way of their prose and spelling would have been in a style familiar to Shakespeare).

Mr Bagot - I received newes by John Briton, that Sir Amias Paulet [2] was at Chartley, to prepare for the Sco Q, whereupon I sent with speede to the Court, to some, who moved the Queen for the stay thereof, which she most willingly graunted; and determined that it was not a fit place to keep her in. My Lord

---

1 Built by Robert Devereux's father Walter, to replace the adjacent castle which was abandoned in 1485. During her progress through England in 1575, Elizabeth l visited the hall. It was destroyed by fire in 1781 as was its replacement. The present hall was built in 1847 and is privately owned.

2 Sir Amias Paulet had charge over Mary Queen of Scots during her imprisonment at Chartley and Fotheringhay until her execution there.

Treasurer, My Lord Leycester, and Mr Secretary [1] *assured that this direction should be given to Sir Amias Paulet. What it is, I know not; but to prevent the worst, and because I will have it lesse fit for that use, I would have you and Sir Thomas Newport* [2] *remove all the bedding, hanginges, and such stuff, to your own house, for a wile; and if she come to Chartley, it may be carried to Lichfield, or els (she being gone to Dudley or els wher) it may be carried back.* There appears to be no record of whether the Earl of Essex's wish was acted upon, and his dislike of the proposal had little effect in the councils of Queen Elizabeth.

MARIE
REINE
D'ESCOS
SE

Mary, Queen of Scots as a young woman

In a letter from Sir Amias Paulet to Richard Bagot it is evident that the Scottish Queen was taken from Tutbury to Chartley on 21st December 1585 where she remained until she was taken to Fotheringhay Castle in September 1586.

On 10th September 1586, evidently just before Mary, Queen of Scots

1 William Cecil - Lord Burghley, Queen Elizabeth's closest and most trusted advisor, Sir Robert Dudley, intimate of Queen Elizabeth, and Sir Francis Walsingham, the Queen's spymaster.

2 Sir Thomas Newport is buried at the church of Stowe-by-Chartley.

transfer to Fotheringhay, Sir Amias Paulet wrote to Sir Francis Walsingham from Chartley, concerning relieving the Queen of her money and jewellery and the need to have an independent witness present. In it he writes...*I thought good to my better discharge in these matters, to crave assistance of Mr. Bagot, who repairing unto me, the next morning we had access to this Queen...*(and declared to her that)...*I was expressly commanded to take her money into my hands, and to rest answerable for it...and advising her to deliver the said money unto me with quietness...*After many vehement protestations from the Queen who refused to hand over the key to her cabinet, she only relented when Sir Amias threatened to break it open. In there, the two men found a considerable sum of money in French Crowns, English coinage of gold and silver as well as a large quantity of gold jewellery.[1] They also discovered another large cache of money in the room of her secretary, Nan, and it was all, Sir Amias concludes,...*bestowed in bags, and sealed by Mr Richard Bagot, saving five hundred of Nan's money which I reserve in my hands for the use of this household.* On 25th September 1586 the Scottish Queen arrived at her final place of internment, Fotheringhay Castle in Northamptonshire. [2]

It is almost certain Mary, Queen of Scots passed through Blithfield at the start of her journey, for in those days there was a road (from Chartley), which ran between Stowe-by-Chartley and Drointon to Dapple Heath in Blithfield parish. Heath Lane then joined the existing road to Abbots Bromley. It is known she paused briefly during the journey in Abbots Bromley [3] from where she would have travelled to Burton, and on to her final destination.

There are many other letters to Richard Bagot, and some contain fascinating first hand knowledge concerning events leading to the eventual fate of Mary, Queen of Scots, three of which follow. They are from the Deputy Governor of Fotheringhay, the first being an account of her trial at Fotheringhay in October 1586-

Marmaduke Darell Esq. to Richard Bagot.

---

1 Thought to have been supplied by her French relations, the King of Spain and subsidized by English Catholic gentry.

2 All that remains of Fotheringhay Castle is its mound, its dry moat and haunting atmosphere.

3 An inscription on a pane of glass, formerly in a house in Abbots Bromley, is said have been written by the Queen to mark the occasion during a time she was supposed to have stayed there. The inscription is not by her but the inscribed date of 21st September coincides with her journey to Fotheringhay. The glass is now displayed in the William Salt Library in Stafford. It reads- translated from the Latin - 'Mary Queen of Scots once stayed at this house, 21 September 1586, on the way to Burton'.

Sir, - Understanding that this bearer is to passe by Blithefielde, in his way from hence homeward; and this place havinge yelded of late suche newes, as may well some worthie of reportinge, I have thought good to signifie thus much to you, brieflie of them. Uppon Wensdai laste, did this honorable assemblie here underwritten, mete together in this castle, as commissioners appointed by her Majesty our Sovraigne, to inquire by all due meanes and proofe, whither this Sco: Queene hath, since the end of the laste Parliament,... attempted, compassed, or imagined any thinge tendinge to the hurte of our Queene's person. - After the end of a sermon made in this Castle to them all, uppon the said Wensdai morning, by tthe Dean of Peterborough; theise Lord Commissioners bestowed the residue of that daye, and the next beinge Thursdaie, in private counselle and consultation, amonge themselves; seeking in that time, by all meanes they coulde, to persuade this Queene to come out into the chamber of state, (where they sit openly and judicially,) and she to sitt before them, to here the proofs to be produced against her; wherein they did assure her, that as the Q's Majesty, our Mistris, had not receaved anythinge, that had happened unto her these many yeres, with greater griefe, than to here now that she should be a procurer of Her deathe;- so woulde nothinge be more joyfull, and acceptable to her, than to heare that reporte to be untrue, and that she had clered herselfe of yt. Which speeche uttered unto her, I thinke by Mr Vice Chamberlayne, prevailed so much with her, as upon condition, that her protestacion (which was that this cominge out to them should not be prejudiciall to the Soveraigntie, and title of her son [1] and others that are to be her successors,) may be accepted and recorded: she would come out to them, the nexte morninge, being Fridaie, which was by their Ho^rs^ after they had considered of it, yelded unto...

The letter goes on to recall the Queen facing her accusers on 11th October 1586 in the great hall at Fotheringhay when her alleged association with the Babington Plot is included. Anthony Babington, along with co-conspirators, were proved to be plotting to kill Queen Elizabeth and rescue Mary from imprisonment at Chartley while a foreign force invaded the country. Babington and his associates were gruesomely executed on 20th September 1586.

Deputy Governor Darell continues -
... And thereupon accordingely, upon ffridaie morning, they being all sett judicially in there places, she came forthe to them, to a chayre placed for her, in the upper ende of the chamber; at which tyme beganne the Queene's learned councell in the lawe, (after the Lord Chancellor's oration had ended,

---

1 James VI of Scotland.

and the reading of the commission,) to do their partes, in layinge open divers bad practises, and plotts, tendinge to the subversion of the whole state; which by the confession of divers and her own letters, which had bene intercepted, did manifestly appere to have been contrived by Her and her Ministers. But the chiefest matter, to bringe her within compasse of the aforesaid statute made the last Parliament, was that she had bothe receaved a letter from Babington touching this late conspired treason, and that she had also, by her answere, animated and incouraged him in it. The proofe whereof was, bothe Babington's confession alledged, and also the Coppies of bothe the said letters shewed, with Nawes and Curles [1] hands to them, avouching them upon their othes to be true; all which notwithstandinge she still stode to her denyall. - In the producinge of their proofes, and answeringe of them, was all ffridaie bestowed, and all the afternoon uppon Satterdai; by which tyme yt seemeth all things bothe againste her, and on her parte had bene handled so at large, as that there remayned no more to be done or sayd in yt at his metinge;- and so first, the Queene and then they, rose and departed; they going from hence after dyner, to their severall lodginge; and the nexte daye, being Sondaie, most of them retourned towards the Corte, where it is said, they have appointed to mete all uppon Sondaie next.- Thus I have brieflie, thoughe rudelye, set downe unto you the substaunce and effecte, of as much as my slender capacitie, and bad memorie would suffer me to carrie awaie; not doubtinge, but you will accept it in good parte, as from one that is your playne, and unfayned frende.
Fotheringhay, 17th Oct. 1586 *M. Darell*

The majority of the written evidence, which secured Mary Queen of Scots fate, was obtained from coded letters written to and from her whilst at Chartley. Sir Francis Walsingham had secured the services of a master forger, cryptanalyst and ex Cambridge University graduate, Thomas Philips. Some time earlier, Walsingham had detained Gilbert Giffard immediately on his return from France, after intercepting his letters [2] to his family, which indicated he was in straightened circumstances due to his being banished to France by his family after an indiscretion with a young lady. Sir Francis seized on this and recruited young Gilbert as his agent and promised handsome payments for his services. As a catholic and member of the prominent Giffard Catholic family from Chillington Hall near Wolverhampton, he proved to be invaluable in Walsingham's efforts to incriminate the Queen in her quest to overthrow her cousin. Giffard had already gained the trust of a loyal and close confidante of the Scottish queen who, in turn, was willing to accept Giffard as someone she could rely

1 Claude Nau and Gilbert Curll, Mary, Queen of Scots secretaries.
2 This was standard practice by Sir Francis against all ex patriot Roman Catholics.

on. Subsequently, Gilbert Giffard visited the Queen at Chartley and set about suggesting to her a method by which she could secretly receive and send correspondence to her outside supporters. The plan, hatched by Walsingham and Philips, involved concealing the letters in a sealed compartment of a barrel of beer delivered weekly to Chartley from Burton-upon-Trent by a brewer, and Catholic, who was also in the pay of the spymaster.

Any letters written to the Queen were handed to the trusted Giffard, who then handed them to Philips to be read and deciphered. They were then secreted inside the barrel of beer and delivered to Chartley Hall where they were passed on to the unsuspecting queen. The process was repeated with her letters to her supporters. All the information they contained was passed on to Walsingham providing all the evidence he required to bring the Queen to her trial and eventual conviction.

Mary, Queen of Scots was found guilty of treason on 14th October 1586 and sentenced to death. She was beheaded in the great hall at Fotheringhay on 8th February 1587 before three hundred onlookers and protested her innocence to the end. She was aged 44.

Deputy Governor Darell writes again to Richard Bagot after the event – in the letter, he hints at the unease he felt in his role:

Sir,- I thanke you, for your curteous letter; as I doe also for sundry other your good frendshippes towards me, for which you shall comande me whyle I live.

I doubt not, but you have longe since hearde, how resolutely,- and in shewe, quietly,- she went to Her deathe, who in her lyfe time, has bene the author of so many troubles; wherein her magnanimitie, and other good gifts, meete for soe great a callinge, no doubt did make us all, that were beholdinge, to pittie her want of grace to use them:- In other points, she shewed herselfe very obstinate, and farre from that, which true religion dothe require at our handes, at suche a tyme, - She hathe nowe ended her last tragicall parte; which by reporte, many doe threaten to revenge;- I beseche God (by the continuaunce of our monstrous sinnes, and wante of repentaunce) we procure not his wrathe against us; and then I hope we shall withstande still, as hitherto, their malyce, well ynough. Sir Amyce, our honourable Governour, (and one to whome for myne own parte, I am very muche bounde,) intendethe God willinge, to returne to London, with his whole famylie uppon Monday nexte. After whose departure, I am comaunded to staye here, with the householde that shall remayne; consistinge most of the Sco: Queene's servaunts, that are now all come together;- the cawse of this there stay, wee thinke to be, because yt is not fully agreed uppon, where the dead body shalbe buried; neather willbe untill the retourne of Mr Carye, out of Scotlande; and untill the funerall be ended, as you knowe, this household cannot be dissolved.- Wee all hope it will be shortlie; for I thinke there is not any of us, that hathe not longe wished to be well freed from this kinde of prisoners lyfe.

Fotheringhay Castle, 25th Feb: 1586-7. *Mar: Darell*

Unfortunately for Marmaduke Darell and his colleagues, it was not for some more months until they received news that the funeral had been arranged and they could see an end to their unhappy predicament, as he writes again to Richard Bagot:

Sir,- Since wrytinge of my former letter, dated also this present daie, I have receaved a full direction from councell, to provide for the byryall of the Sco: Queene; wherewith I am willinge to acquante you as with all and the best newes that this place canne yelde.

The daye is appointed to be the first of August; the place Peterborough, in the Cathedrall Church there.[1] *The manner with greate state and solempnitye. The companye that are to attend yt, very great, and many of them Honorable. As two Earls; three Countesses; five Barons, five Barons wyves; tenne Knights, tenne Knights wyves; twelve Esquires; two Bishopps;. one Dean; thirtie Gentlewomen, to attend the said ladies; three score Gentlemen, to attend the said Noblemen; and two hundred Yeomen, besides the Scottish trayne here, her servaunts. So I am directed to provide for the diett of 300 persons or thereabouts; to have there at Peterborough, twoo meales, at her Majesties chardge.*

Thus have you brieflie, that which came to me, not above an hour sithence; and so beinge nowe withdrawn from this, to more serious cawses, I comende you once again, &c. &c.

Fo: Castle, Sondaie Night, 9th July, 1587. *Mar: Darell.*

The body of the Scottish Queen had lain unburied from her execution until her burial on 1st August.

For her part, Queen Elizabeth put on a great show of grief over her cousin's death and blamed all but herself for it, even though it was she who signed the death warrant. Her fury rested on her secretary, William Davison, who drew up the warrant and he was subsequently thrown in to prison.

It was not long however, according to a letter by Richard Bagot's son, Anthony to his father, before the Queen's thoughts were being directed

1 King James I, Mary's son, had his mother's body moved and reburied in Westminster Abbey in 1612. Her tomb is said to be slightly larger than that of her cousin Queen Elizabeth.

toward her new 'favourite' Robert Deveraux, Earl of Essex who had eclipsed his predecessor Robert Dudley, Earl of Leicester in the role.

Although the Scottish Queen was not destined to rule England, a Scottish King was. On the death of Queen Elizabeth, James VI of Scotland became also, James I of England. He was the son of the ill fated Queen Mary and his succession is said to have had the approval of Elizabeth before she died.

Of the two sons who survived him, Richard Bagot's second son, Anthony, born c.1558, was a close attendant to the Earl of Essex both at home and abroad and as such provides through correspondence with his father, an interesting insight into their mutual acquaintance.

It was Anthony Bagot who penned the famous words (often referred to by historians when trying to ascertain the exact relationship between the Earl of Essex and Queen Elizabeth), in a letter to his father in May 1587. She was 34 years his senior!

... *when She is abroade,- no boddy near her but my Lord of Essex; and at night my Lord is at cards, or one game or another with her,- that he cometh not to his own lodginge tyll birds singe in the morninge.*

It would appear from various letters to Richard Bagot that it was intended for his son to study law or classics in London but circumstances dictated this was not to be.

In a letter dated February 1578 to Richard Bagot, Richard Broughton[1], his son-in-law, relates Anthony Bagot's attendance at the court of the Queen when she was entertaining a certain Duke Cassimir where the Earl of Essex was also present.

He writes:

... *My Lord of Essex, after these shewes are ended, goeth to Cambridge; upon whose going, my brother Anthony (his brother-in-law) stayeth, and in the mean tyme seeth a little of the Cort fassions...*

Subsequently, it is evident that young Anthony began to prefer the prospect of *'the cort fassions'*, for just two days after Richard Broughton's letter, Anthony Bagot writes to his father:

---

[1] Married Anne, Richard Bagot's second daughter, became a Barrister and Welsh Judge and was styled 'The Chief Antiquary of England'. Their infant son, Walter, has his remains buried under a small alabaster slab in the floor of the chancel of Blithfield Church. The inscription is now very worn, although a previous investigator maintains it depicts a figure of Death carrying off a child, with the inscription, "Here lieth Walter the eldest sonn of Richard Broughton Esquier who was borne ye 24 of Aprill 1586 and dyed ye 3 of july folowing, Streight after Birth due is the fatall beere. By death's Sufferance the aged lynger here."

Queen Elizabeth I and the 'Favourite' Robert Deveraux, 2nd Earl of Essex, who's country seat was at Chartley Hall in Blithfield's neighbouring parish.

Here lieth Walter the Eldest son of
Richard Broughton Esquire who
was borne ye 24 of Aprill 1586
& died ye 3 of July following
Strieght after birth one is the
fatall heere by deaths Sufferance
the aged linger here

A 19th century image of the small 16th century alabaster tomb of Walter Broughton. It is in the chancel floor at Blithfield and shows the figure of Death carrying off a child, but is now extremely worn.

As my duty constrayneth me, I am to let you understand, as neare as I can, when my Lord meayneth to take his journey to Cambridge... The cause of his tarryinge so longe at the Cort was to see the cominge of one Cassamyre, a ffreanche Imbassator; whome the Queenes grace doth greatly esteem;- for this February, there was such a shewe of noble men and gentlemen in the Tylt Yard at Whitehall, as the lyke (by every man's report) hathe not beene seene this forty yeares...

A letter from his father to Anthony, no doubt expressing concern at his son's pre-occupation with his new interest over his studies, stimulated this reply:

Right worshipful and good Father. I receaved your letters, wherein I easily perceave and gather the ffartherly, and daylye care you have uppon me, for the applyinge of my studye, and thememploying of myselfe, to please my tutor; which bothe heatherto I trust I have done; and (by the grace of God,) hereafter,(as you shall perceave,) I meane to do.- Also at convenyent times, according to your pleasure, I weate upon my Lord; (Essex) *that is almost every day, eyther at, after dynner, or els after supper; and upon holly dayes, all the daye longe, which lykethe his Lordship very well. I am almost every other daye, either at dinner or supper, with his honor, for he will not suffer me to depart from him untill neene of the clocke.*

Soon after this Anthony Bagot deserts his studies to become closely associated with one of the celebrities of the age.

That the Earl of Essex began to live a life of extravagance beyond his means, which was to continue for the rest of his life, there is no doubt, for he always seems to be in need for money to pay for his expensive lifestyle and in one case, to raise a regiment for foreign service.

This is of some concern to his grandfather, Sir Francis Knollys [1], who, from a letter found in the possession of Richard Bagot, wrote to his grandson as follows:

My Lord, If I should not love you, I should be unnatural; agayne if I should

---

1 Sir Francis Knollys -pronounced Knowles - took early charge of Mary Queen of Scots during her confinement at Tutbury Castle and became Treasurer of the Royal Household in 1572. He was also a Privy Counsellor and Vice Chamberlain to Elizabeth l. His daughter, Lettice married first, Walter Deveraux 1st Earl of Essex and then Robert Dudley, Earl of Leicester, up until then the Queen's favourite. The Earl immediately fell out of favour with the Queen when she learned of his secret marriage to her cousin. She never forgave Lettice, and the rift between The Earl and the Queen led to Robert Deveraux, 2nd Earl of Essex (Lettice's son) becoming her new favourite. Knollys's letter could have been squirelled away by Anthony Bagot to remind him of the excellent advice it gives.

flatter youthful humors in you, I should be guylty of the ruynous race of your undoynge; wherefore you must give me leave to say unto you, that wastfull prodlgalitye hath devoured, and will consume all noble men, that be willfull in expenses, before they have of theayre own, ordynary lyvinge, to beare out such wyllfull and wastfull expences.... You are so farr off from being before hand in land and lyvinge, left by your father to you; that by unhappye occasyons, your father hath not leaft you suffycyent lands for to mayntayne the state of the poorest Earle in Yngland; and you are so farre from goods and ryches, left unto you by your father, that you are left more in debt, than one Qr. of your land, to be sould by you is hable to discharge your debt. Now for you to put yourself to one £M: [1] *charges, (as I hear you have done, by borowinge...) vaynely before hand, for your journey into the Lowe Countryes by levyinge and carryinge with you a furnished band of men, needlesse and causelesse;... which band of men, allso do looke to be recompenced with the spoyl of your leaces and lyvinges:.. I do lyke very well your desyre to see the warres, for your learninge; and do lyke your desyre much the better, that you do take the oportunyty of honoringe my Lord of Leycester with your service under hym... But, this might have been done without any wastfull chardge to yoursealf; for my Lord of Leycester dothe set much by your company; but he delyghteth nothinge in your wastfull consumption. I doe say no more, but I beseeche our Almighty God, so to assyst you with his heavenly grace, that youthfull wyllfullness and wastful youth do not consume you, before experyenced wysdome shall have reformed you.*

Your Lordship's assuredly
F. Knollys

At Rychmond, 14th Nov.1585.

As will be seen, the Earl does not heed his grandfather's warning although in 1592, for a short time, he seemed keen to mend his ways as Anthony Bagot indicates in a letter to his father:

Mr Merrick is rydd in to the contry about my Lord hys Parkes, that are graunted hym by Her Majesty, to make some money, for my Lord is very desyrous to take order hys debts; and now synce Shrove Sondaye, at 4 of the clock, (about which hour he was sworne a Privy Councellor,) his Lordship is become a new man, cleane forsakinge all hys former youthfull tricks, carriinge hymsealf with honorable gravyty, and singularly lyked boath in Parliament and at counsaille table, both for his speeches and judgement.

With the English Reformation by now being consolidated by Queen Elizabeth, another task assigned to Richard Bagot was seeking out recusants - those Roman Catholics who refused to attend Anglican church

1 £1000.

services. They included high ranking families in Staffordshire, among them the Wolseley's of Colwich, Giffard's of Chillington and Fitzherbert's of Swynnerton. Fines were imposed on those breaking the recusancy laws and close confinement was reserved for those who were perceived to be particularly troublesome. Additionally, the threat of invasion by Catholic Spain when they launched their 'Armada' in 1588, raised tension in England. As a precaution against powerful Catholic families taking advantage of a successful invasion by the Spanish and taking up arms with them against the Queen, she sought assistance from Richard Bagot to ensure suspect Catholic families in Staffordshire were denied their armour and weapons.

Richard Bagot was however asked in a letter from one of Sir Francis Walsingham's agents, the forger and cryptanalyst Thomas Philips, to show particular favour, in accordance with the Queen's wishes, to ' *a highly favored recusant*', Mr Giffard, whose son (Gilbert) [1] had given valuable information during the Babington conspiracy- *a thing,* Philips observes, *never to be forgotten.* Richard Bagot was instructed to show himself as Mr Giffard's friend and speak highly of him to others. *Though*, the letter states, *the secrets and particularities be, for good reasons, to remaine between ourselves.*

It is clear that Richard Bagot was very highly regarded and Queen Elizabeth's confidence in him was such that she and her ministers relied on him for all kinds of favours by way of advice, provisions and money.

Of the latter, in his 'Memorials of the Bagot Family' dated 1823, William 2nd Lord Bagot writes that Richard Bagot '*...seems to have been a considerable sufferer, for I find many years after applications made to the Queen's ministers by him and his son for repayment of money so lent, but apparently with little or no success* '.[2]

As well as his duties to his Queen and counsel, Richard Bagot was well read in the antiquities of his family and county. Consequently, he was well aware and knowledgeable of his ancient lineage particularly of that relation to the earls of Stafford which dated back to the 12th century when Hervey Bagot married Millicent de-Stafford.

At some time, Richard Bagot must have publicised this fact, for in 1589 he received an irate and insolent letter from his neighbour at Stafford Castle, Edward, Lord Stafford, grandson of the last Duke of Buckingham.

For a reason only known to himself, he denounces Richard Bagot's superior

---

1 Gilbert Giffard died in a Paris prison in 1590 after being tracked down and arrested by sympathizers of Mary, Queen of Scots.

2 The Queen was notoriously frugal. It was the case that even Sir Francis Walsingham found the need to fund most of his spying activities on behalf of the Queen out of his own money. He died penniless in 1590.

knowledge on the subject in no uncertain terms as follows-

Like as the High Shreef of this Shyre latley told me, that you pretend my name to be Bagot, and not Stafford, which untrew speeches you have said unto dyvers others, although som dronken ignorant Herawld [1] by you corrupted, therein hathe soothed your lying. I do therfor answer you, that I do better know the decendants and matches of my own lyneage than any creature can informe me; for in all records, pedigrees and armes, from the first Lord Stafford that was pocessed of this castle, afore the Conquest, bearinge the verie same coate I now do... - I can not fynd that any Stafford hath married with a Bagot, or they with him. I have faire recorde to prove that the Lords of my hows were never without heirs males to succeede one after another, and therefore your pretens in alledgeinge that Bagot maried an ancestor's wief of mine, (as peradventure she married her servant), yet will I prove that neither she, nor no wydow of my hows did take a second husband, before they were grandmothers by the children of their first husband; and therefore the lady of my hows was too old to have issue by yours.- Beside this, we have been nyne discents Barons, and Earles of Stafford, before any Bagot was known in this Shire; for Busse, Bagot, and Green, were but rayned by King Richard II. And so to prove that you were no better than vassals to my hows, MY STAFFORD KNOT remayneth still in your parlour; as a hundred of my poor tennants have, in sundry Shires of England, and have ever held your lands of my hows, untill thateynder of the Duke, my grandfather. Surely I will not exchange my name of Stafford, for the name of " A BAGGE OF OATES," for that is your name- "BAG-OTE." - Therefore you do me great wrong in this surmyse, as you did with your writing to the Preevy Counseile, to have countenanced that shame-fast Higons to charge me with treason,- whereof God and my trawthe delyvered me.

Your neighbore I must be,
Edward Stafford.

It would seem that the Earl had reason to believe that Richard Bagot had encouraged this *shamefast* Ralph Higgons (' *late of the Town of Stafford* ') in his accusation of treason against him which was not the case. Being a Magistrate, Richard Bagot would have done no more than receive the dispositions of the case to be heard before the Privy Council.

By way of reply, Richard Bagot answers his Lordship as follows-

Richard Bagot, Esq. in Answer to Lord Stafford.

1 Herawld - herald.

Right Honorable,- I perceave by your letters delivered to me, by your Chaplen, Mr Cope, on Monday last, your Lordship is greatly discontented with some, my speeches used to Mr Stanford, in pretending your honor's surname to be Bagot. I do confesse, I spake them;- not offending your Lordship with troth,- I do avowe it.
Not upon any- 'Dronken Herehaught's[1] *report, by me corrupted, to soothe my lieing',- but by good records and evidence, under ancient seales, the four hundred years past. And if it may please you, to send sufficient man, as Mr Sheriff, or Mr Samson Eardswick, Gentillmen, of good knowledge and experience in these ac'cons;- I will shewe them sufficient matter to confirme that I have spoken; being very sorry to heare your Lordship to contemne, and deface the Name of Bagot, with so bad tirmes, and hastie speeches, as you do; more dishonorable to yourself than any blemishe or reproche to me; And if your Lordshipe take it in such disdaine, that I touche you ether in credit, or honor; you may (if you please,) by ordinary proces, bring me before the Right Honorable the Erle Marshall of England, Chief Judge in these causes; when I will prove it- or take the discredyt, with such further punishment, as his Honor shall inflict upon me.*

Thus humbly desiring acceptance of this my answer, in good part, till a further triall be had herein, I do comyt your Lordship to the protection of Allmighty, this first of March, 1589.

Your Lordship's, at camandment
If you please,
Richard Bagot.

Seemingly, the Earl of Stafford acted in a fit of pique in writing to Richard Bagot in the way he did. However it was strange as the earl was in possession of all his family's records and deeds and would have been aware of the truth, for apparently the name of Hervey Bagot has been blotted out in the Stafford manuscripts where it occurs, it is presumed by the earl himself, and at this time.
Additionally, he would well remember his family name suffered during the reign of Henry VIII when his grandfather, Edward 3rd Duke of Buckingham, was tried and convicted of treason (in all probability, unjustly). He suffered the ultimate penalty and all his lands forfeit by the Crown resulting in the family losing most of its wealth and privileges. It suffered again when the earl's brother was executed for treason during the reign of Mary Tudor. It could well be this accusation of treason against him and his family's reduced circumstances touched a raw nerve.
That the Dukedom of Buckingham was ill-fated there is no doubt, for

[1] Herehaught- herald.

during the 136 years from 1383 to 1521 which spanned five generations of the family, either the duke or his eldest son met with a violent death.

Richard Bagot died on 2nd February 1596 and is buried, with his wife, in St Leonard's Church at Blithfield. Their tomb, in the chancel, has Richard in gilt armour next to his wife, Mary. The sallet with the goats head funerary crest above the tomb was carried on his coffin during the funeral procession on the day of his burial. Although it is thought the sallet originally belonged to Richard Bagot's grandson, who was slain at the Battle of Bosworth, it could equally have been provided by the undertaker for the funeral, or for that matter, could have originally belonged to the armour Richard Bagot had cause to confiscate from one the local Roman Catholic families [1].

Considering Richard Bagot's many connections, it can be only guessed at the luminaries of the period who may have been contained within the walls of the Church on that occasion.

He was succeeded by his eldest son, Walter.

---

1 There was armour remaining in Blithfield Hall in the 18th century. William, Second Lord Bagot recalled in the early 19th century that walls of the old Hall were ' hung around with twelve complete suits of armour (parts of which as a boy I remember having seen) '

Along with the Bagot family, the Giffard family of Chillington Hall near Wolverhampton can boast a long family history, and today can joke along with the present occupier of Blithfield Hall as to when they can expect the return of their armour!

The tomb of Richard Bagot and his wife, Mary in the chancel of Blithfield Church.

Above it is the replica Blithfield Sallet with the goats head funerary crest which was carried on the coffin of Richard Bagot at his funeral in Blithfield Church in 1596.

BLITHFIELD CHURCH DURING THE REFORMATION

The 16th century was a turbulent time for the English church.

Henry VIII 's split with the Roman Catholic church and the Pope over his marriage difficulties saw him start to reform the English church to the new Protestant doctrine. This was continued by his son and heir, Edward VI, who succeeded the throne in 1547.

In November 1552, the reforms were carried forward by the archbishop of Canterbury, Thomas Cranmer who produced a new official Prayer Book, the second one since the break with Rome and one which firmly set England on the path to Protestantism. It abolished the Mass in favour of a Communion service. This service was to be celebrated by priests using *' neither alb, vestment nor cope but...a surplice only '*.

The consequences of this order in the Prayer Book gave rise to some who thought to take advantage and take valuable and beautiful items from our churches, for their own use, or to sell.

Edward VI and his Council knew of this, so, for the second time in 500 years, the king sent his commissioners out to English parishes to check the inventories of churches in order to see what items they could appropriate for government finances. Vast sums had been already had from Henry VIII's plunder of England's monasteries 20 years earlier.

In May 1556, they came to Blithfield Church and the return for the parish states:

*' Blithfield. Fyrste on(*e*) chales of silver, with a patent* (paten); *three grett bells*

in the steeple, a sancte (sanctus) *bell; it ^m ii handbells, on cope, on vestment with a shutte* (suit- i.e. stole) *thereto; it ^m ii towelles, on surple* (surplice) *for the Curate, on corporas, ii table clothes, ii cruetts; it ^m on littell bell in Newton Chapell.*[1]

' Mem.- Richard Forsett surveyor, receved of Humffrey Cotton gentilman xxi ^s wh remaaynd as a stoke (a stock or capital sum) *to finde tapers in the churche.'*

The church goods were handed over *' for safe custody ' to Andreue Walker and Thos. Walker, the churchwardens of Blithfield and Newton '*

What, if any items from Blithfield Church were removed before the commissioners visit is, of course, not known. Those in charge only produced what they thought they could not avoid. Some treasures remained concealed from the king's men and some were possibly already in private hands.

---

1 This bell, at some point in time, disappeared, as did the chapel.

In reply to an order by the Kings Council in May 1552 a return was made on 6th September that year as follows:-
Blyfeld Church. The chwds and 4 honest men of the same parish say upon their oathes that there is 5 kyne (kine)[1] *in the hands of Hum. Cotton of Bold, Esq., which did of late belong to the service of the Lady Priest there'* (probably the Chapel of Our Lady at Admaston).
A similar return was made by John Bray, Knt., Lord Bray:-
5 kyne in the hands of Hum. Cotton of Bold Esq., belonging to Our Lady's service in Blyfeld Church.'

It would have been around this time that any painted decoration or other fine embellishments in the Church would have been removed in order to comply with the simpler and less ostentatious form of worship bought about by church reforms. There is very faint evidence of this on one of the carved heads in the nave where red colouring can be seen on its lips. This carving most probably represents a parishioner. The decoration on the tomb of Richard de Blithfield has already been mentioned.

A parishioner immortalised in stone in Blithfield Church?

One thing we do know for certain, is that the three great bells in Blithfield Church are still in the 'steeple'.
These bells date from the late 15th century and are some of the oldest in Staffordshire, with one being inscribed "Ave Maria" and another "Katrinee"

The tenor bell shows several inscriptions, one being the fylfot cross or swastika. The image of this symbol has been tarnished since its adoption by the Nazi Party of Germany in the 1920's, however it is a very ancient one and can be found on all continents.
Swastika, a word derived from the Sanskrit language, means 'well being' and over thousands of years it has been used by many cultures and religions including the Buddhist and Hindu faiths, Norse and Celtic Paganism as well as in English heraldry. It is used extensively as a decorative symbol in Buddhist art and manuscripts and with its arms in clockwise form symbolizes the sun and positive energy.
The example cast into the tenor bell is the Norse version, with its arms in anti-clockwise fashion, and in the Baltic regions it is known as the 'thunder cross. It is sometimes called "Thor's hammer".

1 Kine – an archaic term and plural for cow.

The fylfot or swastika on the tenor bell in Blithfield Church

Centuries ago, church bells were rung in order to quell violent storms and this fylfot was cast into bells as a charm against thunder. No bells, save those cast during the latter part of the 15th and early 16th centuries have it.[1] It has been suggested that this bell came from Burton Abbey which was dissolved under Henry VIII in 1539. It was originally cast by Thomas Bett of Leicester.

The 'Ave Maria' inscribed bell betrays its pre – Reformation origins in that it would have been rung for the Roman Catholic 'Angelus', a set of special devotional prayers which were recited at certain hours, the primary function of church bells being of course, to call the faithful to worship.

The other two bells were cast by the Seliok family of Nottingham who may have operated their business by travelling the country in order to fulfil their commissions. These were the so called itinerant bell founders who would set up their foundry near to the church, or in one recorded instance, in the church itself! Materials not available locally for their task would have been collected along the way.

This procedure would have had the advantage of eliminating the need to transport the finished bell long distances over the atrocious roads of the period and churchwardens would be able to keep an eye on the progress of their order.

The bell founder would have made sure he could make best use of his foundry by obtaining as many orders as possible from the surrounding area before embarking on his journey, and any family travelling with him would have been accommodated at the expense of the parish.

These travelling bell founders did not rely wholly on producing bells. They would supplement this during lean times by producing guns and metal

1 Bells with this fylfot are found only in Derbyshire, Lincolnshire, Yorkshire and Staffordshire. The only other example in Staffordshire being at Ellastone. Could they have been cast by the same itinerant bell founder?

ware and would advertise this by way of suitable markings on their bells.

Although it does not relate to the founding of a bell, there is an interesting account in the Blithfield Church records which details the procedure which was followed when the bells were being re-hung in 1635:-

Februarie ye 15th. 1635

It is this day agreed upon betwixt Edward ffoster and Tymothie Baylie, churchwardens, of Blythefeild on the one part, and George Smythe and Roger Collier on the other part, that the said George Smythe and Roger Collier doth undertake to hang three bells in the Church of Blythefeild as followeth:

First they are to make the frame suffitient whatsoever shall be wantinge, soe that wee are to find them tymber needful thereto. Item they are to make three new wheeles, three yokes, and all other worke whatsoever shall be needful to make them in everie respect suffitient, both for wooden worke and stone, that belongeth either to the Bells the wheels yokes bell-ropes or other, except the brasses and ropes, which are to made good at our charge. For which wee are to paye to them four pounds in money, and they are to have all the wood and stone that now is used or belonging to the bells, £1 6s 8d whereof they are presentlie to receive, 13s 4d when they are finished, £2. a fortnight after being proved suffitientlie performed. They are to finish them before the 25th March next comeinge; wee are to fetch at our charge, the wheeles and other work belonging to them at Stoe. In witness hereof the parties belowe written have put their hands the day above written.

In the presents of

Jon. Beardmore	*Edward ffoster*	} *Churchwardens*
Thomas Walker	*Tymothie Bayalie*	
W	T	
his marke	his marke	
Thomas Lees	George Smythe	
J.B	Roger Collyer	
John Breadburie	R	
his marke	his marke	

A member of the Australian branch of the Bagot family, Hervey Bagot, is owner of Bagot Bell. Established in 1977 it is the oldest established bell business in that country.

the 17th Century

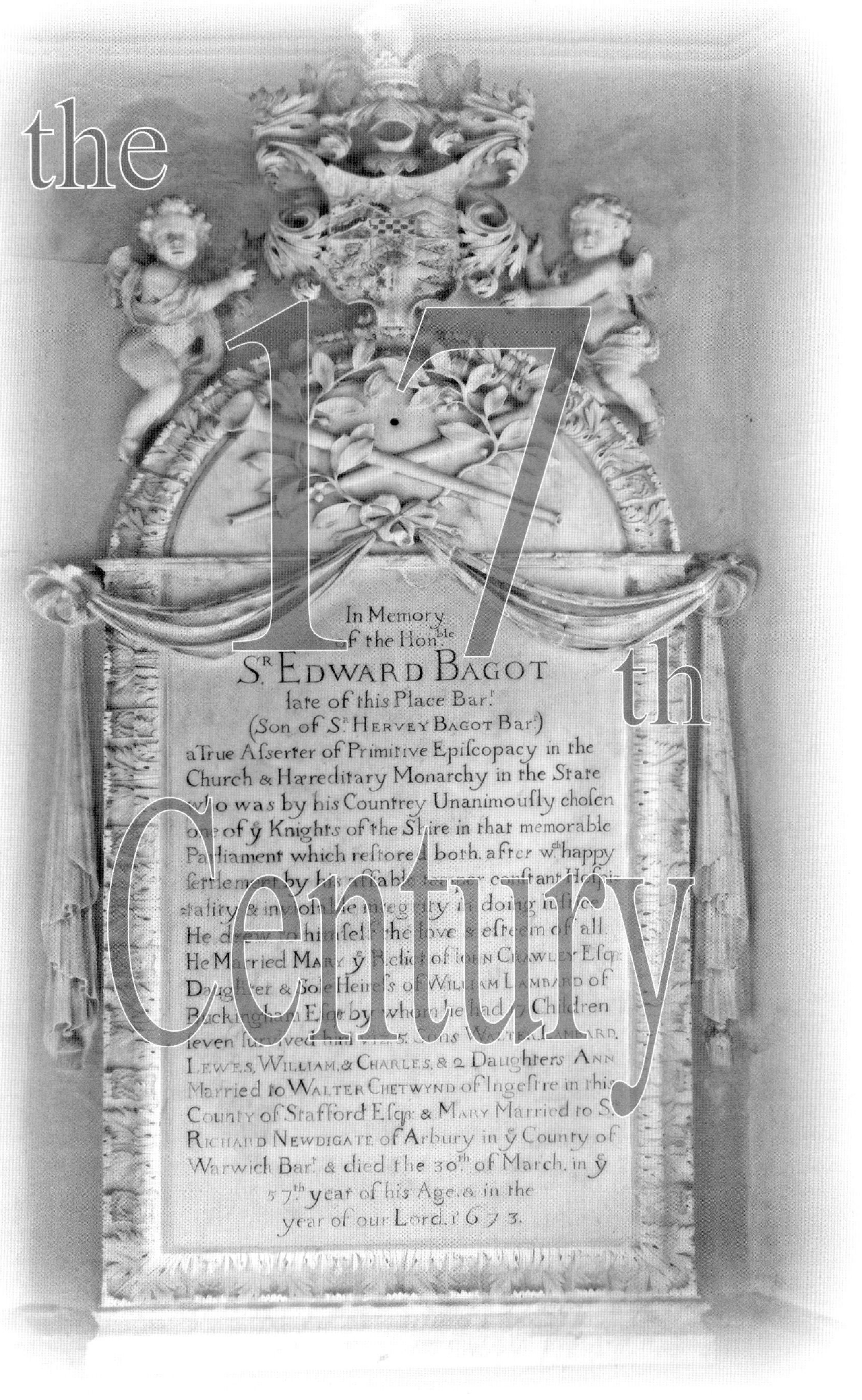
In Memory
of the Hon.ble
S.R EDWARD BAGOT
late of this Place Bar.t
(Son of S.r HERVEY BAGOT Bar.t)
a True Asserter of Primitive Episcopacy in the
Church & Hæreditary Monarchy in the State
LEWES, WILLIAM, & CHARLES, & 2 Daughters ANN
Married to WALTER CHETWYND of Ingestre in this
County of Stafford Esq.r & MARY Married to S.r
RICHARD NEWDIGATE of Arbury in ye County of
Warwick Bar.t & died the 30.th of March, in ye
57.th year of his Age, & in the
year of our Lord, 1673.

WALTER BAGOT 1557 – 1622

Walter Bagot and his wife, Elizabeth. She was niece of Lord Burleigh, Queen Elizabeth I 's closest advisor.

Walter Bagot became Sheriff of Staffordshire in 1600 and 1604 and married Elizabeth Cave, niece of Lord Burleigh, Queen Elizabeth's Treasurer and chief advisor. She bore him eleven children.

Walter Bagot continued to receive correspondence from those close to the Earl of Essex who, during the last decade of the 16th century, became increasingly at odds with Queen Elizabeth. In November 1599, after a series of mishandled military ventures, errors of judgement and indiscretions with the Queen, he was deprived of all his high offices and imprisoned in his London home, Essex House for a month. His 160 servants, including Anthony Bagot, were dismissed.

Two letters give an on-the-spot report on the Earl of Essex's predicament. William Trew was another son-in-law of Richard Bagot and one of the earl's attendants, and the first letter is to his wife. The second is from Ralph Adderley Esq. to Walter Bagot, his uncle, in which he seems to hint that the Queen found at least one member of her court somewhat annoying-

William Treu, to his wife Mrs Treu, at Chartley [1]

[1] Being a retainer of the Earl, William and his wife lived, in turn, at Chartley and Essex House in London

My G.S.M. [1] *- I did write to you by Edw: Mattergent of Utceter* [2] *since when we have lived heare in doubtful expectation, havinge a good daye and a bad one.*
Upon Mondaye and Tuesdaye last, the rumor was all over, that my Lord was gone to the Tower...It was so lamented generally, as I never saw the like. Upon Tewsdaye, at night, there was a letter found upon a payre of stayres in the Courte directed to her Majesty,- for the saffety of her M and her estate.- This letter she had red being twooo sheetes of paper; and not aquaintinge any with the contents of it, lockt it up in her closet. Thereupon, there was a great stir in the Cort that night; and some of the Gard, that gave out they must wayte upon my Lord to the Tower, had theire cotes plucked off.- Yesterdaye beinge Wednesdaye, all went well on our syde; at 4 o'clock, the Queen, my Lady Warwick, and the Erle of Worcester, went privately to York House to my Lord. What is done this nighte I knowe not; - but- we hope well... When the Sheriffs should be pricked, [3] *my Lord Keeper spoke for my brother* (Walter Bagot) *to be spared; but the Queen answered, that "She had hard he was an honest man, like his father, and therefore was sorye she had spared him so longe"... Upon Saterday the ladies come to Essex House to lye there,- they are wearye of the contrye. Let nobody knowe the newes, but my brother...*
Comend me to all, farewell. *Your lovinge husband*
St Andrew's Even [4] 1599 William Treu.

Ralph Adderley, Esq. to Walter Bagot

Sir,- On Thorsday laste, my Lord of Essex was at Yorke House before the Lords of the Counsell, and other Lords... who shewed himself a pretty fellow, and answered them all; wholly without touch but only in some disloyalty towards Her Majesty. They would have had hym confessed those articles, which were agrevated hym in the Starre Chamber; but my Lord yelded to nothinge, but only submytted hymself to Her M. It is doubtfull he shall loose his offices, some of them, but they would have all stand, as yet stand at Her M's pleasure; and he is at his own howse, as he was before,- There were some that said they wold move Her Majesty for my Lord's liberty; and that was Mr. Secretary; and he say'd he did not dout but to havinge a discharge before it were longe;- which God graunt it may be; I doubte he spake not as he ment. My Lord is mery and in helth, thanks be to God. He was at Yorke House, from vii of the clocke in the morng untill almost ix att night, without meate or drinke. He knealed tow hours, by the clocke. They would have had hym stoode, but he

---

1 My Good Spouse Margaret
2 Uttoxeter
3 An archaic term – Marking the name in a list by pricking
4 29th November

wold not, so long so, as the matter was in talke betwixt Her Majestie and hym. *The Lord Grey is gonne over into the Low Countries.- Rawleigh* [1] *is gonne into the contrey, with bag and baggage, as his wyffe and children; and her Majesty call'd hym worse than catte and dogge.*
So my hartie comenda'cons to yourself, your bedfellowe, my Aunt, Cosen Okeover,[2] *with Lettice,*[3] *Mrs Mary,*[4] *Mrs Treu and Mr. Anthony; I leave you to the protection of Allmyghty'-*

London, in haste, this ixth of June,1600.

Assuredly yours
Ralph Adderley

On 5th June 1600 the Earl of Essex was partially reprieved by the Queen and freed from house arrest, but in October the queen decided not to renew his right to customs duties on sweet wines which had been the main source of his income, an action which left him deeply in debt. This action, along with the other indignities his vanity suffered, left him distraught and led him to an unwise and drastic action.
On 7th February 1601, he incited a revolution by parading through the streets of London with 300 retainers in an attempt to gain public support to overthrow the Queen and her court. The plot was a complete failure and he was tried, found guilty and beheaded at the Tower of London on 25th February 1601, but unusually was granted a private, instead of a public execution. He was aged 35.
For his part in the insurrection, Anthony Bagot was pardoned in 1603 just before Queen Elizabeth died on 24th March, after a reign of 45 years.

Two years after the Pilgrim Fathers set sail for America, the Blithfield parish burial register states, *' 1622. - Antonie Bagott, - gent: buryed the one and twentith of dai of June.*

Walter Bagot was keen to continue the glass-making business in Bagot's Park, probably started by his grandfather Sir Lewis Bagot, but certainly by his father Richard. [5] This may have been due to the fact that Walter had

---

1 Sir Walter Raleigh. In 1587, Anthony Bagot wrote in a letter to his father-...Sir Walter Rawley is the hated man of the wourld, in Court, Cytye and Country...

2 'Cosen Okeover ' was the ward of Walter Bagot's wife and was the subject of a legal dispute when, having been betrothed to Walter's daughter, married instead the daughter of a Sir Oliver Cheney when he reached the age of consent of 14 years old. Infant betrothals and marriages were common among the nobility in this period. In the case of the premature death of his father, an infant, unmarried heir could become ward of the crown or a superior lord, resulting in the loss of his estate to his guardian.

3 A daughter of Richard Bagot.

4 Richard Bagot 's wife.

5 See Other Histories - Bagot's Park - A Hive of Industrial Activity. p.280

inherited large debts from his father, largely no doubt, on account of Richard's futile attempts to obtain payment for his services to Elizabeth I.

Later on, in the 17th century, one of Walter Bagot's grand-daughters was to find herself performing a pivotal role in the future of the English monarchy.

Walter Bagot died on 16th March 1622 and is buried along with his wife in the Chancel at Blithfield Church with a monument erected to their memory.

He was succeeded by his second son, Hervey.

THE CIVIL WARS 1642 -1651

Before the story of Blithfield can continue, it is necessary to remind the reader of the single most defining event in England during the 17th century which were the Civil Wars, which shook the country to the core.
The end result of the conflict saw the English people execute their monarch and replace the monarchy with what was called the Republic of England for a short time. The Republic could have remained but for public weariness of the war's outcome.

Civil wars are regarded among the most vicious of conflicts and the English Civil Wars were no exception. It exposed deep divisions within English society pitching family against family, father against son and son against brother. As a proportion of the population killed during the war, more people died than during the First World War as the country was split between support for king and parliament. Groups of people wandered about demanding of those they met - "are you for king or parliament". The wrong answer could lead to a severe beating, or sometimes worse.

The Civil Wars were born from ever deepening divisions within English society, particularly since the accession to the throne of Charles I in 1624 on the death of his father James I.
Charles's belief in the divine right of kings, where rulers consider they are answerable only to God for their actions, began to cause rifts between the King and Parliament.
His Protestant subjects also began to have doubts about the King's Catholic inclinations, which was not helped by him marrying Henrietta Maria, the Catholic sister of the King of France. The reluctance of parliament to give way to the King's demands for money without giving his reason for it and parliament's demands on the king to curb royal power, led to the King attempting a coup against parliament in 1642 which failed.

Another cause of the war were tensions between the newly formed protestant Church of England and puritan groups, noted for their austere way of life, who were wishing to see more radical changes and reform.
The stage for the Civil War, of King, supported by the gentry, Anglican clergy and peasantry, against Parliament, supported by the merchants and much of the nobility, had been set.

By 1645, much of England and Wales was under the control of the Parliamentary forces and, in June 1646, the Royalists surrendered and King Charles fled to Scotland.

The conclusion of this first war however did not bring national unity and the dominant power in the land lay with the 'New Model Army' of Oliver

Cromwell. Formed in 1645, Cromwell had chosen to have it led by professional officers rather than aristocratic amateurs which gave it a distinct advantage during the conflict. However, at the end of the war, some Parliamentary soldiers mutinied through not having been paid, suffering hunger and being ill-clad.

Parliament was deep in debt and looked to raise money from Royalist funds and local taxation. By 1648 the army's grievances still had not been met and they launched a coup against Parliament and arrested 140 of their members leaving only a "rump" of 60 members who were sympathetic to the army's wish to try King Charles for treason.

The King was subsequently arrested, tried, found guilty and executed on 27th January 1649. Later that year, the Parliamentarians destroyed the majority of the Coronation Regalia, including the original St Edward's Crown thought to have been made in the 11th century for the coronation of Edward the Confessor. The gemstones were sold and the gold melted down for coinage.

In February, the monarchy and the House of Lords were abolished by the "Rump" parliament, which now did not represent popular opinion, and by the end of the year England had been declared a republican state. Parliament had become, for the most part, the mouthpiece of the army.

Although the war in England had ended, Oliver Cromwell still found the need to put down rebellions in Scotland and Ireland, and after his successes, returned home to a heroes welcome. His military prowess during the war and forceful character lead him to become installed as Lord Protector of England, Scotland and Ireland in 1653.

Cromwell spent the first 40 years of his life in relative obscurity as a farmer and MP for Huntingdon. On knowing where his allegiance lay at the start of the Civil War, he raised troops for the parliamentary cause and was very successful in clearing the eastern counties of Royalist troops early on, earning the reputation of being the greatest cavalry commander in English history.

The Reformation, bought about by Henry VIII one hundred years before and the now feely available bible, printed in English, had enabled many people to interpret the scriptures for themselves. The victory of the Parliamentarians over the established order had given opportunity for new religious and radical cults to establish themselves.

Among these were the "Ranters", "Levellers", "Diggers" and "Fifth Monarchists", whose doctrines varied from religious freedom, equality between men and women and free education for all, to free love, as well as any other immoral behaviour. Most of these were assumed from each group's various interpretations of the bible!

Parliament itself, largely consisting of Puritans who themselves wished to

regulate and simplify forms of worship, became increasingly alarmed at the real, or imagined influence on public opinion by these radical groups.
The Puritans had, by 1644, already abolished Christmas, and in 1646 the Book of Common Prayer together with the offices of Archbishop of Canterbury and bishops throughout the country were also abolished.
In 1649, they issued an order for Catholic priests to leave the country, forbade Anglican clergymen to teach or preach and censored the press.
As a precaution against insurrection and royalist plots, in 1655 Cromwell appointed eleven major generals to close down ale houses, race-meetings, theatres, bear baitings [1] and cock fights throughout the country which did nothing to improve the government's popularity. The cost for policing this was covered by imposing punitive taxes on moneyed royalists.

The Civil Wars finally ended after the defeat of Charles II at the Battle of Worcester on 3rd October 1651, after he had been crowned in Scotland and attempted to travel to London in order to reclaim his English crown.
After the battle, he fled Cromwell's forces and famously hid in an oak tree at Boscobel just over the Staffordshire border in Shropshire. He then made his way into exile in France disguised as the man-servant of Jane Lane, the sister of one of his colonels and the grand-daughter of Walter Bagot of Blithfield. Jane's parents, Thomas Lane and Anne Bagot were married in Blithfield Church on 8th February 1608.

In 1657, Cromwell declined a House of Commons request to become king and in 1658 he died at the age of 59. He was succeeded by his son Richard who was a politically inexperienced country gentleman. He failed to assert himself as a leader and resigned in 1659.

With the army and parliament being unable to reconcile themselves, the country facing economic hardships, a series of bad harvests and the threat of anarchy bought about by the rising influence of puritan sects and their anti-social practices, the "Rump" parliament was dissolved and a free parliament installed. This re-admitted those who had been purged in 1648 and included many with royalist sympathies. There was no doubt that many people throughout the land wished a return to a settled system of government.

Ultimately, King Charles's son was invited to return from exile in Holland. He was greeted with much enthusiasm and the monarchy was restored in 1661, with Charles II as king. He reigned for 25 years.

It was against this scenario that Sir Hervey Bagot and two of his sons became deeply involved, much to their disadvantage.

---

1 It has been humorously observed that the Puritan objection to bear baiting was not because of concern to the bears welfare, but because people were enjoying themselves.

SIR HERVEY BAGOT 1591 - 1660

Sir Hervey Bagot and his third son,

also Hervey

Sir Hervey was the second son of Walter Bagot and was born at Checkley [1] on 8th February 1590, succeeded his father in 1622 and became a baronet [2] in 1627. Sir Hervey and two of his sons, Hervey and Richard, were staunch Royalists during the Civil War and thereby incurred the wrath of Parliamentarians. Before the war, in 1639, Sir Hervey enjoyed a substantial rental income of £1,400 from his lands, and the woods on his estate were valued at £10,000, but this was soon to be pillaged.

By 1645, when the Parliamentarians had overrun most of the country, they set about to punish Sir Hervey for his Royalist allegiance by sequestrating his property. Sir Hervey was aged 52 at the beginning of the

1 A property of the Bagot family near Uttoxeter. At the time Sir Hervey was born, his grandfather Richard, was still residing at Blithfield Hall. He took up residence at Field Hall in the parish of Leigh, another estate of the Bagot family in Staffordshire, around the year 1620. At that time his mother was still residing at Blithfield until her death in 1638, when it was handed to his eldest son Edward, who succeeded his father in 1660.

2 A title instituted by James l in 1611 who wished to raise money for quelling anarchy in Ulster. He required a sum of money from each of the 200 gentlemen honoured for the maintenance of thirty foot soldiers at eight pence each per day for three years which totalled £1095, the first year's instalment to be paid in advance.

Civil War and upon the sequestration of his estate took refuge in the royalist garrison of the Cathedral Close at Lichfield commanded by his son Colonel Richard Bagot.

There are many letters and notices which Sir Hervey received and replied to concerning this, and the following examples follow the events sequentially and give a clear idea of how the process unfolded.

The sequestration begins as follows:-

To the Constable of Blithfield and Newton.

By virtue of the authorities to us given, wee doe require you forth wth uppon the receipt hereof to give warning unto all the tenants of Sir Hervie Bagot, within your Constable wc^k^, to make payment of all and evrie of their rents, due at Michaelmas last, to us, or one of us, on Thursday the thirtieth day of this instant October, at the house of widdow Dorrington, in Stafford; or otherwise in the meane tyme to pay the same unto the hands of Thomas Aburley, of Newton, so that he may give it to us the day appoynted; Whereof you nor they may faile, upon perill of distresse and payment of those that shall be employed (to distraine) for their paines in that behalfe.

Dated at Stafford, the 20th day of October 1645. Geo. Thorley. Robt Stoakes

It would appear Sir Hervey was ordered to hand over a summary of his income to a 'Committee of Goldsmith's Hall' and judging by this next document, his report was not considered accurate :-

Gentlemen, - The estate given in to the Com'ittee of Goldsmith's Hall, by Sir Ha: Bagott, for which hee desyres to compound, did seeme to them to bee so inconsiderable, being but £134.11s. 8d. paid, besydes what he hath by his Lady, and this estate only for his life;... Wee are not particularly acquainted with this estate, yet it seems strange unto us that a gentleman of his quality and report should receve only £130 per ann: for his own subsistance. Wee have therefore thought fitt to show the particular papers here enclosed to you, and desyre...that you will take a little pains in making a further enquiry into the particular estate of Sir Hervey Bagott,...or can find out any indirect or underhand dealings in the surveyares of the estate of Mr Edw: Bagot [1], or any private resources; - that you will, with convenient speed, certifie the same unto us in writing,...And yf you can make no further discoveries, that you will write your answer to this and enclose those papers in it, that the Com'ittee... may proceed accordingly.

Your affectionate friends and servants
Rich. Skiffington. T Swynfen.

July 7, 1646

---

1 Sir Hervey's son and heir.

In the meantime, Sir Hervey receives a letter from London advising him that although the report he sent to Goldsmith's Hall was considered correct by those sent out by the Committee to check his claim, his correspondent (presumably his council in the matter) warns him:-

...That the Com'ttee of Stafford had nothing to doe to certifie concerning the lands in Warwickshire; also that those lands are undervalued; these things I thought fitt to hint unto you, the use of which I leave unto your further consideration.
I rest
Your humble servant
Tho: Hanwell.

Lincolns Inn, 12th Jan. 1646.

The Committee of Goldsmith's Hall' finally receive the details they requested as follows:-

Right Noble, - According to direc'cons of this Hon[ble.] Com'ttee, to us signified by their letters of the 17th of October last, wee have informed ourselves of the yearly value of the estates of Sir Harvie Bagot, in the County of Stafford and Warwick; and doe find that before these troubles, the value of his lands in Staffordshire were £334. 18s. 8d. per annum; and in Warwickshire, beeinge his Ladies joynture, £200. per annum, and no more that wee can hear off; which wee humbly certifie, and rest
Your humble servants,
R. Skeffington. T Swynfin.
T. Bowyer.

March 4th, 1646

By now, Sir Hervey has earned the title of 'delinquent' from his tormentors and he writes to them:-

To the Hon[ble.] Com'itte for Compositions w[th.] delinquents, setting at Goldsmith's Hall.
The humble Petition of Sir Hervey Bagot, Kt. and Bart.
Sheweth. That your petitioner was unhappilie persuaded to reside within the enimies garrison, and was at Oxford, but never was in armes, nor otherwise assisted in this warr against the Parliament; and was in Lichfield upon the surrender thereof. Now, for that your Petitioner is ready to conforme to all ordinances of Parliament, Therefore your Petitioner is an humble suitor... and that Parliament would be pleased to admitt him to a favourable composi'con for his delinquencie, and discharge of his sequenstra'cons.
And your Petitioner shall ever pray.

However:-

'Att the Com'itte for compounding delinquents, April 29th 1647
ORDERED. That Sir Harvey Bagot, of ffeild , in the County of Stafford, Bart. shall pay the some of One Thousand Three Hundred and Forty Pounds, as a fine for his delinquency;- the one moite in hand, the remainder in three monthes'. *Jo: Leech*

The final particulars of Sir Hervey's Estate recorded by those at Goldsmith's Hall details that:-

Sir Hervey Bagot hath an estate for life in the Manor of Field... and some lands in Uxeter; the remainder to Dame Anne his wife for life;...worth before these troubles, One Hundred Forty Eight Pounds Tenne Shillinges and Four Pence.
The like estate... in Bromley Pagetts, worth per an: Seaven Pounds Five Shillings and Eight Pence... in the Manor of Bromley Bagots,...worth per an: One Hundred and Six Pounds Tenne Shillings and Nine Pence...
of the manor of Leigh, worth per an: Tenne Pounds Foure Shillings and Four Pence.
...of the Mannor of Little Hay, in Colton and Blithbury, worth per an: Twenty Eight Pounds Fourteen Shillings and Seaven Pence...
of the Manor of Newton, worth per an: Nineteene Pounds Six Shillings and eight Pence...
...and in the Manor of Blithfield, worth per an: Fourteene Pounds Six Shillings and Eight Pence.
...Jo: Leeche.

Sir Hervey Bagot hath in right of his wife, for the tearme of hir life, (shee beinge above 76 yeares of age, and very infirme in body) issueing out of the Mannors of Maxstoke at Ryton, in the County of Warwick, worth in times of peace, Two Hundred Pounds.
...Jo: Leeche.

Confirmation follows that all is safely gathered in:-

Wee the Com'ittee for sequestrations for the Countie of Stafford, do hereby certifie that the personall estate of Sir Herv: Bagot, of ffield, in this Countie, Baronett, was seized upon and disposed of by us in the late warrs, for the States' use. In witnes whereof we have hereunto put our hands, at Stafford, this 18th of May, 1648.

Following his heavy fine for delinquency, in 1647, Sir Hervey gains some reprieve:-

'June the 9th 1648

At the Com'ittee of Lords and Commons for advance of money It is ORDERED. That the assessments on Sir Harvey Baggott, Barrt. for his second part be discharged, it appearing that he is much in debt'.

Lady Bagot however seems to have been spared any indignities, as she was granted - '......*quietly and peaceably to have, hold and enjoye the Mansion House of ffield.........and shall enjoy, have and dispose for her own use, all the household goods, corne and cattle which she is now possessed of;- and all persons whatsoever are hereby forbidden to molest the said Lady in the premisses, as they will answere the contrary at their perill.*

An interesting letter to Sir Hervey, briefs him with the goings-on in London when Parliamentary forces act against the House of Commons on 6th December 1648 when they launched their coup and arrested many of those with Royalist sympathies. It is written by a lawyer and eminent antiquary Sir Symon Degge[1] who had considerable property in the parish of Kingstone, which neighbours that of Blithfield. Sir is no doubt keen to learn of any possibility that events may turn in his favour. Sir Symon writes :-

- *I can tell you no good newes, for though the House of Com'ons sate from Monday, December 4, till Tuesday 10 of the clocke, and voted that the King's answere was satisfactory for the setling of a well grounded peace, though there were noe concession for the putting to death of any, ... they also voted that the taking away the King from the Isle of Wight, and removing him to Hurst Castle, was without their consent and privitie; and last of all, appoynted a Comittee to attend the Generall* [2] *to acquaint him with the votes, and to require the reasons for the King's removal &c. What answer this Comittee received, I know not; but on Monday evening a great part of the army came with the Generall to the towne, and placed themselves in Whitehall, the Mewes, St James's, and Goring House, and on Wednesday morning drew a body into the Palace Yard, discharged the Citty Guard, and seized of such Parliament men as they though fit; the number was variously reported, by some 15, the most generall report was 25, but the last and greatest which I received was 50, whereof I heard Waller, Massey, Hollis... and Pryn named, who loudly proclaimed it a breache of priviledge to take him prisoner going to the House: they endeavoured to seize Browne the Sheriff, at the Sessions Howse in the Old Bayley, but hee there, and many more aymed*

---

1 He lived at Blythe Bridge (now known as The Blythe) and died at the age of 92. He is buried in the church at Kingstone.

2 Oliver Cromwell.

at, escaped, having tymely notice. Soe that now Parliament and Citty are both in the power and disposall of the army. What the event will be I must leave to Providence and tyme to produce, for noe man that I mete with can imagine what these men ayme at: the Cittizens and Parliament men look very blanke on the busnesse. This being all the newes for the present I can tell you, I shall only desire my service and best respects may be presented to yourself and good lady, and wish you a merry Christmas, and good newes to succeede these new unexpected things, and rest,

Sir,
Your affectionate servant,
Symon Degge.

December, 1648.

King Charles's removal from imprisonment in Carisbrooke Castle on the Isle of Wight was the prelude to his trial and execution which took place on 30th January 1649.
By this time, the Parliamentary army was being asked by Cromwell to fight in Ireland, and as many still were still in arrears with their wages, dissatisfaction among them led some troops to mutiny, leading to some executions. Dissent was such that, for want of pay, soldiers had been availing themselves by robbing farms of livestock and causing a general nuisance among the general populace.
In this next order, Sir Hervey is assured of protection from the renegade soldiers by Sir Thomas Fairfax, commander-in-chief of the New Model Army:-

These are to require every of you, on sight hereof, that you forbeare to prejudice the howse of Sir Hervie Bagot, of ffield, in the County of Stafford, Bart. or to offer any violence to his person or any of his family; or to meddle with or take away his horses, cattle, sheepe, or household staffe, or any of his goods whatsoever; and you are to forbeare to quarter any officers or soldiers at the howse of the said Sir Hervie Bagot, he providing for them (his right and equal propor'con,) abroad. And further, you are to permitt and suffer the said Sir Hervie with his servaunts, horses, and necessaries, to passe about his occasions, to the City of London or elsewhere, without lett or molestation; as you will answeare the contrary, he doeing nothing prejudiciall to the Parliament or Army.

Given under my hand and seale the last day of Aprill, anno dom: 1649
Thos : Fairfax.
To all Officers and Soldiers under my Com'and

On 16th December 1653, Oliver Cromwell was made lord protector

which gave him wide ranging, although restricted powers.
Even now, the hapless Sir Hervey was still preyed upon by a Parliament in need of funds in order to help shore up the nations flagging economy :-

STAFFORDSHIRE,- By the commissioners appointed by his Highness the Lord Protector and the councell, for securing the Peace of the Commonwealth in the County of Stafford.

Whereas- by instructions from his Highness and the Councell...and to all such within this County which have beene sequestred for delinquency. These are therefore to acquaint you, that they have valued your Estate, beinge taxed att £424. per an:- att Forty Two Pounds,- and to be paid yearely; the one halfe upon the one and twentieth day of this instant December, or within twenty dayes after; the other halfe on the fower and twentieth day of June next following; which summes of money you are to pay to Mr Geo: Brett, in Stafford. Dated this 19th day of December,1655.

Signed by the appointement of the saide Commissioners,

To Sir Hervey Bagot *Will: ff rake, Clarke.*

After submitting to Parliament's demands in money matters, there was one thing above all upsetting Sir Hervey which he was anxious to resolve and he issues this ingratiating plea:-

To His Highness OLIVER, Lord Protector of England,
Scotland and Ireland.
The Humble Petition of Sir Hervie Bagot, of ffield,
in the County of Stafford, Baronet.

Sheweth

That findinge Acts of Grace and Mercy agreeable to your nature, and those of Justice to be forced from you by necessity and the demerits of others, - your Petitioner therefore havinge...yealded both active and passive obedience to your present government, thereby demonstratinge his reall affections to your Highnesse: And whereas you have gratiously declared, that those, whoe shall truly appeare by their lives and conversations to be suche, shall be dealt with according to their integrity; you desiringe reformation even in the woorst of your people, rather than their harme or prejudice...

...May it therefore please your Heighness, to graunt into your Petitioner your destinguishinge grace and favor, not only to discharge his person and estate from the present gennerall charge, but allsoe to obliterate the very title of delinquent, which is more greevous to your Petitioner then all other the concomitants thereof. And your Petitioner (as he is bounden in duty) will ever pray for your Heighnesses health and happiness.

Hervey Bagot.

The sentiments of Shakespeare are echoed in these lines from Othello written some fifty years earlier...*Who steals my purse steals trash: 'tis something, nothing;...'Twas mine, 'tis his, and has been slave to thousands;... But he that filches from me my good name...Robs me of that which not enriches him,... and makes me poor indeed.*

It does not seem to have been recorded if Sir Hervey received his wish but he was now nearing the end of his life. However, in August 1659 after a failed Royalist revolt in Cheshire, he was arrested and detained at Stafford along with other Royalists and only released on a surety of £2,000. One of those detained was Colonel John Lane, who was considered a particular nuisance by the Parliamentary authorities for his surety amounted to £4,000. Colonel Lane was brother of Jane Lane, Sir Hervey's niece.

After all these calamities and persecutions, Sir Hervey died at Field Hall on 27th December 1660 at the age of 70, but not before seeing the restoration of the monarchy of Charles II in May of that year. He is buried at Blithfield with a monument to his memory in the chancel of the church.

Colonel Richard Bagot 4th Son of Sr. Hervey Governor of Lichfield Killed at Naseby Anno. 1645.

COLONEL RICHARD BAGOT was not born at Blithfield, neither did he live there nor was he buried there as will be seen. He was the fourth son of Sir Hervey and took up arms against the Parliamentarian forces under Cromwell.

Richard Bagot began his campaigns in the first major battle of the Civil War, the Battle of Edgehill near Warwick in 1642, where neither side achieved significant advantage, and at the Battle of Hopton Heath near Stafford in 1643 in which the Royalists prevailed.

In 1643 Colonel Bagot raised a Regiment of Foot[1] in the King's cause which numbered approximately 500 men. The following year he was put in command of the King's garrison in the Cathedral Close at Lichfield by Prince Rupert, the king's nephew. His regiment soon gained the reputation for being prolific plunderers and skirmishers. They fought at the Battle of Newark in 1644 and were also involved in some skirmishes at Burton-on-Trent and Hopwas near Tamworth. It was possibly as a result of the encounter with the Parliamentarians at Hopwas, that Colonel Bagot received a contemptuous challenge from the Parliamentary commander at Tamworth, a Captain Hunt:-

Bagot, thou son of an Egiptian Hore, meete mee half the way to-morrow morning, half the way betwixt Tamworth and Lichfield if thou darest; if not, I will whippe thee whensoever I meete thee. Thomas Hunt.

Colonel Bagot met him, and after a brief action it was Captain Hunt who regretted the encounter.

Colonel Bagot's Regiment of Foot also took part in the Battle of Naseby in Northamptonshire on 14th June 1645 when the royalists suffered a heavy defeat at the hands of Oliver Cromwell's New Model Army under Sir Thomas Fairfax.

During the battle, Colonel Bagot received a severe wound from a musket ball to his arm which left a gaping wound and compound fracture. Despite efforts by his surgeons to save him, he died on 7th July 1645. He was 27 years old. He was buried two days later in the south aisle of the badly war damaged Lichfield Cathedral. A monument was erected to his memory. It reads - translated from the Latin:-

Near this place lies the body of Richard Bagot, youngest born son of Hervey Bagot, Bart. a victim of the recent conspiracy of fanatics, Governor of this fortress, who in the fateful struggle in yonder Naseby, while fighting most bravely was fatally wounded. He died unmarried on the 7th July 1645.

In spite of the Parliamentary troops' determination to relieve the Royalists possession of the garrison at Lichfield, the Royalists were sometimes at battle with themselves. Lack of finance led to private soldiers not being paid, officers were divided and refused to serve under rivals and it was reported that... *the Royalist forces by their excesses had made*

1 'Colonel Bagot's Regiment of Foote' is now revived as part of the Sealed Knot, a society formed in 1968 which aims to raise awareness of wars during the 17th century. They re-enact battles which are staged throughout the country and it is one of the oldest re-enactment societies in the world.

themselves more terrible to their friends than to their enemies...

On Richard Bagot's death his elder brother, Colonel Hervey Bagot[1], took command of the Regiment of Foot and the Royalist Garrison at Lichfield. He entertained King Charles I on 15th June 1645 the day after the battle at Naseby.

Between March and July 1646, they endured the third and final siege of the Cathedral Close garrison in which the Parliamentary forces prevailed and the regiment was disbanded soon after. Colonel Hervey Bagot later became a Gentleman Pensioner of Charles II.

Contained in the Blithfield parish records is an interesting account of an unusually large tree which was possibly near to Field Hall, the home, or certainly on the estate of Sir Hervey Bagot. It reads as follows:

AN ACCOUNT OF THE GREAT ELM TREE AT FIELD

An Elm or rather witch hasle was stocked downe at Field wch three good workmen were five days in stocking downe and being stocked downe, three judicious Timbermen did judg^e^ it to containe in timber and firewood fowerscore & seventeen tun.[2] Two saw's were peeced wch had three men at either end of them, to cut the body of it in sunder wch was in compasse seven yards 3 quarters.

There was of ffirewood five and fortie load as much as six oxen could draw, it being a bolt shoot of the house, every 14 inches of the body being a tun of timber. There was fifty seven paire of Nathes [3] made out of it, and as much sawn timber as at three shillings the hundred came to eight pound ye sawinge, the greatest part of it beinge sawen into planks, Table frames, Bedsteds and such like, the rest into wainscott.

---

1 Colonel Bagot's daughter, Anne, was a 'noted beauty' at the court of Charles II. The King was noted for his Mistresses but it was said of Anne Bagot that- *She was the only one that could blush, and the only one that did not need to.* Neither father or daughter were from Blithfield.

2 97 tons

3 The meaning of this word is unclear.

A Blithfield Rector's Advice to His Flock

John Beardmore was installed as rector of Blithfield in January 1610, and it seems he was as keen to instruct his flock on the welfare of their bodies as he was, from the pulpit, the welfare of their souls. This recipe for one of his potions has been left in the parish records:-

A MEDICINE AGAINST SYNEWE SPREANS OR OTHER ACHES IN THE LYMES.

Take a handful of ffether-few, a handful of wormwood, a handful of mugworth, a handful of camamile, half a handful of elder leaves, half a handful of dog-fennel, a little red fennel, put all these together, wash them cleane, but wringe them not, and being washed, chop them with a hackinge knyfe as smale as you can. Then take half a pownd of fresh butter, with new had salt in it, and half a pownd of gaults grease, then sett the hearbes upon a soft charcole fyre, and put to them as much of the butter and grease as will only keep them moist in the boylinge, and so boylinge the hearbes sloly, put in still of butter and grease so much as shall be needful until the liquid substance be made stronge of the hearbes. Then take it of the fyre, and straine the moysture from the hearbes, and take of that moysture and anoynt the place grieved, and when you anoynt it stroake it upwards, having so donne take the hearbes and spread them on a lynen cloath, and bynd that pultisse upon the place where the partie feeleth most paine, let the partie goe to bed and kept there all night and ontill the next daye at noone, and if the patient can endure longer it will doe well to lye until night, and the pultisse will do more good. Then take away the pultisse and anoynt the place everye night with the moysture, after having first warmed it in a sawser, and he shall fynde ease by the helpe of God.

Another of his entries is a form which he no doubt used when helping his parishioners with their wills:-

In the name and the honoure of God Almighty 3 in one and one in three blessed for evermore. I etc. the weakest and unworthiest of all that take on them the profession of God's feare, and knowinge and wayghinge the common condicion of human frailty and not proposing to dye intestate beinge of sounde mynde and perfect memorie (praised be God) doe advisedly and irrevocably make and ordayne this my last will and testament in manner and forme following: First of all I give and bequeath my sinful soul into the hands of Almighty God, that gave it and bought it with a pryce above all pryce, and sanctified it freely, though imperfectly, and will in due tyme glorifie it in his everlasting kingdome. Item I give my body to the earth from whence it came, and to be buried in such seemly and convenient place and manner as my execs. shall think fit, in sure and certain hope of resurrection to life eternal at the last day.

And from my worldly goods &c.

It is to be hoped it was not any of his potions that ever caused any of his parishioners to depart this life!

SIR EDWARD BAGOT 1616 - 1673

While his father, Sir Hervey, was suffering at the hands of Oliver Cromwell and his brothers were crossing swords with the Parliamentarians, Sir Edward Bagot, the eldest son and successor, was safely and unremarkedly ensconced at Blithfield Hall and had been since his father chose to make his home at Field Hall near Uttoxeter.

His reluctance, or refusal, to take an active part in the Civil War could possibly be due to the fact that he was married and had a young child with his wife expecting another.

He succeeded in 1660, the year the monarchy was restored under Charles II, and that year he stood as a Member of Parliament for Staffordshire.

Sir Edward married heiress Mary Lambard from Buckingham, and they had seventeen children. [1] The property in Buckinghamshire which came to him on his marriage was almost immediately sold in order to pay the large debts incurred by the family during the Civil War.

Among many letters he received from eminent men of the time, one which is of particular interest is that from the newly appointed Bishop of Lichfield and Coventry. Immediately after his appointment in 1661, Bishop John Hackett took it upon himself to repair the serious damage done to the cathedral during the Civil War.

---

1 In his will dated 1702, second son Lambard Bagot, left £800 to found a Hospital at Abbots Bromley for 'Six Old Men'. It now serves as two Alms Houses, with the current resident of Blithfield Hall acting as one of the trustees.

On his arrival at Lichfield he "*found his cathedral in an indescribable state of ruin; 2000 cannon shot and 1500 hand grenades having been discharged against it.*"

The Parliamentary commander at Lichfield was Lord Brooke, who was cousin and adopted son of Sir Fulke Greville who Richard Bagot favoured with a grant of land in 1588. Being a zealous Puritan, he swore to raise the cathedral - and all the cathedrals in England - to the ground. Before the bombardment began, he loudly sought Divine providence for his intended action. A contemporary report states...*Lord Brooke came forth from Mr Michael Biddle's house...in a plush cassock with a head piece of steel, having before his face five bars of steel gilt for the securing of his head and face from the fierceness of a sword, and was suddenly shot in one of his eyes by one of two persons placed in the battlements with long fowling pieces* [1] *to make shot at the cannoniers...*

The fatal shot came from the parapet of the cathedral and from the musket of a member of the Dyott family of Lichfield, who was both deaf and dumb and one of those defending it. Bearing in mind muskets were notoriously inaccurate weapons and the distance Dyott's target was some 200 yards away, Divine providence indeed perhaps, to thwart his Lordship's ambitions? Ironically, Brooke also died on 2nd March, St Chad's Day, the Saint to who the cathedral is dedicated. A stone commemorating the event is above that doorway in Dam Street, Lichfield.

The cathedral had undergone three sieges during the war, the third siege, in 1646, saw the central spire brought down. After the Parliamentary forces prevailed, one famous historian says - *'courts of guard were kept in the aisles; they broke up the pavement,* (and) *every day hunted a cat with hounds throughout the church, delighting themselves in the echo from the goodly vaulted roof.* In 1651, with the authority of the Rump Parliament, the walls were dismantled, the lead taken from the roof and the bells broken up. It had received more damage than any cathedral in the country.

In September 1667, Bishop Hackett writes to Sir Edward......

Worthy Sir,- The necessities of the Cathedral of Lichfield, which I am sure you tender, put mee on to sollicite you diverse waies at this time. The much-deplored Sir Seymour Shirley [2] *did promise an hundred pounds, for the reparation of the said Church, before my Lord's Grace of Canterbury, and Mr Topham. He being taken away before the performance of that promise, I have long bethought mee how his good intention might not bee frustrate, which is*

---

1 Fowling piece- a smooth bore shot gun with a barrel of up to 6 feet long, which gave greater accuracy. They were made for shooting birds.

2 Died 16th July 1667.

a debt before God, though the law perhaps will not help mee. I have consulted with the rent gatherer of his lands, Mr. Robert Bennet, whose answer is, That I must sollicit my Lord's Grace of Canterbury, and yourself, whom if it please to give order to him for the payment of that £100, he will do it.
It seems to mee to bee verie just to have it so, and to that end I will write on Satterday to my Lord's Grace, and now do begin with yourself. I decline Sir Fr: Burdett, in some apprehensions of my own discretion. The approbation of two so wel affected Foeffees, will serve. So I represent my humble motion before you, and will expect to heare from you about it; but I beseech you not to put mee off to the Earl of Alsbury, being not willing to goe that way.
My next offer to you, Sir, in the behalf of the same Cathedral, shall be small and reasonable; the Stalls of the Quire to bee erected are 52 in number, each at eight pounds in price. The Benefactors respectfully to be set up in each Stall, with their names upon escutcheons; wherein among the chiefest nobilitie and most ancient gentry I desyre that your memorial may be recorded; a patronage to the Church, and for your own honour, easily purchased.
And my last proposition is your noble ladie: an Organ, with His Maj.^ties approbation, because none but the honorable and most pious of that sex shall contribute to that sum; wherin I have been successfull with some allready; and urging a charitable worke so reasonable no further, I commend it to the furtherance of the grace of God. Noble Sir, you are assured that I am

Your verie faithful servant
John, Lich: and Coven: [1]

Lichfield, Sept, 5th, 1667

To the Honble Sir Edw: Bagot, Kt and Bart. at
his Manner House of Blithfield, Staffordshire.

After starting repairs to the cathedral on the morning of his arrival at Lichfield, approaching every gentleman in his diocese for contributions to the cost and eight years work, the repairs were completed and amounted to £9092.1s.7½d. Of this amount, the good bishop had contributed £1683.12s from his own pocket.[2] He is remembered in the cathedral by a fine tomb and his work in a stained glass window in the south aisle.

Not only was Bishop Hackett a man of great generosity, he was also a man of great courage. It is recorded that, prior to his installation as Bishop of

1 In 1665 Bishop Hackett married Sir Edward's daughter, Mary, to Richard Newdigate in Blithfield Church.

2 Today, these amounts would represent over £2m and £380,000 respectively. (Source for historic inflation figures - The Bank of England)

Lichfield, he insisted on resisting the Puritan persecution of established church practices by conducting his church services accordingly, which could lead to severe punishment. While conducting a service in his London church, he was threatened with instant death if he continued, by Parliamentary soldiers who had entered the church. "Soldiers", said Hackett, " I am doing my duty: do you yours " and proceeded in a louder voice than before. With that reply, the astonished soldiers left the church without harming him.

Being a Member of Parliament, Sir Edward was apt to receive letters from his colleagues, and this letter from William Chetwynd[1] gives some details of the new King's income from taxes levied on his subjects. For obvious reasons, the nations economy had suffered during the Civil War and money for the exchequer was in short supply as William Chetwynd points out....

...The Commons House have seriously sett themselves to inspect the severall branches of the King's revenue His Lands, His Customes, the Excise, the Chymneys, Post Office &c...have (been) *gone through...and worth £400,000... Crowne Lands...have agreed them to bee £100,000 Post Office now set at £21,500, will be raised to £27,000 per an; - but the Chymneys is the thing that amazes us, whose value from the Chequarri is but £162,882 per an; supposed by all never to be lesse than £300,000: this branch is now under hand and besides the grate frauds in the City of London (whose Chymnayes amount but to 18000) many abuses will bee discovered in the country, as leaving out some townshipps...*

The 'Chymnayes' he mentions, refer to the Hearth Tax introduced in 1662 in order to bolster England's finances. The figure of £300,000 mentioned was the sum the tax was supposed to have raised in order to make up the shortfall to the £1.2 million annual income required in order to run the country. It was, in essence, a property tax based on the number of fireplaces a dwelling had and levied '*...for every firehearth and stove...at twoe shillings by the yeare...*' The tax never did raise £300,000 and was eventually abolished in 1689.

In order to claim exemption from the *Hearth-money* a certificate was required by the poor, from the ministers and church wardens of the parish stating that... *we do believe* y^t[2] *(that)* y^e *respective houses wherin* ye p(er)*sons here undermentioned do inhabit are not of greater value yn (than)* 20^s *p annum... neither* y^e *persons hath useth nor occupieth any lands or tenements of* y^r *(their) own or others of* y^e *yearly value of* 20^s *per annum...nor*

---

1 Sir Edward's son-in-law

2 This is a form of shorthand, the 'y' represents 'th'.

hath any goods or chattells of ye value of 10^s...and ye s(ai)^d houses have not above two chimneys, firehearths or stoves in them...

William Chetwynde concludes his letter -

...Theire is a Bill (that you will wonder att) will bee brought in this weeke, to exclude all persons from all civill and military employment, who have acted with the late times; of this theire is thought to bee a greate need...The towne has no newes in it that I heare of... from your humble and hearty servant,

William Chetwind.

Sir Edward Bagot died on 30th March 1673 and he is commemorated with a grand memorial in the vestry of Blithfield Church. He was succeeded by his son Walter.

' THE SCHOLLER '

On the west wall of the chancel in Blithfield Church is the ornate memorial plaque to Hervey Bagot. He was the eldest son of Sir Edward Bagot.

The inscription reads:-

"HERVEY BAGOT, of that noble family, the twentieth heire, more (had he survived) than the twentieth Knight, a youth of excellent hopes, admirable perfections; In morals manly and grave, In wisdom gray haired; Only in age childish; Studious of all good arts, intractable to ill; Not knowing vice but by correcting it in others; Of devotion to God, duty to parents, respect to all. A great exemplar in a little volume, In all huge, rare; In nothing had he not died, coṁon; A S^t though a child; A scholler though an heire; In ye incomparable ornaments of mind and body, a lively express of heavēs power and earths capacity, Deare to his friends, dearer to God, who hasted (as it were) to treasure up this lovely jewell (lest it should be sullied with a long mortality) in his glorious cabinet of eternity: In ye yeare of grace 1655 (of age 13)."

Preserved in the parish records, is this example of his "schollership"-

"Look but about, and you shall plainly see
What transmutations in this world there be;
Those which were once upon the top o' th' State
Are now fall'n low, and made unfortunate:
Those Streames are stopt, which ran from flowing fountains;
High hills are down and Mole hills are grown mountains;
The stately Cedar, and the lofty Pine
Oh! they are fall'n, and Shrubs in splendour shine;
Now doe these Shrubs, seem high by others fall;
But yet, - they may come down, - though ne'r so tall;
The Ivie, that hath lean'd, on Th' Oke for prop,
Proudly presumes, and over-checks the top.
Just so we see, sweet flowers, to fade and perish
Now weeds, and trash, are let to grow and flourish;
Thus will it be, - till time displant those weeds,
And cut them down,- consuming all their seeds:
The greedy Wolfs, will harbour here no more
But Lambs may skip in safety,- as before.
(Signed) Hervey Bagot"

SIR WALTER BAGOT 1644 - 1704

Sir Walter Bagot was born on 21st March 1644.

Sir Walter's marriage was a fortuitous one for the Bagot family but one which began full of drama and was worthy of a romantic novel. According to Bagot family folklore, it came about because of his dog. The story maintains that, when Sir Walter was walking in North Wales, his dog strayed onto the 15,500 acre estate of the wealthy Salesbury family. The incident eventually led him to meet and fall in love with Jane Salesbury, the daughter of the owner, Charles Salesbury.

Charles's father, Sir William Salesbury, was the owner of this large estate in Denbighshire and Merionethshire. Owing to a violent disagreement over his eldest son Owen's marriage, he divided the estate in two, the one part of it, Pool Park, being left to his second surviving son Charles, the other to Owen. The Civil War had caused some animosity in the Salesbury family. Sir William Salesbury [1] was a staunch royalist as was son Charles, while Owen, who died in 1658, tended to lean toward the Parliamentarian cause.

It was Charles Salesbury's only child and sole heiress, Jane, who was to inherit on her father's death, and through marriage therefore to her husband. With Sir Walter Bagot being the favoured suitor, lengthy negotiations began between the two families and, as these progressed,

1 See Other Histories - Friends at War. p.282 Salesbury - pronounced as in Salisbury

Owen Salesbury's son, William and his brother Gabriel's hope that the two estates would be reunited led them to think of sabotaging the marriage by kidnapping the groom on his wedding day. On learning of this, the couple married in secret in July 1670, but Jane's cousins William and Gabriel, were determined this should not be the end of the matter.

Consequently, the bitter rift began a legal battle between the cousins and Sir Walter Bagot, which concluded in favour of Sir Walter and his wife in 1677. This was only after William had died and Gabriel had produced a forged deed [1] in an effort to verify their claim on the lost family lands. Gabriel was obliged to flee abroad for his misdemeanour.

Mrs Salisbury & her Grand-
children Sr Edwd Bagot &
Elizh Bagot afterwards
Countess of Uxbridge

Mrs Elizabeth Salesbury and her grandchildren Edward and Mary Bagot

by John Michael Wright.

[1] Supposed to have been obtained from two London highwaymen.

In 1675, Sir Walter commissioned a set of paintings by John Michael Wright in order to assert his position in this family dynastic clash. The most striking is that of his mother-in-law Mrs Elizabeth Salesbury, wearing the distinctive Welsh pointed hat, with her Bagot grandchildren, Edward and Mary.

It shows the family group before a background of the Clwyd mountains which formed part of the former Salesbury estate, and included Pool Park, home of Mrs Salesbury who was widowed in 1659 and died in 1693. Michael Wright charged Sir Walter £40 for the painting, the original of which hangs in the Tate Gallery in London. A copy of it is displayed in Blithfield Hall. Another painting in the set displayed there (also reproduced above) is that of Sir Walter, in Roman attire with his dog, which is not too convincingly depicted.[1]

Sir Walter's wife, Dame Jane, was a great benefactor to the poor and founded an alms house at Llanfwrog, near Ruthin, in her native county of Denbighshire. She endowed it with £60 per year for ever for maintaining six poor men and six poor women. She died on 20th July 1695 and was buried at Blithfield.

In 1729, two of their daughters, Elizabeth and Jane, founded a Dame School in Admaston which they endowed with 18 acres of land.

Sir Walter Bagot died in 1704 and was buried at Blithfield on 23rd February that year.

Charles Salesbury of Denbighshire, North Wales. His only child and daughter, heiress Jane, married Sir Walter Bagot in 1670

1 In his book, Memorials of the Bagot Family, William, 2nd Lord Bagot describes this painting- *Sir Walter Bagot, Bart, a half length, in a fancy Roman dress, sitting with his arm on a table.*

RECTOR GEORGE ROADES

George Roades M.A. was Rector of Blithfield from 1676 to 1713 assuming the position at the age of 32. He was also Rector of Checkley from 1703, both parishes being in the estates of the Bagots of Blithfield.

He was presented by Sir Walter Bagot and it seems he was a keen record keeper and also was diligent in his care, for not only his new home but his garden and the church too.

However his writings show he was not without his doubts and problems. Here, he records his impressions on first coming to Blithfield:-

"An account of my Affaires Relating to the Parsonage of Blithfield taken ought of my loos papers in May 1711 for the advantage of my successor whoever he be. In May 1676 I was inducted into the Rectory of Blithfield by the Reverend Mr. Wright vicar of Abbots Bromley having been presented to the bishop of ye diocese by the hon^{ble} s^{r} Walter Bagot bar^{t} the patron of the place.

My Predecessor Canon Harrison living at Lichfield I found the whole Rectory (the Easter Dues excepted) let to a Tenant at 80 pound Par annum the Parson paying all Taxes and payments whatsoever. I found the House so very bad y^{t} theere was but one chymney below stares and but one very mean one above staires.

The floors below where dirt and clay and very uneven; and those above of plaister sadley worne to pieces. Above a third part of ye howse had no Floore over it and the spars under ye thaching where so reechy that every body concluded it had bene an ould kiln.

The whole house was thached and carried as mean an aspect as could well be seen.

I had a mind to sould it off ye ground as it stud. I got it at 60 pounds value and was bid but 50 and parswaded not to take it because wee had not Brik mad at that time within les than 2 Miles and those very small and dear."

Rector Roades's Rectory House stood in what are now Blithfield Hall grounds just over the now existing churchyard boundary wall and to the south west of the church.

Brick making at that time and up until the Industrial Revolution, was a cottage industry and, depending on there being a reliable source of suitable clay, local brick makers served customers' needs. There was a brick maker in Abbots Bromley, only a few miles away, and another at Colwich in the Trent Valley around four miles away as the crow flies. Bricks from this source however were prone to contain salt. This brick works continued well into the 20th century.

Rector Roades subsequently decided to make the most of what his house provided and to substantially renovate it:-

"In the year 1678 I began to build y e South west end of y e house. In y e year 1682 I began to repair y e rest of the house all that I aded to ye Bigness of y e house was room for y e best Staircase a passage to y e well yard & a Large Jetty [1] at y e South east end to make itt answerable to that on y e South west Side

"In y e year .... [2] I built from y e ground a new brewhouse adjoyning to y e backside of y e house and well yard

"Laid out in all about my house....... lb350 -: - :
of which I heartily Repented for I might a built a new tile and brick house big enough for Blithfield parsonage & more convenient for y e same money

" Some 3 or 4 years before this I builded 2 bays of building one for a stable with a Loft ouer itt for Hay y e other for either horss or cows house ouer which
I do intend to make loft w ch cost lb s d
24 : - : -

"In y e year 1705 I puled down y e old sorry Tythe barn which Stood Just in front of The house & built a New barn a new Threshing floor a new wainhouse in y e Croft
lb s d
ouer against y e house w ch work amounted to................ 90 : - : -

lb s d
of this 90 : - : - Charge
my Hon e patron Sr Ed Bagot
was pleased to be at
lb s d
40 : - : - Charge
abated 40 : - : -

Rems 50 : - : -

"In y e year 1707 I built a good large hors block w th Stairs att both ends
lb s d
valued to.....................2 : - : -
for Collered Raills on y e side of itt.

---

1 Jetty - a projecting part of a building, especially an overhanging upper storey.

2 It seems he either forgot to enter a date or could not recall it.

"The Summ of ye expenses about ye Repairs of ye Parsonage of Blithfield hitherto by me Geo Roads Rector.........

	lb	s	d
	350	:-	: -
	050	:-	: -
	024	:-	: -
	002	:-	: -
	426	: -	: -

	lb	s	d
"To be aded to ye former a horse house in ye broad field	16	: -	: -

Unfortunately, after all his efforts, although he was not to see it, the Rectory was replaced 50 years later c.1724. This was situated in what are now the hall grounds and a short distance away from the old building.

The present rectory was built in c.1807.

Rector Roades records work he carried out in his garden as follows:-

"In the year 1676 I planted a fair orchard containing about 80 trees & fenced itt about by planting quicksetts Round itt. The quicksetts throve Hugely and yeilded me many crops for Trouse [1] & ye orchard bore what could expect for three or four years but ye soyl prouing Nought & Catbraine [2] I could not gett em to bear any after worth ye while though I was att Charge of Trenching ye ground. In ye same year 1676 I planted a grove of oaks & Sycamores betwixt ye lower end of ye orchard & ye pond ye oaks were sett of acorns and one of them this present year of 1712 is ...." (He probably went out to measure, and forgot to record the result).

In a glebe terrier [3] of 1706, the rectory is described:-

House of 6 Bays with Stable, barn and cowhouse joined together 7 bays; garden, orchard, courtyard before the house and the churchyard all adjoining. 2 acres croft in which the outhouse stands with foldyard 3 acres. The land attached to Rector Roades's rectory amounted to 43 acres from which he derived his 'living'.

Here is an extract from his records concerning the church:-

"The 2 isles of the boddy of the Church are allreddy wainscoted but they are dun very inconveniently for being thay where made to contain 3 persons in every seate there is not rume enough for them to kneel downe but to my

---

1 The meaning of this word in this context is unclear. "Trouse" is an archaic term and the singular for "trousers ".

2 Probably a colloquialism of the time for some sort of invasive weed.

3 Glebe terriers are a record of clergymen's property. Carried out periodically, they are to ensure no encroachment or other intervention is made which would affect his income.

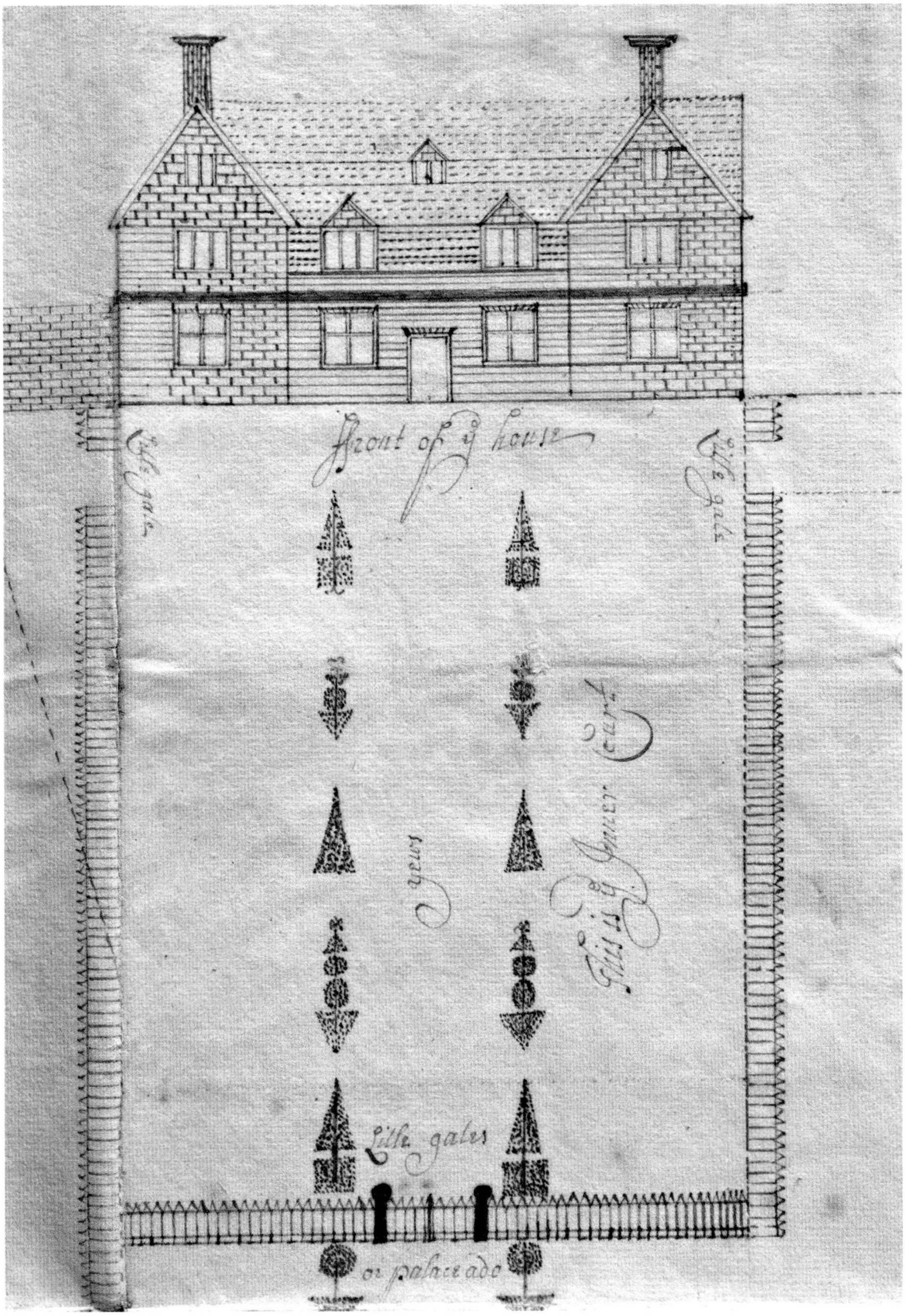
Litle gates

Rector George Roades's plan of his Rectory House with a fenced 'Inner Court' and an avenue of yew trees. The Rectory faced south-west with the front gates opening onto the then existing Moreton to Abbots Bromley/Uttoxeter road which also passed in front of the Hall. The 'litle gate' on the right was 'ye way to ye Church' and opened onto the then, public way to the Church. That on the left opened onto the 'New Road' (Newton to Admaston road). This road now only leads to the Church and the Old Rectory.

great griefe they sit downe jureing all the time of divine servis, this ought to be amended by lessneing the breadth of the seats which would add to the number of them and then by placeing onely 2 in a seat which I hartily desire"

'Parson Roades ' at his writing – as imagined

In 1678, parson Roades oversaw the construction of a new entrance into the Church. A record of this is detailed in an old church account book where he wrote-

In the year 1678 the parish took down an old decaied wooden porch, on the South Isle of the Church, made a fair window of the same proportion with the rest in the place of it; altered the entrance into the Church to the west end, where they set up 2 pair of Large wrought ffolding Doores, erected a Ringing Loft with a Round window in it, and made a handsome Arch of ffreestone [1] at the entrance into the Church.

	lb.	s.	d.
This work came to	*17*	*11*	*02*
Sir Walter Bagot gave			
16 loades of stone unreckon'd			
He also gave ye wood valued at	*04*	*08*	*02*
The lady Bagot his mother gave	*02*	*00*	*00*
Mrs. Kat Lloyd gave	*00*	*10*	*00*
Mr. Rhodes the parson gave	*01*	*00*	*00*
Sum presented	*07*	*18*	*02*
The parish pd. in yr. Levies	*08*	*08*	*06*
Sum	*16*	*06*	*08*
Remr. due to me from the parish	*01*	*04*	*06*

G.R. Rector.

It seems the work carried out may have served two purposes. Obviously the primary consideration was to alter the way of entry into church.

1 Freestone - Stone which can be easily carved and worked with a chisel.

Two images of Blithfield Church as it would have appeared to George Roades in the 17th century. The door-way in the west wall of the tower was inserted during Rector Roades's time at Blithfield. The now existing porch replaced this door-way in the mid-19th century, and around the same time the vestry was built.

Inside the Church, the chancel is shown with a flat roof which replaced the original steep pitched roof. This was re-instated by A.W Pugin in the 19th century as was the five light east window. The large monument on the east wall, to the left of the window, is that to Sir Edward Bagot which is now in the vestry. It is pictured on the opening page to the 17th century.

However, why this should have been thought necessary is not clear, but interestingly, at this time a new pastime was being introduced. The inclusion in the work of a ringing loft suggests this pastime was being made available to people in Blithfield, either by design or accident.

During the early years of the 17th century, bell ringing technology moved forward with the introduction of wooden wheels into the bell chamber. [1] This enabled bells to be 'change rung', i.e. swung through nearly 360°, and in sequence, thereby introducing orderly patterns into the practice. Hitherto, bells were rung randomly, or more accurately, tolled, by members of the clergy. The new method made it possible for lay people to take up a new pastime, which was particularly popular with the aristocracy as it provided physical exercise and intellectual stimulation.

In 1668, the rules for change ringing were laid down and ever more complex ringing patterns gradually introduced. It is still a popular pastime today.

In his book, Notes on the Early History of Blithfield, the Rev. Douglas Murray maintains that when the new entrance was made, the arch in the east wall of the tower was filled in and the smaller 'arch of freestone' inserted, with two folding doors which led into the church. He also says that a staircase led from the floor of the tower and into the ringing loft and then through another door in the east wall of the tower into a gallery - supported by iron pillars - which extended right across the nave. George Roades found the time to marry in January 1705 but died only a few years later in May 1713 aged 69. His memorial plaque can be seen on the south wall of the south aisle in Blithfield Church.

---

1 As has already been mentioned, wooden wheels were introduced into the Blithfield Church bell chamber at least as early as 1635.

SIR EDWARD BAGOT 1673 - 1712

Sir Edward followed his father Sir Walter as head of the Blithfield Bagots, but suffered throughout his later life with gout and died in 1712 at 39 years of age.

His wife, Frances, re-married and moved to Tachbrook in Warwickshire, the place and county of her birth. She took the opportunity to take all the plate, linen and china, diamonds and furniture from Blithfield Hall to her new home, much to the consternation of her son and heir Sir Walter Wagstaffe Bagot. All these items were left to her second husband and were never to return to the house at Blithfield.

On her death, only two years later, she bequeathed certain property left to her by Sir Edward, to her second husband, although it was merely held while she lived. This led to a law suit which eventually terminated in favour of the Bagot family.

Despite these indiscretions she was buried alongside Sir Edward, her first husband, at Blithfield on 20th May 1714.

In 1707 Sir Edward and his wife gifted a fine set of Communion Silver to Blithfield Church.

Sir Edward and his wife gifted these items of church silver to Blithfield Church in 1707.

Consisting of a flagon, chalice with paten cover, and a paten on foot, they are inscribed *The Gift of Sir Edward Bagot Bart., & Frances, his wife to ye church of Blithfield 1707.*

They are in the keeping of St. Mary's in the Square in Lichfield.

the 18th Century

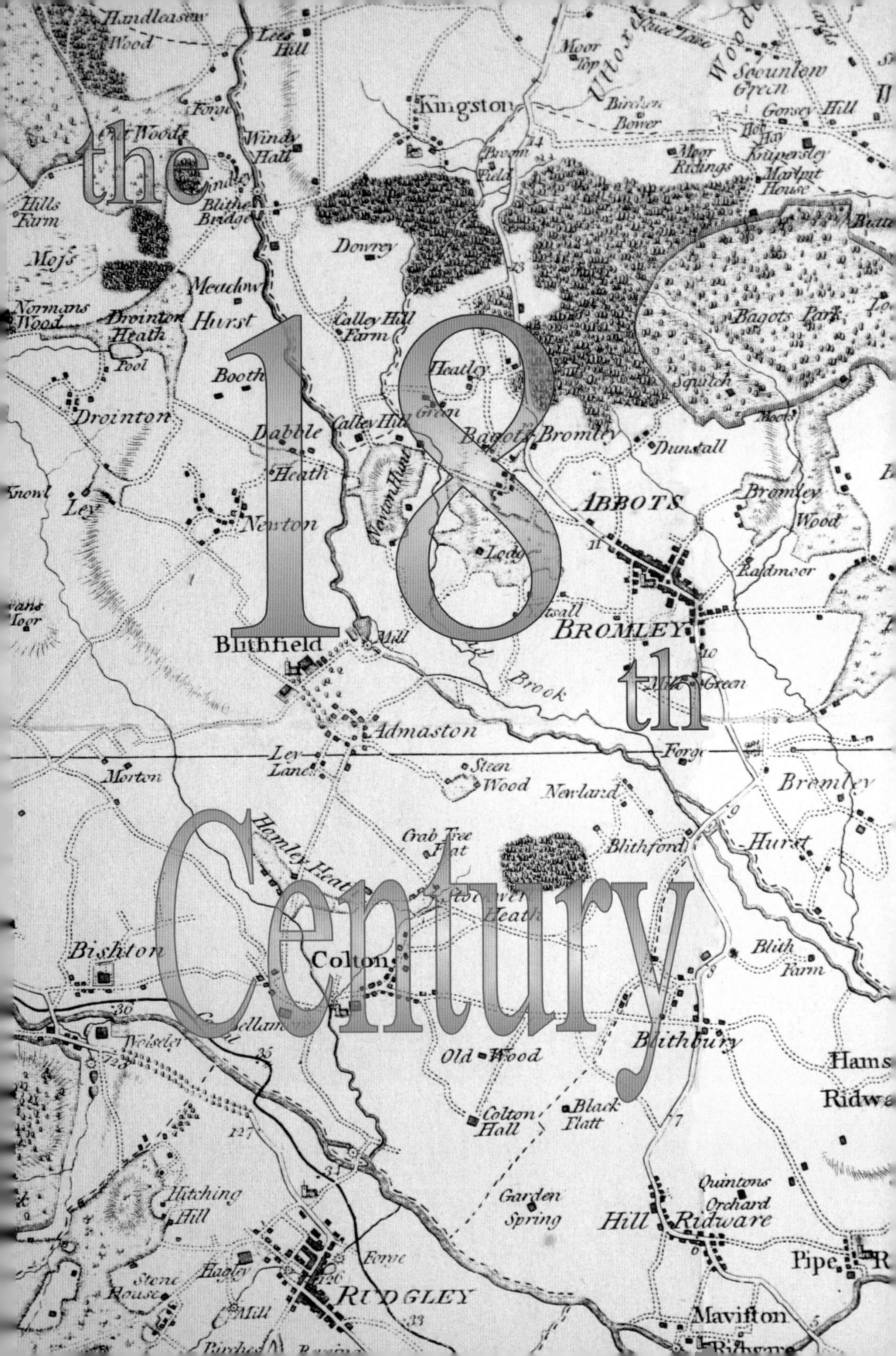

Handleasow Wood
Lees Hill
Moor Top
Uttoxeter
Kingston
Birchen Bower
Scounlow Green
Gorsey Hill
Knypersley
Marlpit House
Moor Ridings
Windy Hall
Broom Field
Blithe Bridge
Hills Farm
Dowrey
Meadow Hurst
Normans Wood
Drointon Heath
Pool
Calley Hill Farm
Bagots Park
Squitch
Booth
Heatley
Drointon
Dabble Heath
Calley Hill
Bagots Bromley
Dunstall
Newton
ABBOTS
BROMLEY
Bromley Wood
Radmoor
Lodge
Knowl
Ley
Blithfield
Mill
Brook
Admaston
Ley Lane
Forge
Morton
Steen Wood
Newland
Bromley Hurst
Crab Tree Flatt
Blithford
Hamley Heath
Heath
Bishton
Colton
Blith Farm
Wolseley
Blithbury
Old Wood
Hams
Ridwa
Colton Hall
Black Flatt
Hitching Hill
Garden Spring
Quintons Orchard
Hill Ridware
Stone House
Hagley
Forge
RUDGLEY
Mill
Pipe
Mavifton

SIR WALTER WAGSTAFFE BAGOT 1702 - 1768

Sir Walter Bagot
J. Richardson

Sir Walter Wagstaffe Bagot 5th baronet succeeded his father, Sir Edward, at the age of 10 years in 1712 and was under the guardianship of his great uncle Charles and his mother, the latter neglecting and depriving her son of his rightful possessions. She had removed many valuable items from Blithfield Hall after Sir Edward's death.

In 1724, he married Lady Barbara Legge, the sister of his school friend Lord Lewisham. That same year he was elected as Member of Parliament for the borough of Newcastle-under-Lyme in the last Parliament of George I. On one occasion for his election, he rode into Stafford at the head of 1500 supporters.

The King died in June 1727 being succeeded by George II, and in a letter to Sir Walter, Lord Lewisham writes...

There seems to be a very generall satisfaction in the people upon the King's accession, and there is hardly any body in town that has not been to kiss the king and Queen's hands, upon this occasion.-

Among the croud, your humble servant had that honour on Sunday last...

He goes on to say....

The common discourse in Town, at present among the young Ladies and Gentlemen, runs the splendors of the Coronation, and it makes a great many Ladies very busie and very happy, and their husbands a little melancholy; for there is no appearing at the best advantage that day, they say, under Five Hundred Pounds....[1]

Sir Walter's family consisted of eight sons and eight daughters. His second son, William, succeeded him and his fourth son Walter, presently became rector at Blithfield and Leigh. Family remembrances a generation later record their father as being a stickler for punctuality for he sometimes rebuked his sons for being late when they assembled at four o'clock in the morning to go hunting in 'Cannock Wood'. These same sons attended Westminster school, and before the invention of the stage coach used to ride to school preceded by a servant blowing a horn.

Sir Walter began improvements to Blithfield Hall and grounds and wishing to extend the same, he had Rector George Roades's old rectory pulled down and replaced with a larger building a short distance to the south west of the church circa 1724. In the glebe terrier of 1766 the new rectory is described-

Newly built away from the old site with convenient brewhouse, dairy, barns, stables, cowhouse, courtyard and garden; the site of the old parsonage is now in the garden of Sir Walter Wagstaffe Bagot in exchange for the part of the Yeld lately enclosed for a garden and lies 'very commodious' to the house,[2] *the exchange judged to be advantageous to the rector.*

Sir Walter continued in Parliament until the General Election of 1754 when he resigned in favour of his son and heir William because of health issues, thereby retiring from public duty.

However in 1762, University authorities called upon him to represent Oxford University in Parliament, which in consideration of his health he was keen to decline. Having studied at the University he must have left with some respect of the authorities there for subsequently he recognised the honour of their offer and eventually accepted.

He duly received this acknowledgement-

To Sir Walter Wagstaffe Bagot, Bart.

Good Sir, I have the pleasure to acquaint you, that this morning, in full Convocation, you was UNANIMOUSLY ELECTED Representative in Parliament for the University of Oxford. We are highly obliged to you for the honor of your acceptance of such an office; and heartily wish you life, and health long

1 This figure would amount to over £94,000 today! The coronation of George II was planned down to the last detail, with even the garments of those attending being considered. The mantle of a baroness could trail a yard on the ground while that of a viscountess had to be *"a yard and a quarter"*. Even the ladies underwear did not escape attention of the organisers. The petticoats were to be *"cloth of silver, or any other white stuff, either laced or embroidered"*. Cloth of silver was woven in the same way as cloth of gold.

2 Blithfield Hall.

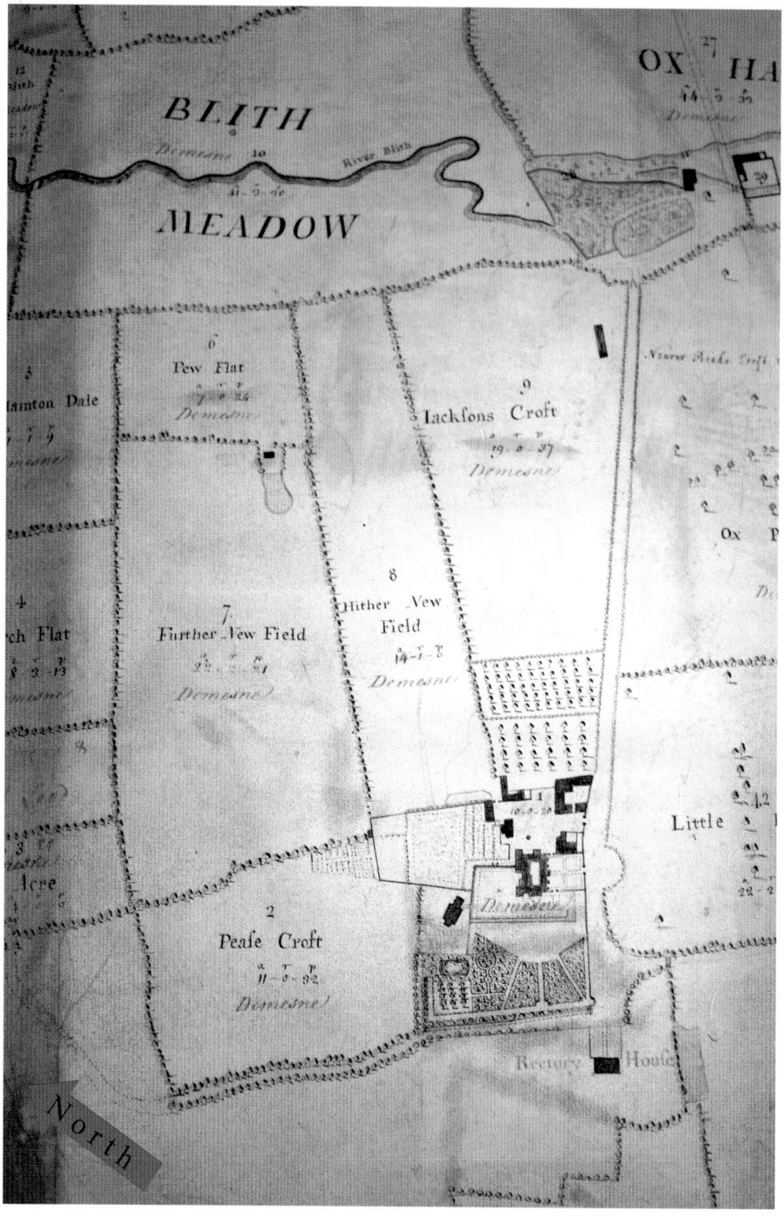
BLITH
MEADOW
River Blith
OX
Pew Flat
Demesne
Iackſons Croft
Demesne
Further New Field
Demesne
Hither New Field
Demesne
Peaſe Croft
Demesne
Demesne
Little
Rectory House
North

Part of a map of the Manor of Blithfield dated 1724. It shows Blithfield Hall, Church and Sir Walter Wagstaffe Bagot's newly extended grounds to his home. His alterations demolished Rector Roades's rectory which stood 60m to the south west of the Church and just outside its still existing boundary wall. The 'new' rectory, shown, was built where the pump house in the Hall grounds now stands. In turn, this rectory was demolished and replaced by the existing building in 1807. At the top of the map, the River Blithe is shown flowing into the mill pond of Blithfield Mill. This has now been submerged by the reservoir as has part the ancient road which passed in front of the Hall and led to Abbots Bromley to the east and Newton and Admaston to the north and south east respectively.

to enjoy the same...

Your most obedient and devoted humble servant,

Queen's Coll: Dec. 16th, 1762 *Joseph Browne, Vice Chan:*

Unfortunately, he was unable to adhere to the sentiment of the last line of the Vice Chancellor's letter.
Three years after his election, in 1765, Sir Walter lost his wife, Lady Barbara and was deeply affected by it. He died three year later at the age of 66 on 20th January 1768 and is buried, along with his wife, at Blithfield.

In 1745, according to family folklore, an incident occurred which exposes intrigue and tensions present in the politics of the time and the dangers they presented to allegiances held by the Bagot family. According to memories related by Harriet Bagot to her niece, Mary Bagot, fifty years later, ...*He* (Sir Walter Wagstaffe Bagot) *was chief of the Tory faction, and perhaps Lord Denbigh was not without some reason for the alarm he felt on hearing a drum beat (which was, in fact, only a signal for dinner) when he halted at Blithfield with his troops on his way to Derby in the '45.* [1]

Nearly 100 years after the end of the Civil War, the issues it raised had still not been satisfactorily resolved, not least that of the exact role of the monarchy and particularly that of its succession. Since the end of the war, King Charles II and his successor James II had had Roman Catholic leanings, and because of these, the latter was ousted from the throne in 1688. Some in political circles wished this to be resolved by introducing a Bill which forbade any Roman Catholic taking the English throne. This was supported by the Whig Party and opposed by some in the Tory Party which included Jacobite [2] supporters in its ranks. Other issues were also involved, but suffice it to say that until these issues were resolved, the undercurrents which resulted were dangerous to the welfare of Jacobite sympathisers, whatever their political persuasion. Anyone who supported the monarchy as part of the government of England had to be careful not to compromise themselves when at this time Protestant King George II was on the throne. The desire for a Protestant succession had already introduced protestant foreigners William of Orange (William III), a Dutch man and German,

1 In 1872, Francis Paget removed this story to the Civil War when he wrote:- *On one occasion it is said that there was a dinner party of Royalist soldiers dining at Blithfield during the Civil War. Consternation was felt by them on hearing the drum beat, and till they were told of the old family custom of announcing meals by drum, they imagined that they had been betrayed into the hands of Cromwell's soldiery.*
Perhaps the reason for this is that a good tale relates better to a part of English history when the antagonists, and the eventual outcome, are well known. The drum is still in -situ at Blithfield Hall.

2 Jacobite- Relating to King James I -Jacobus - Latin for James.

George I, to take the English throne, although they were both connected to the Stuart royal house either through birth or marriage.

It was not until the end of 1745 that this issue was finally settled when, during the Jacobite uprising of that year, Jacobite, Charles Edward Stuart or Bonnie Prince Charlie (known as the Young Pretender) ended all hope of a Stuart succession to the English throne, when his attempt to take it from George II failed due to lack of support as he marched on London from Scotland. He had reached Derby, and there realised he had to return to Scotland in order to save himself and his army. After a crushing defeat in at the Battle of Culloden in 1746,- the last to be fought on British soil- Charles Edward Stuart was forced into exile.

Protestant monarchs have ruled the country ever since.

SIR WILLIAM BAGOT 1728 - 1798
the first Lord Bagot of Blithfield

Sir William Bagot was born at Blithfield on 28th February 1728 and attended Magdellan College Oxford, became an MA and also became an Honorary Doctor of Civil Laws. On leaving the university, he spent time in Paris perfecting his languages of French and Italian before undertaking the Grand Tour of Europe, travelling extensively through France and Italy, as was the case with many of his contemporaries. He was MP for Staffordshire between 1754 and 1780 and was a close friend of Lord North, who became Prime Minister in 1770 and under who's tenure the American Colonies were lost [1]. As a keen and dedicated supporter of his county in Parliament, Sir William declined to be honoured with higher offices in government, but equally did not wish this to be seen being a lack of loyalty on his part to either the King or the Government. To this end Lord North wrote to Sir William:

...I am sorry to find by your letter that my absence from town has deprived me of the pleasure of seeing you this morning. Tomorrow I return to my old quarters, and shall be glad of your company in Downing Street, about two o'clock in the afternoon... as I much wish to have a little conversation with

1 This event was seen as a calamity for the nation at the time, but since has been viewed as the catalyst for the expansion and consolidation of the British Empire to the East.

you, before you leave town... He goes on...*You need be under no apprehension, lest your refusal should be misinterpreted, or misunderstood, in any place; your principles are known to be honourable, loyal, and friendly towards Government; and your motives for declining the Treasurership of the Chamber, will never be thought inconsistent with those principles...*

I am, with the truest esteem,

Dear Sir, your most obliged and faithful humble servant,

North

In 1760, Sir William married the Honourable Louisa St John from Wiltshire, she being of a young age and in a somewhat delicate state of health. They married at Wroxton, Oxfordshire where William Bagot's brother, the Reverend Walter Bagot, Rector of Blithfield officiated.

Portrait of Lady Louisa Bagot

by Sir Joshua Reynolds

In 1773 they suffered the loss of two sons and one daughter to scarlet fever within three days of one another and were left with only one daughter, although a son was born a few months later. Despite this and Lady Bagot's delicate constitution, she went on produce another five children and survived her husband by 21 years, dying in 1820 at the age of 77.

Sir William was raised to the peerage by George III on 17th October 1780 as the First Lord Bagot and he took the title Baron Bagot of Bagot's Bromley.

This, and being a man who was fond of writing verse, prompted him to write to Doctor Thomas Townson his former tutor and rector of Blithfield from 1749 to 1759 -

' Perhaps you will be glad to hear the King has just made me a Peer. I hope you'll think my title comely, t'is Bagot Lord of Bagot's Bromley '

In 1793 he found the need to be almost constantly in attendance at the House of Lords, along with his brother the Right Reverend Lewis Bagot bishop of St Asaph, as news of the French Revolution and it's excesses horrified and frightened the English establishment.

The situation prompted Lord Bagot again to to write in verse to his brother:

Bishop! we live in cruel times,
Portentous! - stain'd with blacker crimes
Than history records
in her long scroll of impious deeds.
To catalogue French crimes exceeds,
By far, - the power of words...

Behold her Capital, - so late
Of arts and elegance the seat,
Sole arbitress of taste
To the surrounding nations; - now -
Her streets with bloody torrents flow;
By murd'ring mobs disgrac'd;

Mobs, urg'd by murd'rers, worse than they;
Assasins hold sovereign sway,
In mischief uncontrol'd; -
Their object plunder;- and the blood
Of all the noble, wise and good;
Ferocious, - blind, - and bold.

Their Queen, - her infant Royal line
Immur'd, - half starv'd, - in dungeons pine;
Behold their Monarch led
With insult to the public square,
High on a scaffold placed there;
Struck off his guiltless head!!!!

O thou Voltaire! - Jean Jacques Rousseau!
... Chiefs of the new Philosophy,
Of this preposterous anarchy
The seeds were sown, - BY YOU:

Which, bursting into monstrous birth,
Now shake the nations of the earth
With universal War;-
But you are the French Philosophers!
Britain may rest secure on hers,
Paine, Priestly, Price, and P - r!!!

This last line seems rather strange in that Thomas Paine and Richard Price were both keen advocates of what Paine titled his book 'The Rights of Man' which was the philosophy of those who were guillotining the aristocrats in France. The last word is illegible - or perhaps, intended to be!

The French Revolution spilled over the borders of France to embroil Europe over the next twenty years in the Napoleonic Wars, which in the early years of the nineteenth century, a young lad from Blithfield was to become involved

During his European travels, Lord Bagot acquired many works of art which he added to those already at Blithfield Hall. He was also no doubt inspired by the architecture abroad which led him to commission Samuel Wyatt to build the Orangery situated to the north of the Hall. It was built from the designs and direct direction of the renowned architect James 'Athenian' Stuart. Lord Bagot also continued to improve the gardens and grounds at the Hall which had been begun by his father Sir Walter Wagstaffe Bagot.

After an agonising illness of some six months, Lord Bagot died on 22nd October 1798 and is buried at Blithfield along with his wife.

Opposite - A William Yates map of 1775 showing Blithfield and surrounding area. The production of this map saw levels of accuracy not seen before, particularly by showing road layouts which were to soon to change during the 19th century when the rapid industrialisation of the country was under way. New roads were then being built with old ones falling into decline. Also shown are water mills (Blithfield, Abbots Bromley and Burndhurst) and forges (Chartley and Abbots Bromley). This map was produced from subscriptions from the main landowners, the nobility, gentry and clergy and consequently it defers to them by depicting their interests. By the end of the 19th century, Ordnance Survey maps of even greater accuracy were in production, showing the newly built canal and railway network.

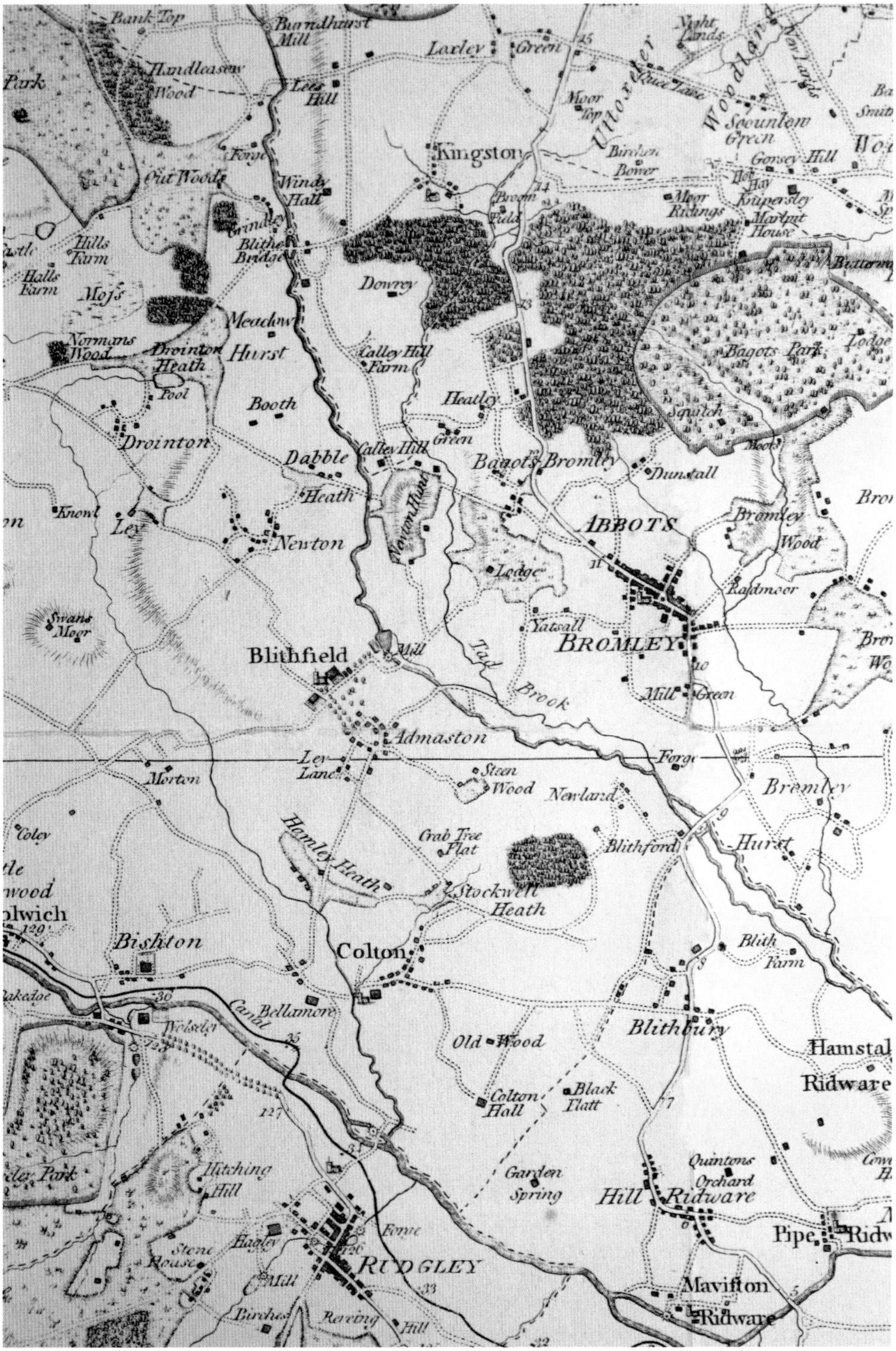
Bank Top
Burndhurst Mill
Loxley Green
Park
Handleasow Wood
Lees Hill
Moor Top
Uttoxeter Woodland
Kingston
Forge
Out Woods
Windy Hall
Birchen Bower
Gorsey Hill
Grindley
Blithe Bridge
Hills Farm
Halls Farm
Moss
Dowrey
Meadow Hurst
Normans Wood
Drointon Heath
Pool
Calley Hill Farm
Bagots Park
Lodge
Squitch
Booth
Heatley
Green
Drointon
Dabble Heath
Calley Hill
Bagots Bromley
Dunstall
Knowl
Ley
Newton
Newton Hurst
ABBOTS
Bromley Wood
Lodge
Swans Moor
Yatsall
BROMLEY
Blithfield
Mill
Tad Brook
Mill Green
Admaston
Ley Lane
Forge
Morton
Steen Wood
Newland
Bromley Hurst
Coley
Hamley Heath
Crab Tree Flat
Blithford
Stockwell Heath
Bishton
Colton
Blith Farm
Canal
Bellamore
Wolseley
Blithbury
Old Wood
Hamstall Ridware
Colton Hall
Black Flatt
Hitching Hill
Garden Spring
Quintons Orchard
Hill Ridware
Stone House
Hagley
Forge
RUDGLEY
Pipe Ridware
Mill
Mavifton Ridware
Birches
Rareing Hill

THE STATE OF WELFARE IN 18th CENTURY BLITHFIELD.

The provision of welfare during the latter half of the 18th century in England was radically different from today's centrally controlled system of benefits to the needy which are distributed from the many and varied taxes paid into national and local government coffers. This system had its beginnings in the early 20th century and was greatly expanded by the post war government of 1945 with the introduction of the fully fledged 'Welfare State' of which we are so familiar today.

Prior to these developments responsibility for these necessities fell on the parishes of England where Parish Rates contributed to supporting the poor and needy. In the parish of Blithfield, and others, Overseers of the Poor [1] were appointed to carry out these duties and for Blithfield, the records they kept are very detailed. Both Blithfield and Newton had their own overseer, each responsible for the people in their Liberty [2]. Overseers were responsible for levying a poor rate and supervising its distribution. A few selected examples of these payments are given on the following pages, together with the total for all entries for the year 1767. All written out in beautiful copper plate handwriting, and in all likelihood with a goose quill pen, they cover a wide range of items, many as payments in kind rather than direct handouts of cash. (In 1767, £1 would be equal to £160 today).

The Account of Joseph Hodgson Overseer of the Poor for the Liberty of Blithfield for the year 1766 & part of 1767.

		£	s	d
Pd	*for a Coffin for Nehemiah Walkeden*	*0*	*10*	*0*
	ale for the funeral	*0*	*5*	*0*
	ale for laying him out	*0*	*1*	*0*
Pd	*for burial fees*	*0*	*3*	*0*
Pd	*for laying him out*	*0*	*1*	*0*
Pd	*for a face Cloth Cap & Jersey for ditto*	*0*	*2*	*4*
Pd	*for him in his illness*	*0*	*6*	*0*
Pd	*to Walkdens Widow*	*0*	*8*	*0*
	Board for Walkdens Child	*0*	*5*	*0*
Pd	*for a pair of shoes for Walkdens Widow*	*0*	*3*	*0*
Pd	*for a load of Coals for Rich*[d] *Bentley*	*0*	*8*	*0*

1 The Poor Law Act of 1601 stipulated that at least two persons were appointed yearly by the vestry, the governing body of the parish. They were from among the parishioners and unpaid. The office was abolished in 1925.

2 A group of manors, the lord of which held certain privileges of the Crown.

	My journey to Kingstone to forbid Asbery's Banns	*0*	*1*	*6*
Pd	*John Lowe for making Parkers Clothes*	*0*	*3*	*6*
Pd	*to Wm Yates for making gown for Parkers Wife*	*0*	*1*	*0*
Pd	*to Mother Hodgson 3 weeks Board for Walkeden's child*		*5*	*0*
Pd	*Mary Lowe for Washing Josh Radford*	*0*	*10*	*0*
Pd	*Thoms Shipley for a Load of Coals for Rd Bentley*	*0*	*8*	*8*
Pd	*Wm Yates for making Walkeden's Widow a gown and Petticoat*	*0*	*1*	*4*
Pd	*for making and mending Shifts for Parker's Wife*	*0*	*1*	*0*
Pd	*for a pair of Shoes for Parkers Wife*	*0*	*2*	*10*
Pd	*for a letter from Widow Boden*	*0*	*0*	*6*
	Total for Period	*21*	*6*	*7*

Receivd of the Old Officer	*1*	*12*	*11*
Gather 65 levies @ 6/4d	*19*	*15*	*5*

Total reciev	*21*	*8*	*4*
In hand	*0*	*1*	*9*

Nehemiah Walkeden was buried on 27th January 1767.
It can be assumed that Mother Hodgson was the Overseers wife who took in young Walkden in order to help its mother.

As well as being helped in bereavement, the overseers record for Newton includes details of support for a case of illness in the village:

Tho: Shipley – Overseer of the Poor for the Liberty of Newton for the year of our Lord 1767

		£	s	d
Pd	*for two shirts John Preston*	*0*	*6*	*6*
Pd	*for Coals Rachel Hollens*	*0*	*8*	*8*
	gave a poor man on his way home	*0*	*0*	*6*
	My journey to Bromley for a Nurse for Eliz Cope	*0*	*1*	*6*
Pd	*Peter Rock for Strike of Malt for Eliz Cope*	*0*	*5*	*0*

			£	s	d
Pd	Sam Cope in cash		0	5	0
Pd	Mary Hill in cash for Coals		0	3	0
	my lad and Horse to Cauden on act of Eth Cope		0	4	0
	Expended on account for searching the pils for Eliz Cope		0	2	0
Pd	for a pair of shoes for Jn Preston		0	4	6
	for 11 weeks Board for Eliz Cope at 3/6d pr week	[1]	1	18	6
Pd	Nurse Barton for Nursing Eliz Cope 11 weeks & two days at 7 (shillings) pr Week		3	19	0
	for attendance for my Self and Servants to Eliz Cope		0	5	0
Pd	Doctor Chadwick his Bill for Eliz Cope	[2]	3	16	4
Pd	Doctor Hordern his Bill Do		1	1	10
Pd	Widow Birchs Rent		1	0	0
	for ten weeks Board & two days at three shillings pr week for Jn Preston		1	10	10
Pd	for mending Prestons shoes		0	0	10
Pd	for Washing Prestons 9 Shirts		0	1	6
	for Keeping and Entering these Accounts for the yr		0	2	0

		£	s	d	£	s	d
Distburst.					24	5	3¼
Receiv'd 65 levies @ 7s/7d per levy	[3]	24	11	11			
Receiv'd of the old officers		1	12	11			
Receiv'd in all					26	4	10
Disburst	[4]	24	5	3			
Pd my partner to Ballance		0	2	3			
Remains in hand		1	17	3			
		26	4	10			

The 'Strike of Malt' for Elizabeth Cope indicates a need for nutrition. Malt is a main ingredient of beer and is the grain which has been steeped in water, germinated and then dried. People of the time could well have been aware of its beneficial health effects, as is the case now, and mixed with warm water it could have been taken as a sort of porridge. Indeed, it was

1 Today, Elizabeth Cope's board would be charged at around £30 per week

2 Doctor Chadwick's bill would be charged at about £650 today.

3 The levies would equal around £60 at today's rates.

4 The total welfare bill would be equal to approximately £4300 today.

small beer [1] - with a very low alcohol content - which was the main beverage in an era when water was invariably unsafe to drink. Alternatively, it could have been this, mixed with bread which was administered to Elizabeth Cope in the case of her being unable to digest solid food.

A strike is a unit of dry measure equal to one bushel, or eight gallons. It would seem however, rather curious that she should have been provided with such a large quantity.

The parish register states that... *Elizabeth, daughter of Samuel and Elizabeth Cope Baptised 23rd March 1766,* and also... *Joseph, Son of Samuel and Elizabeth Cope Baptised October 4th 1767.*

The levies came from the parish rates which were paid by each household.

Unfortunately, the parish rate book for Blithfield is missing. These not only provide rates paid but record family names and the location of the dwelling where they lived.

There is no doubt that the Bagot family took an interest in the welfare of local people for an entry in the diary of Lady Bagot records-J*uly 24th 1815. Harriet and I drove to Leigh Heath and Newton to see the poor folk. Bentley of Newton "sorely handled" with a 'pain' in her stomach, meaning to go to Robert Wingfield, a farrier, to be cured because he had cured Mr Brandrick's leg 'very cheap'*

Most of the tailoring, cobbling, carpentry and other services provided would have been obtained locally. In 1851, Blithfield parish could provide a blacksmith, wheelwright, tailor, shoemaker and shopkeeper. Additionally, in Abbots Bromley, were a nail maker, a baker, a cooper, basket makers, a chemist and druggist, a corn miller, a plumber glazier and painter, maltsters, saddlers, surgeons, joiners and cabinet makers, and drapers.

Other entries, in 1769 by the overseers, include paying £1 for Mary Hodgson's lying in, 5 shillings for the Midwife, payment of 10 shillings for 18 weeks pay for Mary Hodgson, and paying £1 *for the thatching of J^{o} Radford's house.* Ann, daughter of Mary Hodgson was baptized on 21st November 1769.

Another important and unpaid officer of the parish was the Constable who was responsible for a wide range of duties and was also appointed by the parish vestry. An indication as to his duties can be had from the accounts kept during the latter part of the 18th century, and a few of the entries are included here from Blithfield parish records.

One set of accounts are by Joseph Hodgson, who appears to have left his job as overseer and became constable for the Liberty of Blithfield during the year 1767:

---

1 Now a term used to denote something of little consequence.

		£	s	d
Pd.	*the Chief Constable for making an assessment for the Land and Window Tax*	*0*	*2*	*0*
Pd	*for ale when casting snow*	*0*	*5*	*0*
Pd	*for cutting a snowdrift*	*0*	*0*	*4*
	Spent at the highways	*0*	*9*	*2*
	Myself for 46 load of Stones	*0*	*15*	*4*
Pd	*Mrs Kent for 6 load Do*	*0*	*2*	*0*
Pd	*15 men for repairing the Highways*	*0*	*15*	*0*
	for keeping and entering these accounts	*0*	*2*	*0*

Other entries, against the year they were made include:-

1737	*pd for ye Gaoll and House of Correction*	*0*	*1*	*11½*
1738	*Given a soldier with a pass and big bellied wife*	*0*	*0*	*2*
	pd for a warrant for collecting window tax	*0*	*1*	*0*
1749	*Paid for my oath*	*0*	*0*	*6*
1759	*For Repairing ye stocks and Pinfold*	*0*	*0*	*8*
	For passing of Vagrants	*0*	*10*	*4*
1761	*Tho. Harvey a bill for the Stox and pinfold*	*0*	*8*	*6*
1765	*Paid T Harvey for repairing Bridges on Blithe moor*	*0*	*10*	*6*
1768	*Carried 22 load of stones into Steenwood Lane at 4d per load*	*0*	*7*	*4*
	Paid for nine men at the Highway	*0*	*7*	*6*
	Paid Walter Abberley for levelling	*0*	*0*	*10*
	paid toward the County Rate	*0*	*17*	*0*
	My journey to Trentham Court	*0*	*2*	*0*
1770	*Paid John Shipley for the Stocks*	*1*	*2*	*6*
	pd for ale at giving these accounts	*0*	*5*	*0*

The Window Tax was introduced on 1696 and replaced the Hearth Tax. Each household paid a basic 2 shillings and those with between 10 and 20 windows paid a further 8 shillings. New rates were levied in 1747 and in 1825. Homes with less than 8 windows were exempt. The tax was abolished in 1851. It is quite common today to see houses with window openings bricked up, including some at Blithfield Hall, which reduced occupiers' tax liability.

In order to prevent those from outside the parish from receiving its poor relief, vagrants, who did not belong in the parish, were not encouraged to stay and it was the responsibility of the parish overseers and constables to move them on. Various Settlement Acts ensured who had the right of settlement in a parish, which included their place of birth, ability to work, marriage status, and owning or renting property of £10 per annum or more. Anyone who was considered able to work and support their family and refused to do so was considered a vagrant, as were beggars, seasonal workers, the homeless, prostitutes, unlicensed pedlars and criminals. From the early 18th century, passes were issued to vagrants in order that they were able to travel unmolested to the parish of their origin or a particular destination and claim up to nights board or small cash payment from parish constables along the way. By 1824 however, this system was called into question when a parliamentary report suggested as many as 60,000 people were continually circulating the country at public expense. In earlier times vagrants capable of working were very harshly treated and could be whipped, their ears cut off, and for persistent offenders, even hanged.

In her journal, Mary Bagot mentions that her father, Rector Walter Bagot gave work to 'the very old, the very young and infirm' on the glebe farm in Blithfield, for the reason that they were refused employment elsewhere.

By the early 19th century, due to a significant increase in people claiming poor relief, a new Poor Law in 1824 saw the increased use of the workhouse. The very harsh regimes they intentionally imposed on the inmates were seen as a deterrent to those who were able to work and refused to do so. A workhouse in Abbots Bromley for up to 30 inmates is mentioned in a Parliamentary report of 1777.

Soldiers and sailors returning home from the wars also carried passes, or letters, which were issued by their commanding officer or magistrate which indicated their destination and time they expected to be on the road.

Judging by the regularity in which the stocks appear in the accounts, it seems they may have enjoyed some use, which may not be surprising.
Stocks, where offenders were briefly restrained by the legs as a form of punishment, had been in use since Saxon times and were used for the relatively minor misdemeanours such as blasphemy, drunkenness and breaking the Sabbath. An Act of 1405 directed that stocks should be provided in each town and village. By the 1830's they had passed into history.

Churchwardens were other officers who held important positions in English parishes. Blithfield was represented by two, one for Newton and the other for Blithfield. As well as the roles which may be expected to be carried out by them, one in particular, as can be seen from one Churchwarden's accounts, is by today's standards, peculiar.

The Acctˢ of William Bakewell Churchwarden for the township of Blithfield from May ᵗʰ 8 1798 to June ᵗʰ 27 1800

		£	s	d
Paid	*for repairing the light* (Lych) *gates*	*0*	*5*	*0*
	My journey to the confirmation	*0*	*1*	*6*
Paid	*Elizabeth Tooth at Sundry times for Cleaning the Church*	*0*	*4*	*0*
Paid	*for clearing the snow of the church walk at sundry times*	*0*	*4*	*0*
	for attending the church	*0*	*10*	*6*
Paid	*for 4 Days Ringing*	*0*	*12*	*0*
	Carrying Gravel to the Church Walk	*0*	*2*	*6*
Paid	*for Cleaning the Church Walk*	*0*	*2*	*6*
	Repairing the rails and posts	*0*	*5*	*0*
Paid	*for 52 Doz of Rat tails as 1s per Doz*	*2*	*12*	*0*
Paid	*for 5½ (Doz) of sparrows heads*	*0*	*11*	*0*
Paid	*for Parchment to make the Register and terrier and writing out*	*0*	*7*	*6*
Paid	*for three new keys to the Church Cof(f)er and Repairing the Lock*	*0*	*2*	*6*
Wm Bakewells Accts	*Totals*	*12*	*18*	*3½*

Rec'd by 14 Levies	*9*	*5*	*6*
Rec'd of the Old Officer	*1*	*11*	*11½*
Rec'd parishioner to Balance	*3*	*7*	*0¼*
Total Rec'd	*14*	*4*	*5¾*
Total Disburst	*12*	*18*	*3½*
In Hand	*1*	*6*	*2¼*

Seen and allowed by us
this 7th day of Nov 1800

Thº Dennis
Chas Holland

Along with many other responsibilities, including maintenance of the church and representing parishioners in parochial matters, in times past the churchwarden was responsible for the control of vermin. To this end money was paid to those who participated in this pursuit at the rates seen above which at today's values would be equal to about £325.

Churchwardens also collaborated with Overseers of the Poor by supervising relief and education of the poor as well as encouraging parishioners to attend church regularly and ensuring their children were baptised.

The Church Coffer or Chest, was where all church and parochial documents were kept. Usually made of oak, they were furnished with three locks, a key being kept by each of the Churchwardens and the Rector. It could only be opened when all three men were present. It would appear that the Blithfield Parish Chest disappeared from the Church within the last 100 years, for mention is made of it by the Rev. Douglas Murray in his book, Notes on the Early History of the Parish of Blithfield. He implies that in 1919, it was no longer used for its intended purpose and that it was in the passage to the Vestry. There is a fine example of one in the church at Stowe-by-Chartley.

It has to be assumed that William Bakewell's charge of 10/6d *for attending the church,* was not for attending church services!

The rate paid for ringing the bells at 3 shillings per session seems to have been in force for many years. Churchwarden George Holland records in 1760... *Pd for ringing on the Coronation Day, 3 shillings.* (George III on 22nd September) This amount equates to around £27 today, or just over £8 per ringer as at that time there were only three bells in the church tower.

Other examples of charges paid by the churchwardens in 1768/9 include:-

paid – for Cobwebbing the church 3 shillings, for the new churchwardens dinner 2 shillings, for two pounds of Candles 1/2d, for the Bell Ropes 7/6d, and paid John Shipley for mending of seats 1 shilling.

For many years now, most of the day-to-day tasks concerning church upkeep, cleaning, sundry repair jobs, church decorating etc., have been carried out voluntarily and bell-ringers are paid only for their services at weddings.

This short account of welfare payments in the parish does not give a full picture of the total amounts paid by parishioners in levies or rates.

However, a clear indication is given as to the amounts paid in order to alleviate the hardships experienced by local people.

At today's values, the amounts of approximately £4,300 and £3,400 paid out in one year by the Overseers of Blithfield and Newton respectively, totalled nearly £8,000. It seems that the 'in house' care provided by this money covered most aspects of the benefits required.

Additionally, along with other public liabilities, it would appear that a relatively large amount of money was required in order to cater for the overall welfare of Blithfield's population.

MATTERS OF LIFE AND DEATH

The Parish Register for St Leonard's Church, Blithfield extends back to the year 1538. Of all the parishes in Staffordshire, only Alstonefield, Bradley, Burton-on Trent, Church Eaton, and Norbury can equal this.

Taken from the records are these interesting and sad entries:

1682 *A poor travelling boy was buried Apr. 7th*

1725 *Will: ye Bast born son of Temperance Price was baptised Jan 30*

1747 *Sarah and Mary Twin daughters of Richard Brandrick of Newton were Baptised Jan 17*

1747 *Sarah the daughter of Richard Brandrick of Newton was buried Feb 7*

1753 *Esther Daughter of Robert and Elizabeth Heap (Travelling People) was baptised Dec 16*

1754 *Joseph Walkadine (drowned in crossing the Trent at Ingestre Ford) was buried Feb 22*

1755 *John Bast Born son of Deborah Bailey baptised Oct 5*

1755 *John Bast Born son of Deborah Bailey was buried Oct 22*

1759 *Jane daughter of Elizabeth Jones (a Traveller) buried Feb 9*

1763 *Samuel Hodgson (drowned in passing through Blithmoor) buried Decr 4th*

1771 *Thomas son of Thomas & Dorothy Shipley baptised March 6*

Thomas son of Thomas & Dorothy Shipley Buried March 8

Elizabeth daughter of Thomas & Dorothy Shipley Buried March 16

Dorothy wife of Thomas Shipley of Newton Buried July 8

1772 *John Chamberlaine of Newton (whose death was occasioned by being run over by a Waggon) buried Oct r 7*

1777 Thomas son of Thomas and Jane Shipley baptised Aug 23

1779 Thomas son of Thomas and Jane Shipley was buried Feb 10

Two example of gravestones in Blithfield churchyard from an era when sickness and death were ever present

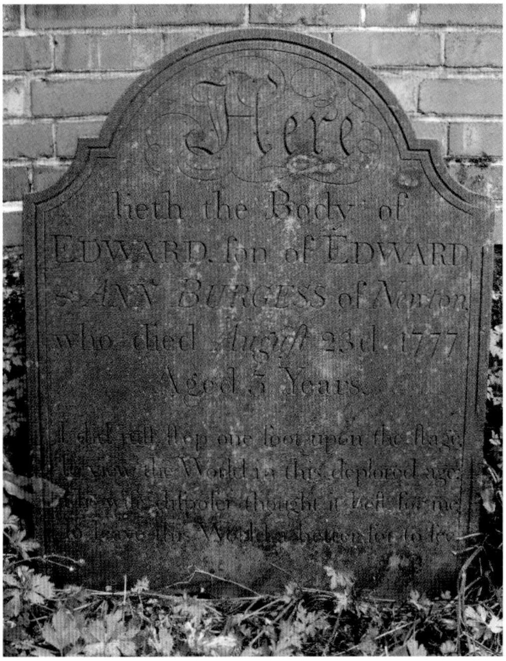
Here
lieth the Body of
EDWARD. fon of EDWARD
who died August 23d 1777
Aged 3 Years

Here
lieth the Body of
EDWARD, son of EDWARD
& ANN BURGESS of Newton
who died August 23d 1777
Aged 3 Years
I did just step one foot upon the stage,
to view the World in this deplored age:
The wise disposer thought it best for me,
To leave this World a better for to see.

To
the Memory of
THOMAS KENT
who died Feb^{y}: 25th 1800
Aged 45
To this thou shalt come
Think and be ready

Also in the churchyard are these inscriptions-

Here Lieth the Body of ANN the wife of NICHOLAS VIRRELS who died March 16th 1804 Aged 32. A loving Wife in prime of life Death quickly snatched away. Sure such a call Bids one and all, Prepare without delay

In Memory of MARGARET, Wife of ROBERT BUCK who died May 13th 1817 Aged 29 Years. Also ELIZABETH their Daughter died June 27th 1817 Aged 2 years 2 months. For this God is our God for ever and ever; he will be our guide even unto death.

Hear this, all yea people give ear, all inhabitants of the world

the 19th Century

MIDSHIPMAN EDMUND BURKE HOLLAND

1789 - 1804

In St Leonard's churchyard Blithfield, is the memorial stone of Midshipman Edmund Burke Holland who died in the year 1804. This can be seen as unusual bearing in mind that Blithfield is as far from the sea as it is possible to be, but there is an interesting story to be told.

The inscription on the head stone reads

SACRED
To the Memory of
EDMUND BURKE HOLLAND
Son of
Capt.WALTER & ANN HOLLAND
Midshipman of
HM Ship Bellerophon
He died of the fatal Yellow Fever
the 1st of July 1804 in the 15 year
of his age on his passage to England
from Jamaica
A more promising young Officer
never... (illegible)...The British Navy

Midshipman Edmund Holland is not buried here.
There is no detail in the parish burial records of this being so, therefore we must conclude that he was, not surprisingly, buried at sea as was the custom up until recent times due to the impracticability of repatriating the dead when ships were at sea.
The stone can be seen therefore as his memorial, placed here by parents proud of their son[1] as the inscription indicates. Mention is also made of his infant brother, Avarne Luke Holland on the stone at the base (barely visible) who is interred here. The burial records state he died on 13th July 1805.
Their parents were from Lee Lane which lies just inside Colton Parish [2] and

1 When the brother of the Duke of Wellington joined his ship as a 'middy' at aged just 11, he was so impressed on seeing the magnificent English fleet, he felt ' *it was a prouder thing to belong to the Royal Navy than to possess any other position in the world* '. In 1809, the Royal Navy consisted of one half of the warships in the world.

2 Inhabitants of Lee Lane have generally always looked to Blithfield Church for their spiritual needs.

Edmund was christened at Colton Church on 12th August 1791.

HMS Bellerophon had been ordered to the West Indies in 1802 and sailed from Torbay on 2 March 1802 and took part in patrol and escort duties in the Caribbean until the Napoleonic Wars broke out 18 months later in May 1803. She immediately went on the offensive against the French and was successful in capturing two of their ships with the help of other vessels in her squadron. It is highly probable that Bellerophon was Edmund's first ship and this his first serious experience at sea.

Whilst in Jamaica, in February 1804, there was a severe outbreak of malaria aboard the ship and 212 crew were taken ill and 17 died. Another 100 were sent to shore based hospitals where another 40 died.

H.M.S. Bellerophon was ordered back to Britain in June 1804, and young Midshipman Holland died at sea on 1st July of yellow fever after surviving the malaria epidemic. His was a young life, full of promise, cut short as so often was the case in the past. This resulted in him being unable to serve his country on the ship which was to become famous for her exploits during the next decade. It was a period which was to define the future of Europe and confirm Great Britain as a world power for the next century.

Another young lad, by the name of Nelson, began his navy career as a midshipman some 40 years earlier, and later his ship Victory, was to join the Bellerophon, and others, in shaping the destiny of Great Britain.

Had young Midshipman Holland survived, he could well have found himself involved in some of the most famous sea battles in English history as well as meeting one of the most renowned military commanders the world has known[1].

The memorial stone to Midshipman Edmund Burke Holland and his brother Avarne Luke Holland in St Leonard's churchyard.

1 See Other Histories - H.M.S. Bellerophon. p.291

SIR CHARLES BAGOT 1781-1843

Mounted on the north wall of the chancel in Blithfield Church is the memorial to Sir Charles Bagot.

He was probably the most influential, on the world stage, of that ancient family who can trace their lineage back to the Norman Conquest.

He was born at Blithfield Hall on 23rd September 1781, the second surviving son of William, the 1st Baron Bagot and was educated at Rugby School and Christ Church College Oxford where he obtained an M.A.

He married Mary Charlotte Ann Wellesley-Pole the niece of Arthur Wellesley, who later became the Duke of Wellington, the famous victor against Napoleon at Waterloo in 1815.

In 1807 he took his Parliamentary seat as the member for Castle Rising in Norfolk and was a supporter of the then Foreign Secretary, George Canning, and formed a close friendship with him. Through Canning's extensive family connections Charles Bagot was soon launched into a distinguished diplomatic career.

He was named Minister Plenipotentiary (invested with the full power to take independent action) to France on 11th July 1814, the year before the Battle of Waterloo, but was replaced by the Duke of Wellington later that summer.

On 31st July 1815 however, he was appointed Minister Plenipotentiary to the United States.

This was only six months after the end of the 1812 American War with Britain when famously, the British attacked Washington, burned down the White House[1] and other public buildings.

This was therefore a difficult assignment as the Americans had grudging memories of the war and the issues which arose from it were complicated.

At aged only 34, and with little diplomatic experience Charles Bagot handled the assignment with aplomb, tact and sensitivity. He won the respect of the American Administration becoming well liked in Washington. He left his name to the Rush-Bagot Agreement which reduced the American and British naval forces on the Great Lakes from the numbers deployed there during the American War.

He was also able to successfully negotiate other disputes concerning fisheries and the border along the 49th Parallel between the US and British Canada which was subsequently agreed, with both countries ceding territory to the other.

The American War (1812 – 1814) is now largely forgotten in Britain, partly in deference to the feelings of our American cousins, but mainly because it was fought during Great Britain's engagement in the Napoleonic Wars which were by far a greater threat to the country and demanded far more resources.

America declared war on Great Britain on 19th June 1812 as a result of the Royal Navy blockading American ports in order to restrict their trade with Napoleon's France. The press ganging of American seamen into the Royal Navy and America's desire to expand its territory into Canada, or British North America as it was then known, were also a cause of tension.

The Americans suffered many defeats at the hands of the British, Canadian and Native American troops, but did along the way, see victories of their own, not least against the Royal Navy on Canada's Great Lakes.

The war ended in 1814 with neither country achieving any significant advantage. With Britain's tussle with Napoleon having ended in 1814 - for the time being -, the trade blockade which was the overriding cause of the war from the American point of view, could now be safely lifted. The British had also secured their aim of preventing any American incursion into Canadian territory.

For her part, America had also successfully repulsed the British in their attacks on New York and New Orleans. America's successes during the war had the effect of boosting national confidence and led the Americans to see the war as their 'second war of independence'.

Charles Bagot returned to England in 1819 and was knighted in 1820.

That year, Sir Charles became ambassador to Russia and took part in the

[1] The White House- So named because, after being rebuilt, it was painted white in order to hide the scorch marks.

negotiations which led to the Anglo-Russian Treaty of 1825 which fixed the boundaries between Alaska and Canada. Alaska was then part of the Russian Empire [1]

In 1824 Sir Charles was appointed ambassador to the Hague where the Dutch king was attempting to unify Holland and Belgium in law, language and religion.

The problems which arose proved this ideal impossible and Sir Charles was to take part in negotiations which led to an independent Belgium in 1831.

It was some indication as to how Sir Charles Bagot was regarded that in 1828, he was offered the position of Governor General of India, but he declined the offer due to worries over his health.

In 1841 however, under prime minister Sir Robert Peel, he became Governor General of Canada. His experience in the United States proved critical in his appointment as at that time the U.S. were again advancing expansionist policies, again threatening Anglo-American relations. Sir Robert Peel endorsed his choice by writing of - *the knowledge that (Bagot) was one of the most popular ambassadors ever accredited to the United States.*[2]

His appointment came at a time of political unrest in Canada, with rebellion and calls for change to the system of government from the English and French speaking settlers.

Under his tenure, and partly due to ill health preventing him from the traditional role of presiding over cabinet meetings, he appointed two Canadians, one of them French, to the governing council thereby paving the way for 'responsible government' by the Canadians themselves in what Bagot called his "great measure".

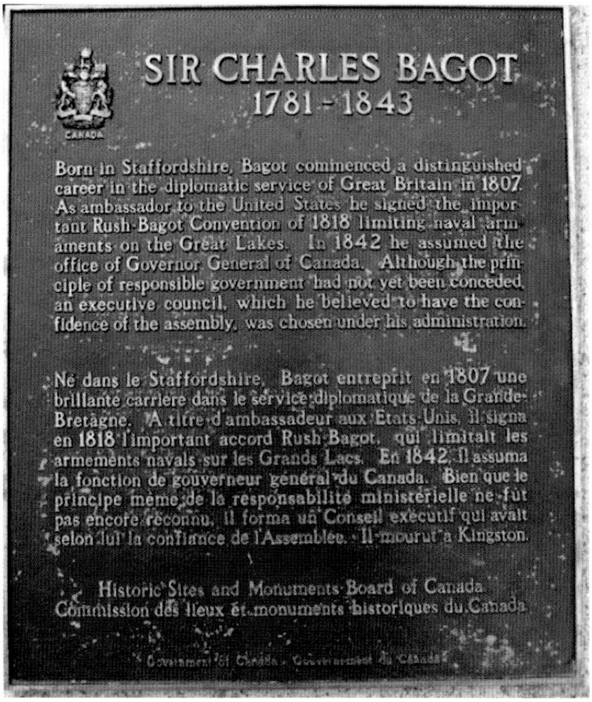
CANADA
SIR CHARLES BAGOT
1781 - 1843
Born in Staffordshire, Bagot commenced a distinguished career in the diplomatic service of Great Britain in 1807. As ambassador to the United States he signed the important Rush-Bagot Convention of 1818 limiting naval armaments on the Great Lakes. In 1842 he assumed the office of Governor General of Canada. Although the principle of responsible government had not yet been conceded, an executive council, which he believed to have the confidence of the assembly, was chosen under his administration.
Né dans le Staffordshire, Bagot entreprit en 1807 une brillante carrière dans le service diplomatique de la Grande-Bretagne. A titre d'ambassadeur aux Etats-Unis, il signa en 1818 l'important accord Rush-Bagot, qui limitait les armements navals sur les Grands Lacs. En 1842, il assuma la fonction de gouverneur général du Canada. Bien que le principe même de la responsabilité ministérielle ne fût pas encore reconnu, il forma un Conseil exécutif qui avait selon lui la confiance de l'Assemblée. Il mourut à Kingston.
Historic Sites and Monuments Board of Canada
Commission des lieux et monuments historiques du Canada

Wall plaque in Kingston, Ontario, Canada to Sir Charles Bagot

---

1 In 1867, Alaska was ceded to the United States by Tsar Alexander II when the U.S. paid the purchase price of $7.2 million (1.9 cents per acre). Critics ridiculed the deal as 'Seward's icebox', named after Secretary of State Henry Seward who arranged it.

2 This proved to be the case for the entire 19th century.

By his action he earned the respect of the Reformers, particularly the French Canadians. This was aided by his fluency in French, his gift of political diplomacy, his charm and respectful manner.

Bagot's reputation in England however was not quite so popular.
Both Queen Victoria and the Duke of Wellington were alarmed by his initiative, as was Sir Robert Peel. Sir Charles was severely criticised by Tory leaders and his policy was repudiated by his successor. Sir Charles's health deteriorated further as a result. It was not until after his death that in 1848 his policy bore fruit and responsible government was introduced in Canada.

He died at Kingston[1], Canada on 18th May 1843 aged 61 after being bed ridden for many months.
From Kingston, his body was transported by barge across Lake Ontario to Oswego in the United States where a newspaper reported that-
All flags were at half mast and all business in the town was suspended. Guns fired from the port and church bells tolled as for a public funeral. At least 4,000 people gathered to witness the departure of the vessel as it departed for New York and then to England.
It has also been written that - *His unquestioned popularity in both Canada and the U.S. received mute witness in the sombre crowds that lined the overland route by which his body was transported to New York City for its long final voyage back to England and the quiet parish church at Blithfield.*

Accompanied by his widow and family, his body was repatriated to England aboard HMS Warspite and buried at Blithfield on 27th June, 1843.

The helmet and brass plate above Sir Charles's memorial tablet in Blithfield Church were G.C.B.[2] insignia placed above his stall in Henry VII's chapel in Westminster Abbey.

Sir Charles had many stories to tell of his experiences abroad, and some found the ear of his daughter-in-law, Sophia Louisa Bagot, who had married his son Charles in 1846.
She writes here of some experiences Sir Charles had while Great Britain's ambassador to Russia:-

Sir Charles on one occasion invited the Czar Alexander to dinner. Sir Charles wishing to do him special honour, had a cup of coffee brought to the Emperor on a most beautiful small, old silver salver, which Sir Charles took from the servant, and presented himself. The Czar refused it, with a look of suspicion; seeing this, Sir Charles drank the cup of coffee himself, and ordered the servant to bring another cup for the Emperor, who then took some. This

---

1 Kingston was then the capital of Canada and the seat of its government.
2 G.C.B. Grand Cross (of the order) of the Bath.

event occurred soon after Sir Charles's arrival in St Petersburg. [1] *The Czar subsequently honoured him with his friendship and confidence.*
Mrs Bagot adds – *It is not to be wondered at that any one of the house of Romanoff in those days should suspect foul play.* [2]

At an official banquet given by Sir Charles Bagot at St Petersburg, a handsome snuff- box was passed around the table and disappeared. The loss was put into the hands of the police. The snuff-box was found, but the head of the police asked Sir Charles to make no inquiries as to who had taken it – of course he did not.

The Emperor Alexander I was godfather to Sir Charles Bagot's son Alexander. The Empress thinking Lady Mary Bagot was cold, at the first visit she paid to the Empress after the christening, took and Indian shawl off her own shoulders and put it on my mother-in-law, who left the shawl to me. The Emperor gave Sir Charles a miniature of himself, and also a very striking miniature of Catherine II.

Colonel Alexander Bagot met with a quite unusual and agonising death in 1874. He had served thirty four years service in the Indian Army and was a keen sportsman. He died, in India, while on a shooting expedition with a party of friends. They were shooting big game and a quantity of arsenic powder had been sent for from their camp which was to be used for curing the skins of tigers and other animals they had shot. At the same time, the cook had sent for a supply of baking powder. The shooting party came in for breakfast, and after eating several chappaties, Bagot and one of the party were taken very ill. Colonel Bagot died after much suffering, however his friend, having not eaten so many chappaties, survived. The cook had not known of the arsenic and mistook it for the baking powder. During the Indian Mutiny, Colonel Bagot commanded a Gurkha regiment.

In 1885, Sophia Bagot's second son, Alan, a Mining Engineer, died at the age of only twenty-nine following an illness caused by an accident in a coal mine. At the age of nineteen, he patented a safety indicator for mines and went on to write several books entitled Accidents in Mines and The Principles of Colliery Ventilation. As an Associate Member of the Institution of Civil Engineers, his work went on to influence improvements in electrical apparatus, agriculture, river pollution and prevention of floods.

---

1 St Petersburg was then the capital of the Russian Empire.

2 In the latter part of his reign, the Tsar became increasingly suspicious and fearful of plots against him. His own succession to the throne was controversial in that his father, and predecessor was assassinated, and Alexander was thought to have been implicated.

It was noted in an obituary that -
Alan Bagot was buried at Blithfield, Staffordshire, where he had passed much time in boyhood and youth. When the body arrived at the Trent Valley (Rugeley) Station, numbers of miners and working men came to show respect, saying they had lost their best friend.

Sophia Louisa Bagot -

the daughter-in-law of Sir Charles Bagot, who she describes as being extremely witty, agreeable and handsome.

In her memoirs published in 1898, Sophia Bagot relates the episode of a brief encounter her mother-in-law, Lady Mary Bagot, had with Napoleon.

In 1814, when Sir Charles was Chargé d'Affaires in Paris, Lady Mary went to Notre Dame to see Emperor Napoleon offer thanksgiving there. She should not have gone, due to her husband's position, and so went as a private person. Sitting in the nave of the Cathedral, Napoleon passed close by her. He had seen her and knew who she was, for Lady Mary had taken care to disguise her visit by ordering her carriage to go to a small door at the side of the Cathedral; when she went for it, it was not there, but had been told to go to the main entrance to the Cathedral, evidently, by command, in order to let her know her presence had been noticed!

She told her son, Charles...*that she never saw such an eye as that of the Emperor. He seemed to see every single person and everything. It struck Lady Mary as something absolutely wonderful.*

Lady Mary Bagot was niece to Napoleon's nemesis, the Duke of Wellington.

She is buried alongside her husband inside the Bagot family vault in Blithfield Church.

There are several people who have left first hand accounts of their memories and experiences of either living in Blithfield, or being associated in some way with the parish during the 19th century.

Mary Bagot was a daughter of the Reverend Walter Bagot[1] rector at Blithfield from 1759 to 1806.

Miss Mary Bagot

Mary Bagot was christened in Blithfield Church on 25th February 1790 and lived in the parish at the Parsonage, with her family, during her formative years.

She is included here on account of her journals, which give a vivid portrayal of life in Blithfield, and Staffordshire, during the reign of George IV and the beginning of the Industrial Revolution which began in neighbouring county Shropshire in the late 18th century. It saw England change for ever and led to the life of our modern age and a process which was adopted by many countries in the world.

It is clear from her writing that she had a deep affection for her place and county of birth and was somewhat perturbed by the rapid changes going on around her from the point of view of her privileged position. She was perhaps aware of the threat they posed to the future of families such as hers.

The following extracts use her own words in describing Blithfield and places in Staffordshire which she would have been able to visit reasonably regularly when calling on friends and acquaintances of equal status in the county. She also gives accounts of encounters with relatives and those involved in the new order which was beginning to evolve, and subsequently started the decline of many families who for centuries been at the heart of power in England. She is quite unforgiving in her descriptions of some of Staffordshire's inhabitants, but she wrote at a time when the class divide had probably never been so wide, showing how insulated she was from the harsh realities of life for most people at the time.

In 1816 Mary Bagot travelled to Italy. On 26th October she set sail from there for Malta, arriving the following month and staying until the end of April 1817. This is where she began her journal. Her writing, perhaps not

[1] The Rev. Walter Bagot was the grandfather of composer, Ralph Vaughan Williams.

surprisingly, seems to reveal a certain amount of home sickness and she begins with this preface:-

"This paper prepared for writing has for several days been lying in my desk – it was the only real step I had ever made towards the execution of a plan, which has long been in my mind, and never so strongly as since my residence in the country from whence I often look back upon England and Home, and not infrequently upon Blithfield, with a degree of affection and veneration which increases with my years; on that subject I wish to write...Every day steals something from the certainty of recollection; our former home (the old Rectory at Blithfield) *is destroyed, some of its inhabitants passed away. I am anxious to secure every vestige of both which remains with me. The time may come when I should in vain attempt to do so."*

THE COUNTY.

... Staffordshire has, I think a sort of pre-eminence over its neighbours. In the days of which I write it was inhabited by a race of ancient nobility and gentry, to whom this honour seemed due, and was in general well deserved. It contained a great variety of country in this respect... The north-west part... is a wild tract, known by the name of the Moorlands, inhabited by a sturdy but uncivilised race.
The farmers grow rich upon their dairy - farms, and, as in patriarchal times, their wealth is estimated by their number of cattle - thirty milch cows and upwards are the frequently the property of one man. The lower orders amongst them lived much upon butter and milk and oatcakes. Uttoxeter (or Uchcater according to the provincial pronunciation),... might be reckoned to be the metropolis of this part of the country.
The dialect has many of the northern peculiarities, and was much broader than that of the Southern people, who were indeed a different race, their manners and morals having been affected by the neighbourhood of Birmingham (Bromwichham).

Along the western boundary adjoining Shropshire is a strange district of coal mines, worked by a set of people more savage in appearance than any I ever saw in England. Their territory is devoid of any recommendation except the wealth derived from its mines...

Wodensbury, in its immediate neighbourhood, is a tract said to be undermined by subterranean fires; in many places the earth has fallen in, to the injury of houses built upon this land, known by the name of "Wedgbury burning-field". The only object of any interest with which I am acquainted is Dudley Castle, once a magnificent baronial residence, and according to print in Plot's "Staffordshire", it was formerly surrounded by fine woods. Adjoining to this country, and stretching into the very heart of the county, is an immense heath, which, though now without a tree, is still called Cannock Wood, and there was a time when a squirrel could have hopped on branches from one end to the other, a distance, I should think, of twenty miles. An eagle was once shot here; my father had one of his wing feathers...

On the north-eastern side of Staffordshire formerly extended Needwood Forest, which once equalled, if not exceeded, in beauty any scenery of the kind in England.

Alas, that I am obliged to speak of this as a thing over and gone! I do remember it in its glory, and can recollect the disturbance occasioned in ye county by its destruction. Almost every one of note objected and deplored, and yet nobody was found sufficiently powerful or active to prevent the measure from being carried in Parliament. How I know not, but Mr Bolton [1] *of Birmingham was said to have been its chief promoter. When the mischief was done and there was no redress the lamentation was universal, and has, I believe, never ceased...*

Of the various Forest lodges one will ever be remembered as the residence of Mr Gisbourne - I recollect Yoxall well, being the first spot I ever saw beyond the immediate territory of Blithfield; it was a time when a journey of eight miles was a great undertaking, and made me considered as a traveller on my return.

This was the first romantic scenery I had ever seen,..I can even now remember how delighted I was in seeing the beautiful holly trees of gigantic size, observing the herds of deer, and looking along ye glades of what appeared to me a boundless wood...[2]

Adjoining the forest and Derbyshire, but I think within the bounds of our county, is Tutbury. The castle is finely situated; every place which poor Mary of Scotland ever inhabited is interesting, and she was for several years a prisoner. I think I have heard of an inscription on a pane of glass in a window at Abbots Bromley, written on the day she passed through that place on her road to Chartley...

Lichfield, I think, is situated in the south-eastern quarter... it is... an ancient and respectable little city, undisturbed by manufactories, and unfrequented now except by its inhabitants, who form a considerable society...Johnson's house (or rather that in which he was born) is pointed out with pride... The window, too, out of which Lord Brooke received that shot which deprived him

---

1 Assumed to be Industrialist Matthew Boulton, who, along with Lichfield physician Erasmus Darwin, was one of the founder members of the Lunar Society of Birmingham in the late 1750's. The society later included Potter Josiah Wedgwood, Engineer James Watt, the chemist Joseph Priestley and latterly, Benjamin Franklin, U.S. president to be.

2 Needwood Forest lies adjacent to Bagot's Park to the east. The reason for it's destruction can be gleaned from further details in Other Histories - Needwood Forest.

of the power of fulfilling his impious wish of seeing all the cathedrals levelled with the ground; he saw no more, and Lichfield still stands the boast and beauty of the county. Its three spires were distinctly seen from the Parsonage (of Blithfield), *and many times I have stood in the nursery window gazing at them, and longing to be nearer to what appeared to me as the most wonderful work of man. Of the wood beyond those spires I had no idea - that distance was greater than my mind could take in...*
In the cathedral is a tablet to the memory of Colonel Richard Bagot, governor of this city during the Civil Wars, and who fell on the right side at Naseby. My father had a ring which had belonged to him and to the third son of the house ever since Colonel Bagot's days; it was unfortunately lost...

I will now mention some spots in Staffordshire, all I am acquainted with,..One of the finest places in the county is Chillington, on the Shropshire border, belonging to the ancient family of Giffard;... The present possessor of Chillington is on some points quite deranged, and in many respects I really think it is an advantage to his estate - he will not suffer a stick of timber to be cut down, and the oaks of Chillington stand unrivalled, except by those in Bagot's Park; Mr Giffard - or the "Old Squire" as he is called - rides over his immense property (followed by a troop of sons he has never suffered to go to school), dressed in scarlet with a great pair of rusty spurs, and sometimes a foxes brush in his hat. Here, and here only, I believe, the old custom of making a feast for the tenants, when they come to pay their rents, is now kept up; quantities of roast beef and plum puddings on that day smoke in the hall at Chillington...

There are still some other places to be mentioned in Staffordshire before we come to Blithfield, which, perhaps because it is best, I keep to the last...

On the Warwickshire boundary is Great Aston, (Aston Hall Birmingham) *now the property of Mr Legge... and alas! to be demolished... This is one of the most respectable houses in the country...but the comfort of the place is sadly impaired by the neighbourhood of Birmingham, whose suburbs come up to the very walls of the parks; its smoke infects the whole country. The sound too of its large hammers and the proving of guns are equally disadvantageous to this place.*
Alas! all England is defaced in some way or other by manufactories. Canals are cut through the most peaceful and pretty parts of the country. Forests are destroyed, old walnut trees felled for gun stocks, and even the beautiful scenery of the lakes is disfigured by the villas of the Liverpool merchants!...

She goes on to give a fascinating description of the place and parish of her birth and describes life there during her formative years which saw out the latter part of George III's reign.

...Blithfield is situated nearly in the centre of Staffordshire, four miles north of the Trent...The climate in this part of the county is cold; patches of the winter snows used to remain longer with us in spring than in any other part of the neighbourhood. To speak first of the Hall, I well remember the time when, according to my childish knowledge and belief, there was not such another magnificent place in the kingdom, and yet, in fact, at that period perhaps there were few so mean, considering the property to which it belonged. The house was situated, like most old ones, in a bottom, with a southern aspect. On the west was a green slope crowned with a grove in which were some limes of size and beauty; to the north was the church, which... had its place in the most honourable part of the parish; to the east were the gardens. In all my wanderings since I left Blithfield such large fantastic old oaks as Lord Bagot's I have never seen...The present Lord Bagot gave the Queen a chair made of his famous timber and finely carved by Westmacott...

I delight to remember and record here what I look upon as a completely English scene: the blazing fire lighting up the great hall on Christmas night, the baron of beef smoking on the table, the black boar's head garnished with evergreens, the great pie ornamented with quaint devices of pastry; old Leonard in attendance, serving all with equal alacrity and respect, from the owner of the feast to his lowest guest: every person in the parish had on that day a good dinner and a good fire to eat it by...

From the Parsonage we had an extensive view of the Wrekin in Shropshire...I do not suppose any little territory afforded more hours of happiness to its possessors. With what eagerness we watched the opening of the first flowers, the green tips of snowdrops and crocuses in January... and hailed the delight of seeing their white and golden faces in February or March. About the same time the rooks began their labours in one of the groves which was exclusively their territory. Great complaints were frequently made by many gardeners but they were my father's friends, and stood their ground against every attack. He took great delight in their building and regular return after an evening's flight...The cawing of these birds is a sound ever associated in my mind with the thoughts of home...the most brilliant and beautiful time with us was early June, when the laburnums and guelder roses were in their glory, and peonies and white naucies[1] *were alternately in blow all along the borders. Just at that time was Rugeley Horse Fair, a great festa with us. The road, which during the rest of the year was chiefly tracked by waggons and teams of oxen, was then crowded with women and children from the northern*

---

[1] Narcissi

Leonard Baker - 'Old Leonard'- described as being "Porter to Lord Bagot", here seen carrying in wood for the fire. In all probability, his military style coat would have been a 'hand me down' from a soldier's uniform. Being very well made for that purpose, it would have given him years of good service and, perhaps, a sense of well being.

villages and hamlets who passed by our grounds to resort to this fair...

Beyond an extensive garden and the glebe was a great hayfield; in the middle of it a gigantic oak, under which my father often sat to watch the work.
His hay-makers were the very old, the very young, the infirm, who for these reasons were refused employment in other places and found it with us.
Not withstanding the lapse of time and this distant situation, I identify myself so completely with the scenes and spots I am describing that, after writing of Staffordshire and Blithfield, on looking up from my paper I start as if awakened from a happy dream on seeing the reality of Malta and the Mediterranean before me...

There were some old customs belonging to the place. On All Soul's Eve our doors were beset by all the boys of the parish shouting:-

"An apple, a pear, a plum or a cherry,
Or any good thing to make us merry"

During the twelve days of Christmas we were sure of a visit from the Morrice-dancers, who performed their antics dressed in ribbons, armed with sticks which they struck to the time of the tune, attended by a fool with a bell and motley coat, and often they danced on the snow in the court...
Since that time I have heard much and fine music; but none, I really believe, ever gave me so much pleasure as the Christmas Carols, the old ditties of the church singers, who used to be ranged in the "Little Hall" on Christmas Day, while we were allowed to look and listen from "the best stairs" On St Thomas's Day all the parishioners received bread and beef for a Christmas dinner, and after the "getting in of the hay" how well I remember the loud shouts of "Harvest Home" before the for supper of the work people on that joyful day.

The Park is distant nearly four miles from Blithfield, and singular from remaining exactly in the same state in which it had been at the time of the Conquest; of course, trees had fallen into decay and others grown up into beauty, but nothing had been cleared away by man. No cultivation had been carried on; the deer were lords of the ground, and, I believe, commanded not less than 12000 [1] *acres. One tree there was of immense size called "Beggars Oak " from a tradition in the family that a poor man under this tree once asked alms of the lord of the domain and was refused. The beggar's curse was*

1 Here she is mistaken. The area was around 700 acres. The adjacent Bagot's Wood is around 1000 acres.

a wish that the first-born of the house might never thrive, and, according to the history of the family, the wish has been granted.
A flock of originally wild goats is kept there. The parish of Blithfield did not contain a meeting house, an ale house, or a workhouse. I do not recollect any instances of poverty such as I have since become acquainted with in other places and later times. Our poor were a laborious, simple, sober race; they were tended and noticed, well instructed from the pulpit and in the schools. One of my first recollections is of the master of the small endowed school for boys; he was also parish clerk, by all the village considered as a learned man and by some as an astrologer; another of the village tailor, to which (for he was a person of ingenuity) he later added the vocation of upholsterer. A better man than he never lived. He fulfilled all the duties of his humble station kindly and well, and to the extent of his abilities and knowledge; his house was his home, and his kindness a support to a numerous family. He was often employed at Blithfield, and from years of faithful service and a certain quaintness of manner he became a great favourite. A sketch of him is still preserved exactly representing his grotesque appearance in his crooked old wig, green baize apron, and great scissors sticking out of his pocket; on Sundays he wore a handsome wig and hat, and drab coloured coat. He survived his old "master," as he called my father, several years...
Our village wake or feast of the patron saint of the parish, St Leonard, was held in September. I well remember the sugared cakes and furmity [1] made of the new wheat...
It is only of the last generation of my family I am anxious to speak one which is now nearly passed away, the last of a class of character which, " take them for all in all, we shall not see their like again."

Sir Walter Bagot was reckoned the most amiable, popular, and one of the handsomest men of his day..." Sir Walter's days " were longed talked of by the old people. He married Lady Barbara Legge, and was said never to have smiled during the two years he survived her. She appears to have been some what feared by children and dependants, but respected by every one; she was the mother of twenty children, of whom fourteen survived. William, the eldest son, afterwards Lord Bagot. accepted the peerage his father had refused; he was plain in person, and had a manner which did injustice to the good sense, taste, and information he possessed. He travelled in Italy and was all his life enamoured of the country.

Walter, the third son, was my father; the world did not possess a character which stood more fair- in every way he was above it. Like all the rest of the family he was educated at Westminster and Christchurch, and to the last

[1] Furmety or frumenty - a kind of wheat porridge made from hulled wheat boiled in milk and seasoned with sugar and cinnamon, with raisins.

retained a strong attachment to both; at school he was the chosen friend and companion of Cowper.[1]
His virtues had their foundation in that which is only stable – our holy religion.
His divinity was of the old school... The last book we saw him read was Butler's "Analogy"; he much prized his Polyglot Bible, and bequeathed to the living at Blithfield.
He had a relish for humour... In early life he was a good rider, a bold hunter, and excelled in the sport of fly-fishing; in his youth, too, he had been handsome. Of his dress he was neglectful, but had " Parson Bagot " been clad in rags and tatters there would still have been something in him to " show the world he was a gentleman... "

...Mary Bagot, St Julians Malta, March 1817.

The Reverend Walter Bagot was born on 2nd November 1732. He married twice, first, in 1773 to Anne Swinnerton with whom he had eight children. She died in 1786 soon after the birth of her last child and is remembered by way of a plaque in the south aisle of the church at Blithfield. In 1789 Walter married Mary Ward with whom he also had eight children. She also has a memorial plaque in the church. Mary Bagot was the first daughter of the second marriage and born when her father was aged 58 and her mother 21 years old.
Rector Bagot died in 1806 and is buried in the church yard at Blithfield.

The Rev. Walter Bagot's younger brother, Lewis, baptised in Blithfield Church on 15th January 1740, also chose to join the clergy and became Canon of Christ Church in 1771, Bishop of Bristol in 1782 and Bishop of Norwich the following year.

In 1790 he became Bishop of St Asaph where he rebuilt the palace. He is recorded as having been "amiable, gentle, benevolent, humble and laborious" and "that he lived on intimate terms with his clergy and the 'common people'."
He died in 1802 and is buried at St Asaph.

On the 18th April 1817, her last day on Malta, Mary Bagot wrote -
... a bright shiney morning the last of any kind which I shall spend at St Julian's. A spot to which I shall always feel indebted for it has afforded us repose, I may say comfort at a time when we much needed it – To write these

---

[1] William Cowper, the poet and hymnodist whose hymns, "God moves in a mysterious way" and "Oh for a closer Walk with God" are well known. His, are the lines, "Variety's the very spice of life, That gives it all its flavour" and "I am the monarch of all I survey" He collaborated with John Newton, who composed the hymn, " Amazing Grace".

TWO BAGOT MEN OF THE CLOTH -

The Reverend Walter Bagot, father of Mary Bagot, was Rector of Blithfield for 46 years. He married twice and had sixteen children. Both his wives have memorials erected to them in Blithfield Church. The The Rev. Bagot is remembered in the churchyard by an unpretentious headstone, away from the traditional Bagot burial area, which is adjacent to the south wall of the chancel.

Younger brother of the Rev. Walter Bagot, Lewis Bagot was alternately Canon of Christ Church, Bishop of Bristol, Bishop of Norwich and Bishop of St Asaph, where he is buried.

few lines I take my eyes from a last look at our fine Mediterranean view. Farewell to St Julian's!...

After a very stormy, arduous and frightening crossing of the Bay of Biscay and many months away from home, her ship arrived in Falmouth on 30th May where with relief, she wrote:-

...We were safe. We were in England. We were out of a ship!
In short we had so many causes for happiness that it was quite overflowing – I felt it to be so -
Arrived safe and well at home on Tuesday the 3rd June.

The changes of which Mary Bagot writes did not affect Blithfield, although in 1845 a railway was proposed to run along the inside of the western edge of the parish. The route of the Manchester to Birmingham Extension Railway as it was to have been, was passed by Act of Parliament but never built.

From her writing, it can be assumed that by 1827 she was living - or staying - in the Cathedral Close at Lichfield, for she continues in her journal with this description of an event at Blithfield Hall given by William, 2nd Lord Bagot. The event also gives her chance to reminisce on her childhood at Blithfield and she pulls no punches on her acute observations of some of her fellow guests -

...September 1827

At Lichfield, where we arrived at about nine o'clock, I most thankfully left the coach, and not often has any one more nearly verified the expression of being " tired to death ".
Nevertheless, between two and three o'clock next the day, I found myself in the midst of a splendid crowd and of ostrich feathers, assembled in the halls of my fathers to attend an archery meeting [1] *given by Lord Bagot, who on such occasions spares no expense or trouble. When the guests were collected, leading out Lady Shrewsbury himself, he requested all to follow to the shooting ground, which was done to the sound of the excellent band, and halted on the very spot where stood the old Parsonage, where, notwithstanding the gay* [2] *crowd and lively airs, " Auld Lang Syne " alone filled my head and heart. The principal target was placed in the centre of the green walk which I used to gaze at from the nursery window, scarcely*

---

1 Archery parties (Mary Bagot writes) were the great fashion in the Midland counties &c., and meetings, bye-meetings; costumes, the great subject of conversation amongst the young ladies- an archery hat, though made of the coarsest straw, and containing two green feathers, was to cost one of the young ladies <u>five guineas.</u> (At today's prices, nearly £500).

2 gay - In this context, light hearted and carefree.

supposing the country had anything to compare with it in wealth and beauty!

One of the great pear trees, which formerly grew at the end of the house, which was cut down, has thrown up a stem, which is now in its turn a tree, and I saw it loaded with fruit, and thought of the pleasure my father used to have in it. Many trees have been planted, many others removed, but I recognised some old familiar forms with pleasure. The was the gigantic Portugal laurel, on whose boughs we used to ride, under whose shade we built houses; the lignum vitae, on whose bough the thrush always sang his evening ditty; the high holly trees, in whose lower branches birds' nests never failed the eager seekers who, however, would have as soon have cut off a hand as have wilfully disturbed or destroyed one. The waving grove of beech and elms, once thickly peopled by my father's friends, the rooks; the large firs, picking up whose cones was a pleasure, and burning them afterwards another, at that age, and those bygone days when pleasures were simple and thoroughly enjoyed!

For the Strangers' Prize, the target was fixed on the very spot where, with poor Hervey and Humphrey [1]*, I shared a little garden, and even now I believe remember nearly all that it contained, I was able to ascertain the place by reason of a holly tree which is left, and whose summer shower of leaves have heretofore occasioned me much labour and vexation. In the midst of such recollections, I was carried away from the really splendid scene, striking and beautiful as it was, and to which I must return.*

A quiet observer of numbers collected for such a purpose, must be dull indeed, not to be amused by observation -at least, that is a source which never fails me, and it certainly did not at Blithfield. I saw some real enjoyment, natural, genuine; I saw some acts of disinterested kindness – but I also saw the extreme of vanity unabashed and undisguised, setting even common decorum at defiance, and making a beautiful little girl little better than a disgusting object. I saw love of rank leading to all that is mean; and heard heartless attempts at merriment from some who have lived for the world, and from whom it is beginning to pass away.

The dress, generally speaking, was superb. Such hats - such brilliant colours - such flounced petticoats and such gorgeous bracelets I never before saw. The archery uniform for the ladies I did not think was in general very becoming, consisting of a dark green pelisse [2] *and hat of the same colour, ornamented with gold and white feathers.*

The prizes were very handsome; a gold chain, cameo brooch, garnet and gold

---

1 Her younger brothers. They died in 1816 and 1815 respectively aged 23 and 22. Humphrey died of wounds received while fighting the Gurkhas in India.
See Other Histories - The Gurkhas. p.296

2 pellise - a cloak, with armholes or sleeves, reaching to the ankles.

clasp, gold wrought bracelet, gold earrings. These were adjudged by Lady Harriet Bagot, Ellen Anson, Miss Boothby and Caroline Gresley. The gentlemen's prizes were a chased snuff-box, a gold pencil, and silver sandwich case. They were won by Heneage Legge, Colonel Newdigate, and Richard Gresley. At six the shooting ended, and after a weary hour of total idleness and almost darkness, dinner was served in the Hall, and a temporary room a hundred feet long; it was sumptuous and abundant, and except turtle, venison, fish and game, everything was cold.

The decorations were of laurel, mingled with the emblems of archery, and such a multiplicity of lamps that the whole scene was light as day. The fruit formed the most beautiful part of the show, and nothing could be more picturesque than its arrangement. Pines, melons, grapes, and peaches, piled in silver vases placed on the centre of every table, alternately with pine trees, about three feet high, in pots, and laden with bunches. (of grapes) [1] *This sight was really worth a journey to witness. After dinner was over, and the rooms cleared, the ball began, before eleven o'clock, and was kept up up till two. A little before four o'clock we were again in the Close at Lichfield....*

A few years later, Mary Bagot entertained, and was entertained by her cousin. She includes this first hand report from him on a similar event but in a different country with an extreme climate. The comparison is interesting, but this event is organized by someone occupying the pinnacle of a feudal society, one which England had all but abandoned in the Middle Ages.

...November 6th, 1829.-

Sir Charles Bagot dined here. He was naturally clever, strikingly handsome, always agreeable, notwithstanding the extreme finery of his earlier days, but that has given place to better things. He has spent many years abroad, and is returned one of the most agreeable, conversible, and entertaining of travelled men. His situation as our Ambassador at St. Petersburg, enabled him to witness the splendour of the Empire of all the Russias, in the Court of Alexander - whose state banquets or suppers are given in a salon as large as Westminster Hall. The tables are pierced to admit the immense stems of the orange trees (which are brought from the Taurique Palace), the guests are literally seated under their shade, in all abundance of fruit, leaf, and flower.

...and this is done when the outside temperature of the outward atmosphere

[1] Fresh fruit of this kind was one of the status symbols of the age. At a time before it was possible to transport such items from overseas, the advent of coal fired boilers enabled aristocratic families to grow their own, by the use of large walled gardens and hot-houses. It was an expensive undertaking. Another luxury available to the Bagots of Blithfield was ice. The underground ice house at the Hall is still well preserved.

is perhaps twenty-five degrees below zero!...

She again touches on the subject which must have been a constant part of the conversation at dinner tables of many, regardless of their upbringing:-
...December 11th 1829
Went to Newcastle, (under Lyme - most likely Keele Hall) *where we dined. The light of the furnaces and factories, which now surround the place, glared over the snowy surface of this wintry landscape.*
We hear much of the struggle which is carried on between canals and railroads, or rather which will be if success attends the latter scheme, and probably that must be the result when thirty miles an hour has been accomplished with safety, and much more is promised!
Should this project answer, the change which must take place in the state of the country, the situation of its inhabitants, and alas! in its own fair face, is beyond all calculation. It is possible that those who live ten years longer may survive green fields, retired lanes, and how many other enjoyments! [1]
In the present state of conveyance, the potter of this neighbourhood pays as much for the carriage of his crate of goods from hence to Lichfield as is afterwards necessary for its transference to America. Upon such facts are founded the hopes of railroads!...

Mary Bagot's journal entries conclude – in this book - with her encounter with one of those whose positions, in due time, were to overhaul that of the then established order, and bring about the changes of which she showed so much alarm:-

...October 20th 1830
We dined this day with one of our few neighbours, a mercantile person, who returned from London with an alarming account of the depressed and fluctuating state of the funds, occasioned by the convulsed situation of the Continent, and still more perhaps by the prospect of affairs in Ireland where the repeal of the union is loudly, and, may be violently demanded...The papers announced what seems to be the certain establishment of railroads. The change which such a system may effect cannot be foreseen in all its bearings, but the tremendous fluctuation in property (so much of which is vested in canals) which it must occasion is certain.
What awful times are these, when the topics I have mentioned form the conversation of one afternoon!
Mary Bagot spent her later years living in London and died there at the

[1] The proposed new HS2 (High Speed) rail line, if approved, will take a route which skirts the southern boundary of the parish of Blithfield and is facing stiff opposition. It promises to whisk passengers along at 150 mph.

age of 73 on 5th June 1863.

Another observer of happenings in Blithfield 175 years ago was Sophia Louisa Bagot. She was the daughter-in-law of Sir Charles Bagot and has left these details of her memories of Blithfield, again in her own words:-

I shall never forget the impression made upon me by my first visit to Blithfield, Lord Bagot's fine old place in Staffordshire. As I am not a Bagot by birth, I may be forgiven, perhaps, for attempting to record these impressions; the more so as they were formed before I had any idea that I should marry into the family and become a Bagot myself.

My first acquaintance with Blithfield was on the last night of the year 1839. My parents and myself...were staying...at Milford, about five or six miles from Blithfield, and drove over to dance the New Year in at a ball given by Lord Bagot to his tenantry, to which any of his neighbours who cared to do so were cordially invited to come, and bring their guests with them. It was a beautiful sight, and even after a lapse of sixty years the scene remains vividly before my eyes. The Bagot's were all so handsome- famous in those days for their good looks- the old lord so high bred and courteous in his manners...

All the country houses in the neighbourhood of Blithfield were filled and brought their guests to the ball, besides the tenants for whom it was given, and servants and retainers of all sorts. As the clock struck twelve the dancing ceased, and in came the head forester, Henry Turner, with the magnificent bloodhounds from Bagot's Park. Everyone admired the dogs, and shook hands with everyone else and their partners. Mine was a Grenadier, my future husband Captain Charles Bagot. One dance more, and the "quality" went to supper, and left the old hall to the servants, tenants etc.; and they kept the ball up till morning.

There was an an indescribable charm in old Blithfield as I knew it first at the age of eighteen. A sort of feudal attachment to it of all ranks; so respected by the county, and all branches of the family received there with such hospitality, kindness, and old world courtesy by the dear old lord, who at eighty welcomed every one on their arrival, and took them to their carriage when they left, after visits of weeks or more.

The drive from Blithfield through Bagot's Woods to Bagot's Park struck me, and all new comers, immensely. Lillies-of-the-valley grow wild in these woods and flowers of many kinds....The great features of Bagot's Park are the oaks and a herd of wild goats. The Beggars oak...is still a mighty tree; the girth of its trunk so large that a carriage and four horses are almost concealed from view when drawn up behind it. The " King's " and the " Venison " oaks are also enormous trees, and, could they speak, would tell strange tales of centuries long passed.

CHANGING FORTUNES AND ASPIRATIONS

The last 50 years of the 19th century saw the high water mark of grand living in many of the country houses of the landed aristocracy in England, including that of the Bagots at Blithfield, described so well by Mary and Sophia Louisa Bagot.

The end of the Napoleonic Wars had brought an economic slump to Britain as prices and wages fell and unemployment soared. In a measure to maintain the incomes of landowners during this time the Corn Laws, introduced in 1815, imposed high tariffs on cheap imported grain in favour of the more expensive locally grown commodity. This had the effect of maintaining farmers' and landowners' income but also increased bread prices, which placed a heavy burden on the poor. The measure was also designed to enable farmers to pay the high taxes imposed by the government in order to affray the cost of the recent wars. However, it did not altogether achieve the desired higher grain prices, as prices fell to 9 shillings per bushel from 12 shillings in 1812.

The 1845 famine in Ireland, when their potato crop failed, greatly influenced the need for agricultural reform as there was insufficient grain to export to the beleaguered population. Reformers argued a similar situation could follow in England if the planting of potatoes, instead of cereal crops, were to occur. The landed aristocracy were bitterly opposed to any reform which would damage their interests and incomes, and being a major influence in the house of Lords and Parliament, were a formidable opposition.

Nevertheless in 1846, the reformers, among them many of the new industrialists who were gaining more political power, eventually won the argument. This led to the Repeal of the Corn Laws, championed, along with others by Prime Minister Sir Robert Peel, MP for Tamworth and led to the resumption of cheaper grain imports. However the associated benefits of cheaper prices did not occur for another 25 years.

In 1870, a slump in grain prices was caused after the opening up of the vast prairies to grow cereal crops in America, and the new steamships enabling easy transport of grain across the Atlantic. In 1869, the Suez canal opened which also enabled agricultural produce from Australia to be economically imported into the U.K. These factors started a depression in British agriculture, leading land prices and rental incomes to fall dramatically. British agriculture did not fully recover from this until after the Second World War.

The industrialisation of the country was bringing about radical social and economic changes by way of the mass migration of country dwellers seeking work in the rapidly expanding towns. The population of the country too, was greatly increasing.

Mary Bagot's 'mercantile' people and industrial entrepreneurs soon became rich, enabling them to challenge the established order in the corridors of power, and a new middle class of aspirational people was being created who wished to see political reform.

Agriculture, which had been the mainstay of the British economy for centuries past, was on the wane and new forces were at work. The mould which would shape the politics and economy of Great Britain for the next 100 years had been set.

WILLIAM, 2nd LORD BAGOT 1773-1856

William, 2nd Lord Bagot succeeded to the title in 1798. He was the first of the family in his position to experience the first decades of the 19th century which began to see momentous changes in England, with the Industrial Revolution beginning to change the economic and political landscape of the country. The Bagot family, as well as other landed aristocrats throughout England, had been the economic and political masters for centuries and now, other contenders for these positions were waiting in the wings to take their place.

Around the year 1807, Lord Bagot had the Rectory House, in which Mary Bagot had spent her happy childhood years, pulled down making way for the archery ground and a pump house, which drew water for Blithfield Hall from Blithfield Mill on the River Blithe.

At the same time a new rectory was built by Lord Bagot for his brother, Hon. Richard Bagot M.A. the then Rector of Blithfield, which is some distance away to the west of the Church. It was devastated by fire in 1962 and converted into apartments in the 1980's.

By 1827 financial difficulties began to surface for Lord Bagot, for that year the Bagot Estate and family were in debt to the tune of £60,000[1] and selling part of the estate to clear this was considered a possibility. In the event timber from the estate to the value of £20,000 was sold '*as this was not*

1 This figure would equate to an amount of about £5.6 million today.

yielding any money'.

Blithfield Hall was built by Sir John Bagot in 1394, and over the centuries, as was the case with many ancient country houses, successive generations of the Bagot family added to, and improved the fabric of their home to suit the prevailing tastes and conveniences of the period.

The responsibility for the way Blithfield Hall looks today is that of William 2nd Lord Bagot, who undertook the work in the 1820's. Somewhere at its heart lie the remains of that medieval structure of Sir John's.

Blithfield Hall as it appeared before it was re-modelled by William, 2nd Lord Bagot during the early years of the 19th century.
At that time a road passed in front of the Hall which led to Abbots Bromley.

At sometime, Lord Bagot took out a loan for a considerable sum of money, presumably in order to carry out this work. By November 1832 he had appointed three trustees to manage the Bagot Estate, among them his brother, Richard, who by now had become Bishop of Oxford.

Records show that the trustees had inherited loans to Lord Bagot amounting to £116,041 8s. 8¾d. In June 1835, the Trustees had a balance in hand at the Lichfield Bank of just £534 6s. 1½ d. It is not clear whether the Bagot debt included, or was in addition to the 100 year loan.

It is probable that the loan was taken out by Lord Bagot soon after he succeeded the title in order to fund his building works, which were not inconsiderable. If this was the case, then he would have done so when the British economy was buoyant and his income such that repaying his loan would have been possible. However, Britain's wars with France concluded at Waterloo and thereafter, an economic slump took hold of the country which would have made Lord Bagot's situation very precarious.

In September 1838, Lord Bagot wrote to the Trustees of the Bagot Estate appealing for occasional lump sum payments in order to bolster his annual allowance of £2,100, which would not allow him to save for emergencies. He begins his letter:-

' When I first entered upon my allowance of £2100 per annum I found in the house at Blithfield such stores of all, wine, wax candles, and stores of different kinds, that I was enabled to save a sum during the first 4 years 1833, 4, 5 and 6 amounting to £1000.

He explains to the trustees that out of this £1,000 he now only has £150 which is insufficient to pay for the upkeep of his daughter, Eleanor and for... *keeping this large House of Blithfield in a mere state of absolute habitation... to furnish rooms... in the way of curtains, chair covers, Hangings for beds, papering the rooms...which I cannot now accommodate'...This certainly is (out of my allowance) a strong measure and certainly ought to be considered by those who manage for me, particularly as every article I put into the house at once becomes the property of my trustees...The only thing I should crave of my Trustees, a small sum of money might be given me from my estate to keep up what I call my Nest egg...to keep my mind at ease as to extraordinary and unavoidable expenses, which I cannot control. If at the present moment my Estate was perfectly come round, and everything in the most prosperous state, I declare and vow I wou^{d} not write to alter... my present situation or require...more than the sum I now receive...*

He concludes:-

The price of almost everything, and every article of living has much greatly increased within the last four years as well as wages (in my small establishment) to servants - for as people grow from boys to men additions must be made to them...I pay every common thing every week, and every extra every quarter, my wages every half year and at this moment outstanding bills are few...

Bagot

Blithfield
September 24 1838.

Exactly three years earlier, in 1835, Lord Bagot had received a plea from one of his tenants whose situation was significantly more precarious than that of his landlord.

Sampson Walkeden occupied one of the farms on the Bagot estate near Abbots Bromley and found himself and his family threatened with eviction for non-payment of rent. Instead of appealing directly to Lord Bagot, his letter is addressed to his son and heir, Mr William Bagot for, as will be seen, sentimental reasons if no other -

Bromley Hurst Septr 23 1835

Honoured Sir,

I humbly beg you will pardon my great presumption in addressing you to solicit your kindness to entreat you to intercede in my behalf with your most Honoured Father, for whom I have so great a veneration that I dared not address him fearing it might be too much for his Feelings to find that a Tenant whose Father, Grandfather and self had lived more than a Century on his Estate, was so far reduced by misfortunes to be compeld to supplicate his compassion. It is impossible for me to express my grief at the great arrears I again owe to his Lordship, and the impossibility of paying them at present, but should my Lord vouchsafe to allow me to continue a Tenant and my endeavours blessed with success, it would be my first wish to pay the arrears I now owe. It is my intention to pay his Lordship 50% of arrears in the course of a few weeks.

I beg leave Honour'd Sir to state my unhappy Case to you, which causes me to take this great liberty, Having made out a statement of my affairs according to Mr M Turnor's desire and sent it to him to lay before his Lordship's Trustees, he requested me to sign a writing he had drawn up for me to promise I would send a Notice Paper that I would leave the Farm I now hold at Lady Day [1] next, the thoughts of which pray on my mind very much to think that I am constrain'd to turn myself, my wife, and children out of doors, at my time of life, without any capitol to enter into business of any kind. My wife has been a sufferer with bodily infirmity for the last three years, and have had long and expensive illness in my Family for many years.

My three sons are all dependent on me, two are Apprentices and my eldest son is with me. Honoured Sir I am induced to take this great liberty with you from the condescending kindness you showed me the Day you, and your noble Father Honour'd the Party at Abbots Bromley with your presence. I shall never forget your kind manner of questioning me whether I perfectly understood Sir Chas. Bagot's speech, and you saying it exactly accorded with your Father's and your own Feelings.

I humbly pray Honour'd Sir, that my entreaty may find favour in your Sight - and beg leave to subscribe myself

Your most Humble,
most obedient Servant
Sampson Walkeden

1 Lady Day - 25th March, the traditional start of the farming year.

addressed to The Honble Mr Bagot M.P. Blithfield.

P.S. I will most gladly submit to any measure my Lord may think proper for his own serenity, should he be pleased to let me remain.

From the records, it would appear Mr Walkeden's heart felt, ingratiating plea was unsuccessful, for in 1841 he was an agricultural labourer and living in Blithfield parish with his wife and two of his sons. He was about 57 years old.

His landlord was successful in his plea for his 'nest egg', for in November 1841 the Estate Trustees had voted in favour of it, but of the £200 his Lordship requested, only £100 was forthcoming. This amount was not extra to Estate expenditure, but by courtesy of two of his children, Hervey and Alfred, who agreed to forego part of their annual allowance from the income of the Estate.

Michael Turnor, Agent to William, 2nd Lord Bagot, with the Beggars Oak and Bagot Goats in the background.

This frugality on the Trustees part was entirely due to their alarm at the extent of the debt which still amounted to £100,000. On 16th November 1841, with this in mind, they sent a letter to Michael and Thomas Turnor, Lord Bagot's agents, stating in no uncertain terms ordering that they co-operate in order to redeem the situation.

They write,...*it is by a system of severe and stringent Economy alone, that any sinking Fund can be established, which holds forth a hope of lightening the dead weight of Debt. The most rigid abstinence from every expense, however trifling, which is not absolutely essential... becomes therefore an imperative duty... and the salvation of an Estate which has been handed down through so many generations...* The trustees go on to highlight areas where excessive expenditure has occurred, on the Home Farm, planting (trees) and repairs to the Hall. They direct that...*the expenditure of the Parks and Woods...be limited to the lowest point indispensable for the proper management and good husbandry...and the necessity of giving employment to the labouring poor*. They also request that...*no ornamental planting or Building to be carried on...without an express written order from the Trustees.* The agents are instructed to make it clear to every person employed by the Trust...*that they will be retained in their places only so long as they punctually adhere to them.*

Signed Dartmouth [1]
R Oxford
Ralph Sneyd [2]

Again, in 1844, the situation had barely improved and the Trustees ordered timber to the value of £1,000 to be sold and that the preservation of game be curtailed to the sum of £250 on the Staffordshire Estate and that no corn whatever to be used on the Welsh Estate.

Another interesting document in the Bagot archive is a letter written by Lord Bagot to his tenants on his Welsh Estate of Pool Park, Denbighshire. This refers to his tenants experiencing some hardships from a downturn in the agricultural economy, and especially those being experienced by agricultural workers country wide.

In this letter dated November 1830, he again addresses the issue of the *labouring class* and indicates he is willing to take a reduction in rent from his tenants... *thereby showing that I am perfectly ready to make every reasonable sacrifice, to promote the welfare of a tenantry for whom, throughout my life, I have felt the greatest regard*...although he stipulates that...*for one important duty on their part, which is that all my tenants should take into their employ such a number of Labourers, as the size of their Farms requires, and upon such wages as they may then be fairly entitled to. By thus promoting the necessary comforts of the Labouring Classes, my Tenantry will not less advance their own interests, than prove their attachment to myself, by cooperating with me, in what is so manifestly for the advantage of the Country.*

Your sincerely attached
Landlord
Bagot.

1 The Earl of Dartmouth
2 of Keele Hall near Newcastle-under-Lyme

Alongside the Industrial Revolution, agriculture too, was experiencing a revolution of its own during this period and the authorities and landowners were becoming increasingly concerned by the effects of this on Lord Bagot's 'Labouring Classes'. It would appear from this letter that Lord Bagot was providing for those rural workers who were unemployed and thereby trying to avert any upset in the prevailing rural order.

Ever since the early 18th century, agriculture had been changing in Britain by way of advances in animal breeding, crop rotation, the invention and introduction of agricultural machinery and, not least, the advancement of land enclosure [1], all of which greatly improved the efficiency of British agriculture. These innovations led to more food being produced and began a rapid increase in the population which led many country dwellers to migrate to the ever expanding towns and cities. It has been argued that this Agricultural Revolution was the catalyst for the Industrial Revolution.

Enclosure Acts had forced many cottagers and subsistence farmers off common land where they had hitherto eked out a living. By the 1820's and 30's this became a serious issue when soldiers released from army service after the Napoleonic Wars and those of the expanded working population flooded the labour market. Inevitably wages fell and unemployment rose resulting in great hardship for agricultural workers.

In 1830, in protest at their plight, some farm labourers struck out and the new machinery being used on the larger farms became the target of saboteurs who also set fire to farmers hay ricks in what became known as the Sling Riots.

Centred mainly in south eastern England, the targets of malcontents were mainly farmers and landowners who were exploitative and unsympathetic to the situation of the farm workers.

Additionally, trade unions were being formed in order to address the grievances of the working classes, and famously it was the intended formation of a trade union which led a group of Devon farm workers, the Tolpuddle Martyrs, to be tried and deported to Australia.

All these factors greatly alarmed the authorities and landed classes, who resorted to various actions in order to maintain order. Lord Bagot's contribution to this end was to ensure his tenants employed as many labourers as practicable, at some cost to himself, but also through philanthropic self interest.

With no resort to a Welfare State, the unemployed received some respite from the 1601 Poor Law, from which also the aged and sick were able to receive money from the parish rates as detailed in a previous chapter.

A new Poor Law was enacted in 1834 which resolved to ensure help for the

---

1 See Other Histories -- Needwood Forest. Land enclosure also brought about the familiar patchwork fields we see today though now they are very much larger. p.293

deserving poor while discouraging the undeserving and at the same time trying to ensure that wages were not reduced as a consequence.

By 1850, matters had improved to the extent that agriculture entered in its 'Golden Age' which was to last until 1870.

Lord Bagot was the first of his family since his forbear, Richard Bagot in the 16th century, to take a serious interest in his family's history when he took an inventory of the extensive Bagot records which were kept in the Muniment room at Blithfield Hall. From these, which extend back to the 12th century, he wrote his book, "Memorials of the Bagot Family," in 1823 which he had printed at Blithfield.[1]

Lady Louisa Bagot, second wife of William, 2nd Lord Bagot and their second son, Hervey. Lady Bagot died in 1816 aged 28.
Lord Bagot's first wife, Emily, died in 1800 leaving an infant daughter who died the following year.
Hervey Bagot became Rector of Blithfield in 1846 and remained so for thirty-three years. During that time he oversaw the work which restored Blithfield Church and made additions to it which included the porch and new chancel roof by architects Street and Pugin.
He also reduced the size of the Rectory by removing the top story from the west wing. This was done in true no nonsense Victorian style, by raising the roof bodily and replacing it when the walls had been lowered.

---

1 All the documents were labelled by Lord Bagot which proved to be a great help when they were found in a very damp condition by Lord and Lady Bagot in 1946 and subsequently transferred to the William Salt Library in Stafford for restoration. This vast archive is now held by the Staffordshire Record Office in the adjacent building. Many interesting letters and documents were acquired by the Folger Library, Washington D.C.

William, 2nd Lord Bagot is detailed in official records as being - *well versed in Natural and Antiquarian Studies, a Fellow of the Society of Antiquaries, and of the Linnaen, Horticultural and Zoological Societies.*

Lord Bagot was mindful of the service provided by his household staff. In 1825 he erected a monument in Blithfield Church to Mrs. Frances Tooth who died in May that year aged 71:-

TO TESTIFY TO HIS GRATEFUL SENSE OF THE AFFECTIONATE ZEAL, THE UNWEARIED DILIGENCE AND THE STRICT INTEGRITY WHICH SHE ENVINCED IN THE SERVICE OF HIS FAMILY AND HIMSELF FOR MORE THAN FIFTY THREE YEARS

Servants at Blithfield were not averse to erecting monuments in church to their fellows. Above the memorial stone to Mrs Tooth in the north wall of the south aisle is one erected, and inscribed to -

LEONARD OAKES WHO DIED 11TH OCTOBER 1825 AGED 82 YEARS.
THIS TABLET TO HIS MEMORY WAS ERECTED BY T RUTHERFORD
FELLOW- SERVANT WITH DECEASED FOR 27 YEARS.

Also, in the churchyard, a gravestone remembers -
John Harding - after an honest and faithful service of 52 years
in the gardens of Blithfield,
died 23: April 1869; aged 73 years.

Lord Bagot died at the age of 82 and was buried at Blithfield on 20th February 1856.

THE RIGHT REVEREND RICHARD BAGOT D.D.

1782 - 1854

Richard Bagot[1] rose to become one of the leading clerics in England during the first half of the 19th century. He was the sixth son of William, First Lord Bagot and brother of William, Second Lord Bagot and Sir Charles Bagot and like him, was educated at Rugby and Christ Church College Oxford where he obtained an M.A. In 1803 he became a Fellow of All Souls' College, Oxford. He took holy orders in 1806, and the next year became rector of Blithfield and Leigh at the age of 24. His rise in the Church of England saw him become a Prebendary of Worcester Cathedral in 1817, Canon of Windsor in 1822, Dean of Canterbury in 1827, and in 1829 he became Bishop of Oxford when he also received his degree of Doctor of Divinity.

It was in his position as Bishop of Oxford that he became reluctantly involved with the Oxford Movement, a group of Oxford University Anglican intellectuals who were questioning the ability of the Protestant Church to arrest the spiritual decay in the country and were calling for a return to High Church traditions. The leader of the group was John Henry Newman

1 Bishop Bagot is great-great grandfather of Charles (Charlie) Bagot-Jewitt, the present occupier of Blithfield Hall.

who published many 'Tracts' on the subject which aroused passionate objections from Bishop Bagot's clergy and latterly, the Oxford University authorities. Eight years later, the Bishop diplomatically steered the controversy to a close when he persuaded Newman to cease his publications, which he duly did. Although Bishop Bagot disagreed with the 'Tractarians' proposals he did continue to defend them against their fiercest critics while pointing out errors of judgement in their writings. He also spoke of his respect for the leaders of the group but felt little sympathy for their disciples and when Newman controversially converted to the Catholic Church, the ways irretrievably parted for him and Bishop Bagot.

John Henry Newman was enthusiastically received into the Roman Catholic Church and during his life was the author of hymns including Lead Kindly Light and Praise to the Holiest in the Height. He was canonized by Pope Benedict when he visited this country in 2012.

In 1832, when he was Dean of Canterbury, Richard Bagot was party to a strange experience. According to the memoirs of Sophia Louisa Bagot, her husband, Charles, was invited along to the Cathedral at Canterbury after a discussion had taken place as to whether Henry IV was really buried there. It was subsequently decided to open the tomb of the king to whom, in the early 15th century, Bishop Bagot's ancestor, Sir John Bagot, had been associated and loyally served.

Sophia Bagot records that... *This was done in the middle of the night by torchlight, in the presence of a few of the cathedral authorities and specially invited spectators.*

The body of the king was found wrapped in lead and leather. For a few moments after this covering was removed the face of the king was revealed in a state of perfect preservation as though still endued with life.

As the spectators looked, all crumbled away into dust, and my husband declared that it was a most weird and impressive scene; which indeed, with the flickering torches and solemn surroundings of the ancient cathedral, it must have been.

Mrs Bagot continues:- *A portion of the king's beard, which was of a reddish colour, was cut off before the tomb was closed, and my husband was given a piece of it by his uncle. He gave this piece to the Duke of Northumberland of that day, feeling that the hair of the monarch whom the Percys placed on the throne and then helped overthrow, would find an appropriate place among the historic relics of the family...*[1]

In 1845 Richard Bagot became Bishop of Bath and Wells although soon

---

1 In fact, Henry Percy, Earl of Northumberland, in turn fought for the king against Richard II, but in 1403 was defeated and killed by the king at the Battle of Shrewsbury when Percy tried to claim the throne. Henry IV died, as king, in 1413. It is thought that Sir John Bagot fought for the king in the battle.

after he became ill due to the stresses brought on him by the Tractarian disputes. After recovering, in 1854 he was involved in another controversy with an Anglican clergyman over church doctrine which was not satisfactorily overcome before the bishop's death.

Bishop Richard Bagot died in Brighton on 15th May 1854, leaving his wife with eight sons and four daughters. He was buried at Blithfield on 23rd May, the officiant being his nephew, the Rev. Francis Paget.

WILLIAM, 3RD LORD BAGOT, 1811 – 1887.

An important preoccupation for aristocratic families was always to ensure that their children married well. For the young ladies of the household this was especially important, for female emancipation was a movement which had not yet found its time and parents were always keen to ensure a suitable match for their daughters. Consequently, any prospective suitor who at least could afford to maintain the lifestyle of his heart's desire, had to be carefully cultivated.

The Honourable William Bagot, as he was correctly titled before his accession to the barony, found himself one such target for an aristocratic family's daughter's affections.

At aged 20 in 1831, Mr Bagot spent some time hunting at the country estate of some relatives to the Duke of Northumberland. After his departure he received the following letter from the lady of the house – it is an episode which could have been lifted directly from a novel by Jane Austen -

Dear Mr Bagot

You have made so unusual a conquest of my daughter, that I think it but fair to inform you of it; and shall transmit you a copy of a conference with her Maid, which I heard of this morning.

I have written Harriet such a volume of reports at your departure that I will not repeat them to you.
As I don't think I can be accused of superlatives, you will believe when I assure you that we miss you very much.
In want of your guidance today, I tumbled very deep into the mud! This weather will do well for your hunting, I hope you have had good sport, I have not had a run since you left us.
Charles and Walter charge me to give you their blessings.
Believe me,
very sincerely yours

Maroline Bertie Percy

The 'copy of a conference', reads as follows -

Addressed to
The Honourable William Bagot

Dialogue between Isabel and her Maid
"Caroline, do you like Mr Bagot?"
"I don't know Miss Percy, he is a gentleman. I have no means of knowing whether I like or dislike him."
"But you have your likes and dislikes I know, however as you do not seem inclined to answer me, I will say as we are on the subject, except that I love him very much. When he went away he desired me not to forget him, and I am sure I never shall."
"It would be very wrong if you did, after his having been so kind to you and that beautiful work Box will remind you of him, when you look at it.
"Oh no it would not, if I did not like him besides."

Unfortunately for Miss Percy, William Bagot married the Honourable Lucia Caroline Agar-Ellis and they had seven children. One daughter, Louisa, married Hamar Alfred Bass of the Burton-upon-Trent brewing family.

William Bagot attended Magdalene College, Cambridge and a bill for his three months term attendance to Christmas 1830 amounted to *£107. 2s. 6d*, (£10,820)[1] which included *£10* (£1,010) for his tutor, *£6. 2s. 6d* (£618) for coal, his rent was *£39. 15s. 1d*, (£985) his cook cost *£36. 10s. 4d* (£3,686) and his bedmaker cost him *£2.10s* (£252), and the bill also states that it is...*to be paid before the next Quarter day at farthest.*

On his succession to the barony in 1856 and soon after his father's death, William, 3rd Lord Bagot sought to perpetuate his fathers memory by

1 The amounts are adjusted to 2017 prices - in brackets.

building a new school in Blithfield parish.
In 1851, the yearly income of the old school was £31 (£3,850) which fell far short of the annual expenditure. The master and mistress received £80 (£9,920) a year for teaching 40 boys and 30 girls who were provided with books and other necessities by the 2nd Lord Bagot. He also made up the excess school expenses. He had also been personally interested in the school's progress for in January 1815, his wife Lady Louisa noted in her diary ...*Lord Bagot and I walked to the school and found it going on very well. The girls did a sum in addition very well.*

There had been a school in the parish since 1729, founded by daughters of his great, great, grandfather Sir Walter Bagot. Since then, the 2nd Lord had built two schools, one in Admaston and the other in Newton, but by his death they were in need of replacement. They are now desirable residences.
His son duly arranged a fund to be set up in order that his friends, relatives and tenants should contribute to the new building and a letter was sent to them by the Rev. Francis Paget [1] of Elford:

MEMORIAL TO THE LATE LORD BAGOT

It is proposed to raise a fund for the re-construction of these Schools, with Teachers' Residences, etc., on a better site, intrusting the choice of plans, and of all other details, to the present LORD BAGOT, to the present RECTOR OF BLITHFIELD, and to the HON. ALFRED BAGOT, with a stipulation that a Tablet, affixed in some conspicuous place in the new buildings, shall record the circumstances of their erection...
I am authorised to state that such a work will be highly gratifying to the late LORD BAGOT's children, and that such gratification will be much enhanced by the knowledge that all ranks and classes of those connected with him have contributed to it.

Elford Rectory, Lichfield
March 12th, 1856

---

1 The Rev. Paget was grandson to William 1st Lord Bagot and nephew to Sir Henry William Paget, 1st Marquis of Anglesey, of Waterloo fame. His mother, Frances Bagot, fourth daughter of William, 1st Lord Bagot, died at the birth of her son, aged 21. He is recorded as being a 'divine and author', became rector at Elford near Tamworth in 1835 and maintained a strong affection for Blithfield throughout his life. His mother has a memorial window in the south clerestory of St Leonard's Church. The inscription reads, "This window was made to the memory of Frances, wife of the Hon. Edward Paget, and daughter of William Lord Bagot, who in child-bed departed out of the miseries of this sinful world on the xxx day of May, MDCCCVl" (1806)

At some point, a decision was taken to build only one school, in Admaston, for following the Rev. Paget's letter, a total of 286 donations came in amounting to over £100 (£12,400) from richer contributors to a shilling (£6.20) or two from poorer tenants which was sufficient to build the new school and adjoining schoolmaster's house.
Lord Bagot chose the renowned Victorian architect G.R. Street to design the new school, a man who had already been employed to make additions and alterations to Blithfield Church. Mr Street was paid £80.4s (£9,500) for his work. The total cost of the building was £1025.2s.6d. (£127,114)
The tiles adorning the walls inside the school were donated by Herbert Minton the famous Stoke-on-Trent manufacturer. He was a keen benefactor to many in the Stoke area, particularly hospitals and schools and there are vast quantities of them in Lichfield Cathedral, The House of Commons, The Capitol Building in Washington D.C. as well as a fine set in the chancel at St. Leonard's Church Blithfield.

In the era before State sponsored compulsory education, the parents of pupils paid for their education according to their income. In 1880 the fees were raised to:

2d (£1.24) per wk in the case of parents earning less than £1 (£124) per wk,
3d (£1.86) per wk in the case of parents earning more than £1 per wk.
In the case of farmers, 6d (£3.10) per wk.

The poorest children were provided with bread at lunchtime under the following rule:

Admaston School.
Orders for the present Direction of the School at Admaston.

No child is to be admitted to partake of the Charity but such whose Parents are poor and inhabitants of the Parish. The bread to be distributed according to the will of the Founder of the School, to those children only who come from the greatest distance. The children before Admission to be approved by the Patron or Minister of the Parish.

It was also directed that-

No Child to be Admitted before the Age of Six years.
No Child admitted at Six years of Age to continue longer than eleven, without leave again obtained.

Blithfield
School,
1909

Pupils at Blithfield (Admaston) School in 1909

Children were, of course, required to walk to school in all weathers and those living at Newton and Dapple Heath chose the easier option of taking the short cut across the fields, some now submerged by the reservoir. Poorer children were not always adequately clad and Lord Bagot helped them by providing cloaks to wear and he also contributed toward their footwear.

The children's education was basic, the emphasis being on reading, writing, arithmetic and bible studies. Admaston, being a church school, Blithfield's Rector saw to it that the children received a good grounding in their religious education in which they were required to learn and recite parts of the Bible and prayer book by heart.

The children used slates and chalk to write down their work and it was not until 1905 that this method was discontinued in favour of pencil and paper. In 1880, there were a total of 82 children on the school register although the school had a capacity of 120 which was never attained, and by 1892 the average attendance was 46. In 1906 however, the school received the accolade of sharing with one other school, the highest attendance in the county.

Blithfield school closed in 1944 and the children from the parish were transferred to St Mary's Church School in Colton.

William, 3rd Lord Bagot in his later years

Blithfield Hall and its estate required Lord Bagot to maintain a large household.

In 1871, Blithfield Hall was home to 53 people, and included the Bagot family with a staff including a butler, footmen, valets, governess, coachman, 'helpers in the stables', gardeners, housemaids, nurse, groom, usher, ladies maid, schoolroom maid, kitchen and scullery maids. Many others were employed as game keepers, foresters, dairy workers, bricklayers and maintenance workers. These would have lived locally, away from the Hall, but on the Bagot Estate.

As well as the Hall, Lord Bagot maintained a London residence, Dover House in Whitehall, where he would stay when on city business and where some of his Blithfield staff would follow.

Lord Bagot was M.P. for Denbigh in North Wales from 1835 until 1856 when he succeeded his father and entered the House of Lords. He then became Lord-in-Waiting, (government whip in the House of Lords), during the administrations of Earl Derby and Benjamin Disraeli in the 1860's.

As well as his political career, he was Gentleman of the Bedchamber[1] to Prince Albert, and a colonel in the Staffordshire Yeomanry.

The Blithfield Hall 'Kitchen Book' reveals details of the dietary requirements of the household for the month of February 1871.

During that month a total of 912 persons were catered for and included 253 'gent', 499 servants and 160 'strangers', an average of 33 people per day.

Food purchases for the month amounted to 543 lbs mutton, 435 lbs beef, 52 lbs pork and 81 lbs of veal. Poultry purchases were 2 ducks, 6 geese, 22

[1] A royal appointment which gave Lord Bagot regular access to the Consort to Queen Victoria. His duties included waiting on the prince when he ate in private, helping him dress, providing companionship as well as guarding the bedchamber and water closet. This position therefore was a relatively important one with potential for a close mutual friendship.

chickens as well as dairy products and eggs. The record also shows more exotic fare was consumed: grouse, partridge, pheasant, snipe, woodcock, hare, rabbits wild duck, venison and pigeons.

Interestingly, the Bagot family did not appear to have been heavy drinkers, for during the Christmas period of 1873, the kitchen book records only two bottles each of brandy and sherry and one of port- and, additionally, '2 old fowls'! The fact remains however, that there was a well stocked wine cellar at Blithfield Hall. The book does not record any other alcoholic beverage purchases such as beer, which in any case was most probably brewed on the estate, or it may be proof positive that Lord Bagot was showing, by example to his staff and tenants, his disapproval of alcohol. Anecdotal evidence has long since had it that the parish of Blithfield does not have a pub due to Lord Bagot's insistence.

In 1859, Lord Bagot determined to improve the condition of the farms on his Blithfield and Pool Park estates in North Wales.

Along with many other aspects of British life during the 19th century, agriculture had been evolving and adopting new techniques and practices in order to feed the growing population of the country.

A report commissioned by the government encouraged landowners to upgrade the facilities on their farms to modern standards by providing money for loans in order to do so. This, it was argued, would improve the value of the land and the letting potential of the farmsteads concerned as well as the added benefit of increasing rental values.

After an expert appraisal of his estates, a total of £23,000 - £2.7m at today's values- was allocated to Lord Bagot for both his estates which then amounted to over 10,000 acres. Over the next ten years Lord Bagot achieved his goals, the benefits of which are still enjoyed by farmers in Blithfield today. [1]

In the south aisle of Blithfield Church is the brass memorial plate to -

William Stonebridge
Born January 1813
Died 13th July 1892
For over 50 years the faithful Servant
and friend of
William, 3rd Lord Bagot.

Lord Bagot died in January 1887 and was succeeded by his son William.

1 See - A Thousand Years of Farming - The Mainstay of Blithfields Economy p.232

the 20th Century

WILLIAM, 4th LORD BAGOT 1857 - 1932

The closing years of the nineteenth century also brought with them the closing pages to a long chapter in the history of the Bagot family.
William, 'Billy', 4th Lord Bagot, was 22nd in an unbroken line of male descent which stretched back directly to Simon, Lord of Bromley Bagot at the time when Richard the Lionheart ruled England during the late 12th century.

His tenure at Blithfield Hall was to see personal misfortune and family tragedy which would see the Hall, the Estate and the Bagot family undergo radical change, as indeed would the parish of Blithfield and the country.

Lord Bagot was Deputy Lieutenant for Staffordshire and Derbyshire, a Gentleman Usher of the Privy Chamber and Lord in Waiting to Queen Victoria[1] and formerly A.D.C. to the Governor General of Canada. He also held the rank of Lieutenant Colonel in the Staffordshire Yeomanry.

---

1 These titles, respectively, involved the holder being a servant to the sovereign, who would wait and attend the king or queen in their private apartment and representing the sovereign on engagements when their absence was unavoidable.

Lord Bagot did not marry until 1903 when he was 46 and his wife, Lilian Marie May, 35 years of age. She was the daughter of lawyer Henry May of Baltimore U.S.A. and they married at the Brompton Oratory Catholic Church in London by license and one of those present was the Secretary of the American Embassy.

Their daughter, and only child, Barbara was born on 1st January 1905 although, even well before this time, the marriage was unfortunately experiencing difficulties.

From Lord Bagot's point of view, it appears that his wife was of a somewhat feisty nature who tended to demand a separation at any time she did not get her own way. His refusal of her wish to have a diamond tiara sent to Paris to be re-set, upset his wife, he maintained. Some forty six years later, Lady Bagot confided to her successor, Nancy Lady Bagot, that- *when I wanted new curtains for the drawing room at Blithfield, my husband told me that these curtains were good enough for his mother, so they are good enough for me.*

Lady Lilian subsequently left Blithfield Hall for Paris in May 1904 but later returned to Folkestone.

After twelve months of receiving solicitors letters from his wife, and having been very ill, on 2nd of July 1906, Lord Bagot wrote to his wife explaining the misery she had made of his life and that her suggestion of her returning to the family home was impossible. He began his letter -

Dear Lily,

I was somewhat surprised receiving a letter dated 29th June, from you, and more so at the contents. What you suggest is impossible. Surely you can not forget that almost from the first week of our marriage you commenced the cry of a wish for a separation, and you know well the misery you made my life...

He claimed that in letters to friends she had...*spread abroad the most infamous, cruel and heartless untruth that any wife could invent against her husband...*

After she had informed him that any letter he sent to her would be unopened and forwarded to her solicitor, he informed her in his letter that he had decided to inform his solicitor on the state of affairs between them and insisting on an immediate separation. He continues his letter -

...You have ruined my life and my health...nothing in the world will ever permit of my living under the same roof with you again. It would be a life of the most utter misery both for yourself and for me, and you know it...and it is far better for you and for me that we should never meet again. As you are perfectly aware, I am prepared to do all in my power for you and your child. You are perfectly aware of the fact that the House at Blithfield is completely

shut up, and very deeply do I regret, that for the rest of my life there is no hope of my ever being able to afford to open it again... He goes on to advise his wife to avoid court action and settle the matter privately, as he continues -*...I can only tell you that the costs etc. will so utterly impoverish this Estate that it will be very hard indeed, if possible at all to find the income you now have...You have made a good deal of your belongings being sent to you from Blithfield. It was this day last year, the 2nd July 1905, that you wrote insisting that everything that belonged to you at Blithfield should be at once packed and sent to you in London, and that you should send a "Paris packer"! to Blithfield to pack your dresses and clothes.*

I cannot understand your constantly writing to Mr Neighbour [1] *that you are pressed for money - you have all there is - and an income of £800 a year* [2] *(20,000 francs) is no small income.* He concludes his letter -

I expect to be in London this week, as I am obliged to see my doctor -

Yours sincerely

Bagot.

On 10th July 1906, Lady Bagot filed proceedings in the High Court against her husband for the restitution of her conjugal rights, for as she was a Roman Catholic, a divorce would have been out of the question. It is certain, particularly under the circumstances, that Lord and Lady Bagot's daughter would have been christened into the Catholic church, which, as it was against family tradition and he was a staunch Protestant, would have upset his Lordship further

It is said Lady Bagot was a friend of King Edward VII and that he tried to reconcile the pair, but there was no resolution to the rift between them and their separation became permanent. He continued to live alone in Blithfield Hall, and she took up residence in Hove, Sussex with her mother and daughter, Barbara. Here, Lady Bagot was able to maintain a household staff of eight servants.

In 1911, and possibly for the first time in it's history, Blithfield Hall was not home to a Bagot family, and at the age of 54 Lord Bagot had been obliged, for practical purposes if no other, to drastically reduce the number of household staff at the Hall to a total of nine.

It would be only a few years later when the Bagot family would suffer further tragic misfortune, for dark clouds were beginning to appear on the horizon.

Lady Lilian Bagot died in 1958 at the age of 94 at her home in Hove.

---

1 Lord Bagot's agent. Lancelot Neighbour's demeanour was such that local people- amongst themselves - used to refer to the two men as Lord Neighbour and Mr. Bagot.

2 This figure would equate to nearly £90,000 today.

American, Dowager Lady Lilian Bagot, seen here dressed in her robes for the Coronation of George VI in 1937. Although by this time her husband had died, being the wife of a peer of the realm, she was perfectly entitled to attend.

Her successor, Nancy, Lady Bagot wore these robes at the Coronation of the Queen in 1953. They are now displayed in The Potteries Museum, Hanley.

THE WORLD - AND BLITHFIELD - GO TO WAR

1914 - 1918

The beginning of the 20th century (1901) saw the last year of Queen Victoria's reign, the second longest to date of any British monarch. The British Empire was at its zenith, but storm clouds were beginning to gather.

The First World War, which began in 1914, traumatized Blithfield as it did the majority of parishes and communities throughout the land as they sent their men folk off to fight a war which at the outset was judged would, 'be all over before Christmas'. This as we know, was not to be and the four year conflict brought grief to many families from all social classes.

Great Britain declared war on Germany on 4th August 1914.

The First World War, or Great War as it was known in the inter-war years, did not have one single cause. It was born out of many years of international political machinations, rivalries, suspicions and jealousies, particularly over the last decades of the 19th century.

France and Germany had been suspicious of each other for a thousand years and the Franco - Prussian War of 1870/1 had produced unreconciled differences. European Powers, particularly Germany, became jealous of Great Britain's domination of world trade and its Empire, and the Austro-Hungarian Empire was on the wane, with Austria losing its power and influence in the Balkans.

Kaiser Wilhelm II became Emperor of Germany in 1888, and it was not long before Britain, and the rest of Europe, became increasingly concerned over Germany's military preoccupations and ambitions.

An 'arms race' began in the first decade of the 20th century when Germany determined to equal Britain's naval strength, by building more and more large battleships and cruisers.

These tensions resulted in alliances being forged. France allied herself with Russia, Great Britain with France, Germany with Austria and Russia with Serbia.

Britain for her part, saw these tensions as being primarily a problem for the Continental countries and had no particular quarrel with any of them, secure as she was in her position as the dominant world power.

The tinder box was lit when Franz Joseph, heir to the Austrian throne, was assassinated at Sarajevo on 28th June 1914 by a Serb nationalist. Austria used this as an excuse to declare war on Serbia.

In a domino effect, the respective aligned countries followed each other into declaring war. The last European Power to join the fray was Great Britain.

In 1839, a treaty had been signed in London by the five European Powers, Britain, France, Russia, Austria and Germany, which protected the neutrality of Belgium. Belgium had been formed as an independent country from Holland in 1831, after the Napoleonic wars, when Sir Charles Bagot, as ambassador to the Hague, was involved in the negotiations.
It was the violation of this treaty by Germany, that brought Britain into the war.
By the end of it, out of a total of nearly 8 million killed, nearly 1 million were from this country and the Empire. Seven were from Blithfield. Here are their stories.......

Every year at the annual Remembrance Day service in Blithfield Church, the names on the War Memorial therein are read out to remind us of their sacrifice.
To most of the congregation 100 years since the end of the war, they are just a name. These names are now unfamiliar to local people as their families have long since moved away from the parish and locality. The following accounts detail as much as possible where they lived, worked and where their families originally came from as well as giving them a context into a world which is now long gone, largely brought about by the very war in which they lost their lives.
Their stories are presented in the chronological order of their deaths so as to indicate the progress of the war from March 1916 - the date of the first death - to March1918, the date of the last, not, of course, forgetting the parish's one loss in the Second World War.
Included is just one of the 26 servicemen listed on the Blithfield Roll Call, who fortunately, returned from the war.
The following accounts of those lost from the parish are not all complete due to records of their service being sparse, or in many cases non existent. This is due to the fact that during the London Blitz in September 1940, the archive in Arnside Street was hit by an incendiary bomb and of those records which were not destroyed in the fire, many more were lost due to water damage from firemen's hoses. Of 6.5 million documents, only 1.25 million were saved.
Consequently, while most of the information here is correct, some has been conjectured from the facts that are known and therefore can only give a plausible account of what could have been the truth.
Servicemen's records from the Second World War are still classified and held by the Ministry of Defence.
The servicemen's stories are interspersed with a brief history of some of the battles and armed services in which those from Blithfield were involved.

PRIVATE WILLIAM JOSEPH STONHAM

Private Stonham was killed in action on the 5th March 1916. He was aged 20.

By the time he reached the front line, the war had degenerated into trench warfare, bought about by the stalemate between the rival armies caused by the use of highly mechanised and devastating weapons which had never been used before in a major conflict.

William Stonham left home early and aged 14 was living at the Newton Hurst farm of Mr Tudor Roe[1] and employed there as a 'farm servant', although he was born in the neighbouring village of Abbots Bromley, where his parents lived. His father, Joseph, was gardener at Blithfield Hall and had moved to the area from Sussex with his wife. It seems young Stonham yearned for the prospect and 'adventure' of fighting for king and country. Before conscription began in 1917, many young men volunteered and answered Kitchener's call 'Your Country Needs You' with enthusiasm. After all, at the outbreak of the war in August 1914, 'it was going to be all over by Christmas'.

There is an anomaly in William Stonham's age of 20 given above and noted in official records. This it seems was his age assumed by the authorities and proves his determination to 'join up'. In April 1911 he was 14 and so at the time of his death he was 18 and therefore must have lied about his age when he enlisted, which was quite common for some headstrong young men.[2] The enlistment officers were not too diligent in wishing to verify the age of a potential recruit, although they were, by not doing so, flouting the law, for the enlistment age was 18 and the lawful age for overseas service was 19.

He was in the 6th Battalion of 'The Buffs' Regiment which finished the war earning 48 battle honours including 1 VC and losing 6000 men during the duration of the conflict. They mobilised for war and landed in France in June 1915 and were involved in the Battle of Loos in October.

The 5th March 1916 found Pte Stonham's battalion in Annequin, a small French mining village near the Belgian border and on the front line.

---

1 Mr Roe's family still do.

2 The youngest lad to enlist during the First World War was only 12 years old! He was tall and heavily built and no doubt as far as some of the Recruitment Sergeants were concerned, if someone looked old enough they were old enough. He was eventually found out and returned home

British troops taking over a crater during the Battle of Loos in September 1915 after the explosion of a mine before the main attack.

They were to relieve the 11th Middlesex Regiment who were occupying one of the forward trenches and three craters[1] which were in poor condition due to the weather and enemy shelling.

They achieved their objective but it was necessary to relieve one of the craters at night due to it not being connected to the trench network and by reason of a *'deadly German sniper* ' who claimed three English killed and three wounded. It can be assumed that one of those killed was William Stonham

He is interred at the Loos Memorial about 14 miles from where he fell. Private Stonham is also commemorated on the War Memorial in Abbots Bromley.

1 These craters were formed by shell fire or deliberately blown by mines in order to destroy the opponents trench system as was the case here. In order to advance sufficiently near to the enemy trenches in order to lay the explosives, it was necessary to tunnel underground some distance and deep enough to prevent damage from shell fire. Miners, many from the Staffordshire coalfields, were employed for the task. Any craters large enough were effective protection for attacking, or retreating troops and could be linked to a previously dug trench network in order to advance either side's front line. Many did however, soon fill with water and many soldiers were drowned in them.

2nd Lt. EDWARD LUKE HENRY BAGOT

2ND LT E. L. H. BAGOT.
Welsh Guards. Only son of
Major the Hon. Walter and
Mrs. Bagot.

On 10th September 1916 at age 19, 2nd Lieutenant Bagot was killed in action at Ginchy in France during the Battle of the Somme. He was fighting over the same soil for King George V, as his illustrious ancestor, Sir John Bagot, had fought for King Henry V, 501 years before.

He was the son of Major the Hon. Walter Bagot DSO (Grenadier Guards) and Mrs Bagot and heir to the Bagot Barony through his uncle William, the fourth Baron Bagot. [1] The family lived in London. His father served on the staff of General Sir Henry Rawlinson, commander of the British 4th army and responsible for the main attack on the Somme on 1st July 1916.

Second Lieutenant Bagot held a probationary commission (special reserve) with the Coldstream Guards from August 1914, at the outbreak of war, until March 1915.

Interestingly, Edward Bagot's school reports and training records with the Coldstream Guards emphasise his determination for a military career may not have been wise. Nonetheless, for whatever reason, determined he was. He had attended Eton school from Easter 1909 to Summer 1913 and while there was in the Officers Training Corps from February 1912 until he left school 'early'. Whilst in the OTC he gained no qualifications and left with the rank of Private, although one report states...*he has plenty of pluck.*

Edward Bagot joined his battalion with the Coldstream Guards on 16th

---

1 William, 4th Baron Bagot married an American lady - a Roman Catholic - and their first and only child was a girl, Barbara. Her mother had their daughter baptised a Catholic, unknown to her husband and against his wishes. Edward Luke Henry's father pre-deceased his elder brother the 4th Baron and therefore on Edward's death the direct line of the heredity was broken and the Barony passed to cousin Gerald Bagot who became the 5th Baron in 1935. Many aristocratic landed families were decimated by the slaughter in the First World War. Many sons - being officers - were disproportionately killed as they led their platoons 'over the top'. All three sons of the family at Tatton Park in Cheshire were killed in that conflict.

September 1914.
However, by December 1914 reports to his superiors detail that... *he is not a competent officer...*and that... *he has not gained the confidence of men under his command'....* On the 16th December 1914 he is given another month's trial with further reports on his progress requested.
These reports detail that he is... *constitutionally unfitted for command...* and that... *he is a continual source of anxiety to the captain of his company...,* but they also state...*he may be fit for a less strenuous profession...*and...*he does his work to the best of his ability....*
One final report states that...*soldiering does not appear to be his metier.*
On 21st January 1915 he was called to resign his commission and before doing so, in March 1915, he applied for a cadet-ship at the Royal Military College, Sandhurst.
However, he subsequently joined The Welsh Guards, 1st Battalion Prince of Wales Company and went to fight the Germans. [1]

The Welsh Guards were formed as a foot guards regiment on 25th February 1915 by King George V and they were mobilised for war on 18th August that year having joined with the 3rd (Guards) Brigade of the Guards Division. They won 20 Battle Honours and 1 VC during the war and they lost a total of 860 men.
During 1916 they fought in the battles of Fleurs Courcelette (which began on 15th September 1916) and Morval, two of the many fought as part of the Battle of the Somme.[2]
These battles were part of an Allied push on their entire front and included the Battle of Ginchy which began on 9th September.
The 16th Division succeeded in capturing the village later that day, denying the Germans valuable observation posts of the surrounding area, although there were still many Germans taking refuge in cellars.
Previous attempts to capture the village on 3rd September had been repulsed by German counter attacks.

It was early evening on the 9th September when 2nd Lieutenant Bagot's Prince of Wales Company were ordered to move up, under cover of darkness, into the captured village in order to relieve troops already there

1 It could be that as with many other young men, Edward Bagot's determination to fight was due to his quest for 'adventure' which made him oblivious to his shortcomings. Alternatively, family pressure -and reputation - from his Guardsman father- could have played a part, particularly as the army was desperate to recruit young officers. The newly formed Welsh Guards were no doubt keen to oblige those wishing to join their regiment now that, at the end of 1915, the war had begun in earnest and the realities of it were being faced. Additionally, there were outside pressures which persuaded young men to join the fighting. The practise of young ladies presenting white feathers to those who they considered should be 'doing their bit' for King and Country is well known.

2 See Other Histories - The Battle of the Somme. p.299

and prepare for the inevitable counter attack.
In the early hours of 10th September, unable to locate their objective, they were caught in the German counter attack and before they could reoccupy their trenches all the officers became casualties. Second Lieutenant Bagot and his Company Commander were killed.
In the bitter fighting that day The Prince of Wales Company suffered a total of 88 casualties including 13 killed. The total casualties for all the Guards companies involved in the action was 205.
The towns of Morval and Lesboeufs, just beyond Ginchy, were captured by the Guards on 25th September.

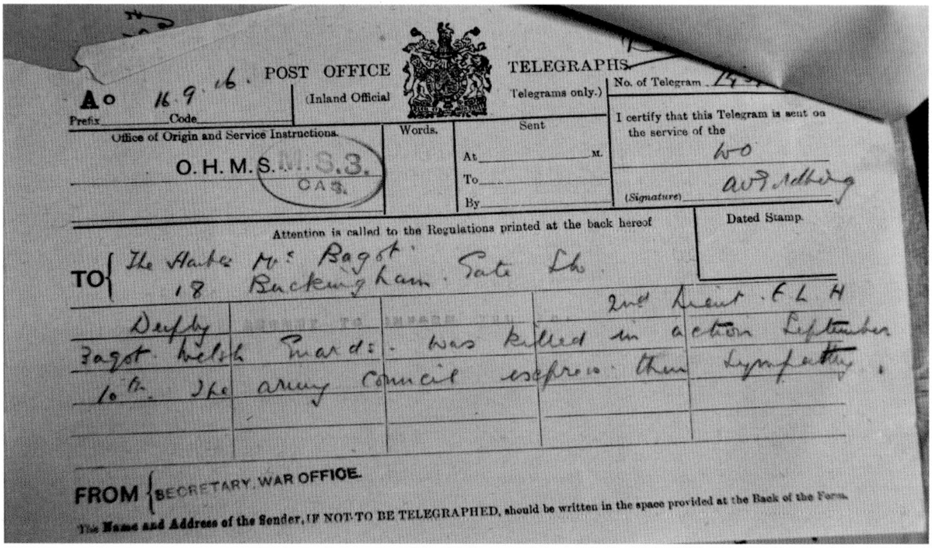
POST OFFICE TELEGRAPHS
(Inland Official Telegrams only.)
Ao 16.9.16.
Prefix Code
No. of Telegram
Office of Origin and Service Instructions.
O. H. M. S. M.S.3. CAS.
Words. Sent At M. To By
I certify that this Telegram is sent on the service of the WO
(Signature)
Dated Stamp.
Attention is called to the Regulations printed at the back hereof
TO The Hon'ble Mrs Bagot 18 Buckingham Gate SW
Deeply 2nd Lieut. E L H Bagot Welsh Guards was killed in action September 10th. The army council express their sympathy.
FROM SECRETARY, WAR OFFICE.
The Name and Address of the Sender, IF NOT TO BE TELEGRAPHED, should be written in the space provided at the Back of the Form.

The telegram every relative of a serving soldier fears.

Whatever the reason behind his will to fight, given the outcome, it is as well to commend it, after all, he paid the ultimate sacrifice.
Consequently it can be considered an act of bravery, rather than one of foolhardiness.

Second Lieutenant Bagot lies in the Guards' Cemetery, Lesboeufs, only a few miles from where he fell. As well as being commemorated on the War Memorial in Blithfield Church, there is also a brass wall plaque in his memory on the south wall of the chancel.

In February 1917, it is recorded that Edward's father was resident in Johannesburg, South Africa, while his wife, living in London, was dealing with the aftermath of their son's death.
Also in the chancel at Blithfield, a large brass plate informs that his father:-

WALTER LEWIS BAGOT
BORN AT BLITHFIELD APRIL 22 1864
DIED AT ADMASTON,[1] JOHANNESBURG SOUTH AFRICA MAY 26 1927
MAJOR GRENADIER GUARDS D.S.O. 2nd SON OF WILLIAM, 3rd LORD BAGOT
AND HIS WIFE, LUCIA
SERVED SOUDAN 1898, SOUTH AFRICAN WAR 1900, A.D.C. TO LORD
RAWLINSON GREAT WAR 1914-1915
GENERAL MANAGER TO VICTORIA FALLS POWER COMPANY 1910-1927

The Guards Cemetery, Lesboeufs, France.

1 Named after Admaston, Blithfield?

RIFLEMAN BERTIE GEORGE PYE

Bertie George Pye was born in July 1892, the son of George and Harriet Pye of Dimsdale Admaston. He found employment on the farm of Mr Houldcroft of Stansley Wood Farm, in the parish, as a *'general farm lad '*
His father was born in Norfolk and was employed as a gamekeeper at Blithfield Hall.

On 26th December 1912 he married at Abbots Bromley and on 3rd August 1913 a daughter was born.
On 26th February 1914, six months before the outbreak of the First World War, he set sail for Australia intending to settle there and landed in Melbourne, Victoria on 10th April 1914.
However, he was motivated to move on to New Zealand and in 1915 he was living near Auckland where, on the 12th January 1916, he enlisted with the New Zealand Expeditionary Force and joined the New Zealand Rifle Brigade on 1st May 1916.
After training at Trentham near Wellington and settling his affairs, he embarked for Europe on 19th August 1916 and arrived at Devonport on 25th October 1916 as Rifleman Pye, 4th Battalion 3rd New Zealand Rifle Brigade. From here the battalion was transported to Sling Camp on

Salisbury Plain where it was prepared for action in France. There is no doubt that Bertie would have had leave from here in order to visit his family back in Blithfield when the photograph, above, would have been taken.

He left England for Etaples in France on 15th November 1916 and joined 'A' Company of his battalion on 4th December *' In the Field of France'.* On the 1st February 1917 the 4th Battalion was near Ploegsteert [1] ('Plug-street ' to the British Tommy), near the Belgian border, in a forward position and in a salient of the British front line, surrounded on three sides by enemy positions. This was regarded as a 'quiet' sector where no set piece battles had been fought and therefore ideal initiation for soldiers new to the Western Front.

On the 3rd February, the Germans launched a gas attack on the 4th Battalion's trenches with a *'considerable number of gas shells'.* The battalion suffered 18 casualties but no fatalities.

A few quiet days were followed on the 6th and 7th of February by an artillery duel between the opposing forces, each replying in kind for the other's actions.

It was on the 6th February that it is recorded that two fatalities occurred as a result, one it can be assumed being Rifleman Pye at aged 24

He is interred at the Rue-Pettillon Military Cemetery, Fleurbaix, Northern France.

During the month of February, the NZRB 4th Battalion lost 16 men killed.

Rifleman Pye left his entire estate amounting to £33 16s 10d (£33.84) [2] to his father, George, at Stansley Wood, Admaston.

The 5th Battalion of the New Zealand Rifle Brigade was famous locally when they were transferred from the Western Front to Cannock Chase Military Camp in September 1917.

They had distinguished themselves during the Battle of the Somme in 1916 and the Battle of Messines Ridge in 1917 and were seen as being a valuable source of combat experience and therefore capable of training freshly recruited soldiers.

Brocton Camp on the Chase, was to be their home and headquarters for the rest of the war until they returned home to New Zealand in May 1919.

The good relationships formed between the NZRB, other army units and

---

1 One year earlier, Colonel Winston Churchill was posted here after losing his position as First Sea Lord. Although still a Member of Parliament, he held the rank of major in the Territorial Army and 'joined up' to command a battalion. The experience reinforced his view that it would be machines - tanks and aircraft - which would help to win the war, a view which was to be fulfilled. He subsequently left the army and became Minister of Munitions when David Lloyd George became Prime Minister.

2 This figure would amount to around £2,200 today

the local civilian population saw to it that the Brigade presented its colours to the town of Stafford before they left for home. The photograph below, shows the ceremony taking place in Stafford Market Square.

Bertie George Pye's home, 'Dimsdale', Stansley Wood. It was demolished in the early 1950's to make way for Blithfield Reservoir

Lt. LEONARD MURRAY

Lieutenant Leonard Murray was the son of Rev. Douglas Stuart Murray and Mrs Harriet Georgina Isabel Murray and was born at Blithfield where his father was Rector from 1879 to 1919. His mother was the grand-daughter of Emily Mary Bridgeman, nee' Bagot, daughter of the Right Reverend Richard Bagot, Bishop of Bath and Wells.

Lt Murray obtained a commission as 2nd Lieutenant with the Lancashire Hussars Yeomanry on 10th January 1916 and was promoted Lieutenant on 20th December 1916.He became attached to the Royal Flying Corps in January 1917, which he was very keen to join when he told his C.O. that '*he felt he would be doing more real work there than staying on with us*'.

He began training with the RFC [1] at Harlaxton near Grantham and was killed in an accident there on 13th March 1917 at age 20.

The Commanding Officer at Harlaxton said that Lt Murray was *'one of his keenest and most promising pupils'.*

Records differ in their account of his death. The Commonwealth War Graves Commission burial record states he was killed 'while flying'.

Another document from the National Archive at Kew records his death from an 'aero accident' which coincides with anecdotal evidence - and the truth - that he was struck by a revolving aircraft propeller [2].

---

1 See Other Histories - The Royal Flying Corps p.302

2 These anomalies are not uncommon when referring to the fallen. In some cases the actual cause of death is not disclosed in deference to the feelings of loved ones due to the banality of some incidents and tragedy in others. Some fatalities occurred through self inflicted accidents.

Accidents of this kind would have been a common occurrence with aircraft of the period and a fate not easy to avoid. Many fatalities arose from flying accidents and mechanical failure of the fledgling technology.
Lt. Murray lies buried in the churchyard at Blithfield and his grave is maintained and cared for by the Commonwealth War Graves Commission.

Two of Lieutenant Murray's older brothers fought both in the First and Second World Wars. Walter achieved the rank of Lieutenant Colonel in 1916 and was awarded the Military Cross in the same year. He was awarded the O.B.E. in 1918. Major George Murray served in the Royal Engineers and died on active service in 1940. Both men were born in Blithfield and are listed in the Blithfield Roll Call of those who served during the war, their names being carved onto a board which presently is displayed in Admaston Village Hall. Their father died on 19th March 1920 after serving as Rector at Blithfield for forty years.

A De-Havilland 5 aircraft after a hard landing at Harlaxton airfield in March 1917. Undoubtedly of the type flown by Lt Murray, the pilot of this 'plane most likely survived the incident. It is being reclaimed here by Australian members of the R.F.C.

PER ARDUA AD ASTRA
LIEUTENANT
L. MURRAY
ROYAL FLYING CORPS
13TH MARCH 1917 AGE 20

The Grave of Lt. Leonard Murray at Blithfield on the 11th November 2018, the Centenary of the end of the First World War.

It is cared for by the Commonwealth War Graves Commission.

PRIVATE CHARLES SAMPSON GRETTON

Private Gretton was killed in action on the 9th April 1917.

He was the son of George Gretton and Annie Gretton of Admaston, his father being employed as a stableman at Blithfield Hall. Charles was born in the neighbouring parish of Stowe-by-Chartley.

At the age of 14 Charles Gretton was employed as a 'Waggoner's Lad ' on the farm of the Wint family at St Stephens Hill Farm in Admaston.

He enlisted with the Kings Own Yorkshire Light Infantry and he fought in their 6th Battalion. The K.O.Y.L.I were awarded 26 battle honours and 8 VC's during the First World War.

On 21st May 1915 the 6th Battalion was mobilised for war and landed in France at Boulogne and in April 1917 they were in Beaurains, a small village just 2 miles south west of Arras, in northern France.

Between the 1st and 8th April 1917, the battalion carried out intensive preparations for the Battle of Arras, one of the main offensives by the British Army that year. Along a front of 14 miles, two British Armies confronted their foe and were to pour some 5 million artillery shells onto their positions.

At midnight on 9th April parties of 20 men from 6th Battalion K.O.Y.L.I were sent out to cut the barbed wire in front of their first objective while being continually sniped at, and at 7.15am, six tanks arrived at the KOYLI assembly trenches. At 7.34am, the creeping artillery barrage began and companies of the battalion moved forward in two waves and the first objective was taken without difficulty and they took 35 prisoners. Their next objective was a redoubt which was heavily wired and consisted of a deep and strong trench system. Under cover of the barrage and with the help of three tanks they took the redoubt along with another 31 prisoners, a trench mortar and two machine guns.

Two platoons were left to consolidate their gain while the rest of the battalion battled on to another trench system under machine gun and shell fire from enemy positions. They pressed on and captured their third objective where they met some resistance when searching it. Another 15 prisoners were taken. Beyond, yet another trench was denied the Germans and they took another 35 prisoners.

At 1.30pm a German counter attack by 150 of their soldiers was successfully driven off.

The last two trenches formed part of the Hindenburg Line, and after consolidating their position on the 10th April, they were ordered to attack a nearby village. They succeeded and at 5.30 pm the 6th battalion KOYLI were relieved by another Brigade.

The Battle of Arras April 1917. British troops with their German prisoners who carry one of their wounded

So, sometime during that Easter Monday of 9th April, amid a freezing wind, driving sleet, mud and a hail of flying metal, the waggoner's lad from Admaston lost his life. He was one of 28 who were killed from his battalion in those two days, out of a total of 169 casualties. He is buried two miles from where he fell, in the C.W.G.C. cemetery at Tilloy - Les - Mofflaines.

In two days, more than 11,000 prisoners and 100 guns had been captured but soon the Germans began to bring up their reserves and checked the British advance, which in some places had been three miles. From then on, the familiar stalemate situation was the result of the offensive which officially ended on 23rd May. Again the casualties on both sides were horrendous, with over 158,000 British and 130,000 German soldiers being killed or wounded.

The most famous victory in the battle was in the capture, by Canadian troops, of Vimy Ridge, a bastion of the German defence along the Hindenburg Line, which had defied a previous French attempt in 1915.

PRIVATE GEORGE RUSHTON

Private Rushton was killed in action on the 27th April 1917 aged 24.
He was the son of Isaac and Sarah Rushton of Yeatsall, Abbots Bromley. His father was a bricklayer on the Bagot estate.

At the age of 18, he was a '*pupil teacher at an elementary County Council school*'. Although his family home was at Yeatsall in Abbots Bromley parish and is commemorated on the War Memorial there, it can be assumed that the school in question was Admaston school [1] in Blithfield parish.
Yeatsall is close to the boundary of Blithfield parish, and some of the properties there were on the Blithfield estate of the Bagot family. Admaston school was originally endowed by the third Lord Bagot, and thereby perhaps encouraged Blithfield to claim George as one of their own.

He enlisted in the Sherwood Forester's Regiment, 2nd/6th Battalion - Territorial Force - and during the war his regiment was awarded with 57 battle honours and 9 VC's. It lost 11,410 men.

In February 1917, the Germans began a strategic retreat along part of their line to well prepared and defended positions known as the Hindenburg line.
It was in the pursuit of the Germans to their new line that Private Rushton's battalion was involved.

Private Rushton's battalion landed at Boulogne on 27th February 1917 and spent the next month in reserve and support roles. On 31st March they were in Bernes where they launched an attack on the enemy and came under heavy shell fire. They successfully captured the village of Veniselles and went on forward and captured Veancourt and took ten prisoners. On 22nd April the battalion marched on to Roisel a small farming village and important railway junction in Picardy, where they were held in reserve.
From here, on 27th April, another attack was launched against rear guards of the German retreating troops, the objectives taken and a new line successfully established. Seven prisoners and one machine gun were captured.
It seems Private Rushton was the only soldier killed in this attack.

By First World War standards, these first experiences of the battalion fighting the enemy were small skirmishes, attacking a foe who had no wish to hold his territory and who were merely covering the retreat of their comrades.
In between these actions, the battalion even had time to entertain their

1 The school now serves as the parish Village Hall. It is the only listed village hall in Staffordshire.

Corps commander who visited to award two Military Crosses and two Military Medals to those who had distinguished themselves in their first battle on 31st March and to commend the battalion on their *'smart appearance'.*

It was not until 6th May that Private Rushton's CO wrote *' no incidents of any importance occurred during this tour. Casualties one. Other rank slightly wounded '*

Private George Rushton lies buried at the British Cemetery at Bellicourt, five miles from where he fell.

The British Cemetery, Bellicourt.

PRIVATE JOSEPH WILLIAM JOHNSON

Private Johnson was born in Eccleshall. He married at Uttoxeter in 1905 and lived in Fradswell with his wife Sarah Ann. He worked as a farm labourer and they had three children. He was killed on 21st March 1918 at aged 35.

By the time he enlisted in the army at Uttoxeter on 6th December 1915, he had become a gamekeeper for Lord Bagot on Bagot's Park near Abbots Bromley and was living at 'The Spintel ' in the park.

On 13th June 1916 he was posted to the Army Reserve of the 6th Battalion, Territorial Force, North Staffordshire Regiment and left England for France on 24th December 1916 and was transferred to the 2/5th battalion (Prince of Wales's).

At the beginning of 1918, the war was no nearer a conclusion than it ever had been. Military planners were preparing for the conflict to continue into 1919, and soon the Allies were to begin a mighty struggle with their foe.

The British army had just fought the Third Battle of Ypres - or Battle of Paschendale as it became known - fought during the end of 1917, and was much in need of rest.

Since then, the Germans had been planning a major offensive in which they hoped to drive a wedge between the British and French armies thereby preventing any further interaction between the two. If successful this would have achieved a French capitulation and victory over the allies before the American Army became an effective fighting force. The US had joined the war in 1917.

On 20th March 1918, Private Joseph Johnson with his 5th Battalion North Staffordshire's were brought up from reserve to the front line at Bullecourt, 10 miles south west of Arras.

This heavily fortified village originally formed part of the German Hindenburg Line and was captured by the British during the Battle of Arras 11 months before, during which Private Johnson's comrade from Blithfield, Private Charles Gretton was killed.

The German Spring Offensive was unleashed on 21st March 1918.

Just as the weather conditions had favoured the Germans during the battles of late 1917, that morning they were ideal for the attackers again, and a nightmare for the defenders. A low mist hung over the 50 mile front preventing the British from seeing their foe's advance and poison gas utilised by the Germans in their heavy artillery barrage, hung close to the ground. After their barrage had done it's work, the Germans attacked at 9am and in the onslaught the Staffordshire men were decimated, taking the loss of 22 officers and 539 other ranks, including the battalion Headquarters and Staff.

Private Johnson was initially listed as missing but was later found to be one of those killed. At the end of January 1918, the battalion's strength was noted by it's C.O. as consisting of 53 officers and 1,214 other ranks. The battalion had lost nearly 50% of it's strength within a few hours.

On the afternoon of 21st March the remains of the battalion were moved by motor transport and route march ahead of the German advance and, side stepping it, were given the chance to rest, train and replace those soldiers lost.

On 30th March the battalion was inspected by King George V and by 2nd April, the battalion was based at Watou, just over the French border in Belgium, 70 miles from Bullecourt.

Private Johnson lies buried at the Commonwealth War Graves Commission Arras Memorial in Arras, northern France and only a few miles from the CWGC cemetery of Tilly-Les-Mofflaines where Blithfield lad Charles Gretton rests.

With effect from 25th November 1918, Private Johnson's widow and their three children were awarded a Pension of 29/7d per week (£1.47).[1]

The Arras Memorial Cemetery

1 An amount which would be the equivalent to nearly £100 today.

.....Ebbs out life's little day......

We do not know the exact circumstances of how those from this parish died, but here is an account of how one man faced death on the battlefield......

Soon after 2nd Lieutenant Bagot was killed, on the 15th September 1916, a soldier from another English Regiment - the Sherwood Foresters - was engaged in the ferocious fighting around Ginchy. He was not from Blithfield but from Swinefleet, near Goole in Humberside, and he was Private John Duesbury.

His parents received a letter from him on 3rd September 1916 and this could well have been his last, but this was not the case as on the 15th September he wrote these lines......

Dear Mother,

I am writing these few lines severely wounded. We have done well. Our battalion advanced about three quarters of a mile. I am laid in a shell hole with 2 wounds in my hip and through my back. I cannot move or crawl. I have been here 24 hours and never seen a living soul.

I hope you will receive these few lines as I don't expect anyone will come to take me away. But you know I have done my duty out here now for one year and eight months. and you will always have the consolation that I died quite happy doing my duty.

Must give my best of love to all the cousins who have been so kind to me the time I've been out here. And all the best of love to Mother and Harry and all at Swinefleet. *x x*

His body was eventually found and hastily buried on the spot and his note eventually passed on to his family.

Subsequent artillery bombardments however obliterated his grave and his name is now engraved on the Theipval Memorial as one of those hundreds of thousands of soldiers whose bodies were never found.

There is no doubt that this scenario would have been played out many thousands of times during the war.

This unique and heart rending letter however is proof, if it is needed, of the courage, heroism and suffering caused by this, or any war.

There is also a supreme irony here. Private Duesbury's family was of German origin, their name having been changed from Duesburg.

OF THE 33 SERVICEMEN WHO LEFT BLITHFIELD TO FIGHT IN THE WAR, CHARLIE KENT WAS ONE OF THOSE WHO RETURNED.......

DRIVER CHARLES FREDERICK KENT
and the
ARMY SERVICE CORPS

Charles Frederick Kent was born on 21st December 1879 at Newton in Blithfield parish where his father was a farmer and wheelwright who instructed his son in the trade.

In the First World War he enlisted with the Army Service Corps, in the horse transport section, as a driver/wheeler and arrived in France on 18th December 1915 at age nearly 35. He initially trained at the Military Barracks in Clonmel, near Waterford, in what is now the Irish Republic but then, part of the Union.

His company of the ASC was part of the 16th Divisional Train and came under the direct orders from that army division which mainly consisted of Irish Regiments.

The ASC was one the unsung heroes of the war.

By April 1916 the British army in France numbered one million men distributed along a front of 83 miles. If they were to stand shoulder to shoulder in Britain, the line would have stretched from London to Edinburgh. At the time it represented the number of the male population greater than that of Ireland of those aged between 15 and 45.

To supply such numbers with food alone required a huge effort. Every day, each man had over one pound of fresh or preserved meat, over one pound of bread or biscuit, four ounces of bacon, three of cheese, four of jam, three of sugar, eight of vegetables and half an ounce of tea. Only butter was in short supply which amounted to two ounces a week.

This meant transporting 600 tons of meat, 600 of bread, above 100 tons of bacon and jam and nearly 100 tons of cheese and sugar every day.

This was the task assigned to the ASC. It became the Royal Army Service Corps in 1918 and was the forerunner of what is now the Royal Logistical Corps. By the end of the war the RASC consisted of over 10,000 officers and

315,000 men.

In addition to the army's nutritional needs, units of the ASC were responsible for moving infantry, thousands of tons of munitions and artillery, timber for the construction of trenches and underground bunkers, coal and not least, medical supplies.

The British army at this time were fortunate in leading the world in motorised petrol driven transport although horses and mules were indispensable for hauling artillery and times when the breakdown of motors occurred.

The ASC were trained as infantry and responsible for their own local defence if the need arose. They also maintained army vehicles. Charles Kent being a trained wheelwright,[1] would have been well suited to this task.

Men of the ASC relax for a photograph which was probably taken during their training at Clonmel near Waterford in Ireland. Charles Kent is not in the picture

Among other actions, Driver Kent's company provided for soldiers fighting during the battles of the Somme in September 1916 - including the Battle of Ginchy where 2nd Lieutenant Edward Bagot fell-, the Battle of Messines in June 1917 and the Third Battle of Ypres in August 1917, also, known as Passchendaele. This was the defining battle for many British and Commonwealth soldiers, not only for the fierce fighting, but for the exceptionally muddy ground conditions.

Men, horses and mules were drowned in the mire and the ASC's task was made almost impossible.

On the 11th hour of the 11th day of the 11th month of 1918 the war ended, and the Army Service Corps 16th Divisional Train was stationed in

1 See Other Histories - Trench Art of the First World War. p.304

Taintignes, Belgium.

The following extracts from their War Diary emphasise what was uppermost in the minds of their commanding officers:-

Taintignies 11.11.18
...Feeding strength 13,414........RUM was issued to the whole division by order of GOC on the occasion of cessation of hostilities.......

Avelin (France) 23.12.18
Supply arrangements as usual. No Christmas Puddings having arrived the Commanding Officer went to Army Headquarters to see the D.D S & T. [1] *Very wet all day.*

Avelin 24.12.18
Supply arrangements as usual......at 2pm Plum Puddings arrived on the Pack Train and balances drawn by MT [2] *from Army Headquarters. Weather bright and fine.*

Avelin 25.12.18
...........Each Coy. held a Christmas Dinner, the Commanding Officer and Adjutant visited each Coy. in the evening, all very happy. [3]

We can imagine Driver Charles Kent at one of these dinners and can wonder if he was involved in transporting the Christmas Puddings.

Bearing in mind the essential services they provided, units and companies of the A.S.C. would have been among the last servicemen to be de-mobilized. Available evidence suggests that Driver Kent de-mobilized on 8th March 1919, after 4 years at war, and returned home to the Rectory Farm near Admaston rejoining his father there. He married Blithfield girl Mary Deakin from Newton Hurst in 1925 and took over the farm on the death of his father in 1931.

Charles Kent died on 21st July 1945 and is buried in the church yard at Blithfield along with his wife, daughter and son-in-law.

---

1 D D S & T - Deputy Director Supplies and Transport

2 M.T. - Mechanical Transport

3 Author's Note - Charlie Kent was my grandfather and he died before I was born. Edith Lucy, my mother, was his only child. She confided in me not long before she died in 2012 that her father never, at any time, addressed her by her first, or second name. She never knew why her father always called her "Tye-nt". Taintignes was where, it would seem, Charlie Kent was stationed on Armistice Day. Having come through the conflict since 1915 unscathed, the day would have come as an enormous amount of relief and joy.

It was Napoleon Bonaparte who famously declared that an army marches on its stomach. The degree to which soldier's nutritional needs were catered for is detailed in this despatch from the Brigadier General commanding the 47th Infantry Brigade suggesting changes to regiments' rations. Dated 29th January 1916 this image is reproduced from the A.S.C. 16th Divisional Train war diaries. Jam tomorrow?

To The Supply Officer attached to the 47th. Inf. Brigade.

I should like to make the following suggestions as regards rations.

(1). The men of the 6th. R.Irish Regt and the 7th. Leinsters do not like cheese, this probably applies also to the 8th. R.Munster Fusl and the 6th. Connaught Rangers. In fact I think it is probable that all Irish Regiments do not care for it. I would therefore suggest that, in any rate, in the case of the first two named Battalions they be given something in lieu of cheese, I would suggest Jam.

(2). The present allowance of Potatoes is I understand from you 6 ozs.(the Quartermaster of the Leinsters told me he was only receiving 2 ozs.) of Potatoes, and 2 ozs of Carrots or Turnips. I would suggest that an arrangement be made with Quartermasters for an issue of 8 ozs of Potatoes either every day or on days instead of the present mixed vegetables ration. I have just given up command of a Welsh Batt. where cheeseX was a special luxury, and I think perhaps exchanges might be made.

(3). In the first Division my Battalion had a special issue of Flour and Yeast. We had two bakers, and they used to bake XX extra bread which the men appreciated very much.

Could we have extra flour in this Brigade for that purpose it is also useful for making puddings. If we could have currants or sultanas at the same time it would be a great advantage. In my late Battalion we had " Plum Duff " 2 or 3 times a week for each company.

(4). The man do not care for biscuit and if we could have a full ration of 1½ lbs. of bread per man, whilst at rest, it would be much appreciated.

29/1/16. (sgd) G.Pereira Brig. General

Commanding 47th. Brigade

THE LAST MONTHS
of the
FIRST WORLD WAR

The German Army's Spring Offensive, which began on 21st March 1918, created much alarm for the Allied Command. It had succeeded in making great in-roads into the allied lines on three fronts and was determined to seek a victory before the American army was able to become an effective fighting force in terms of numbers and experience.

The German success was enabled by the release of hundreds of thousands of German soldiers to fight on the Western Front after the capitulation of the Russian threat on the Eastern Front, which became effective in January 1918. The British and French armies had few reserves to call upon and could only hope that they would be able - weary as they were after their battles of 1917- to at least slow the German advance until the Americans were able to even the balance.

By April 1918, the situation had become critical for the Allies, to the extent that Sir Douglas Haig, the British Army Commander issued this statement to his troops...

......*There is no other course open to us but to fight it out. Every position must be held to the last man; there must be no retirement. With our backs to the wall, and believing in the justice of our cause, each one of us must fight on to the end.....*

In June, the German forces had reached the River Marne and were in striking distance of Paris, a position they had achieved in the early months of the war in 1914. They had overrun most of the territory the allies, including all the men from Blithfield, had shed so much blood for - as had the Germans- and it was at this point that, ready or not, the American army had to be deployed in order to help stabilize the grave situation.

However, by the end of July and sometimes outnumbered five to one, by sheer determination, tactics and over stretched German supply lines, the Allies held on and checked the German advance.

On 8th August 1918, the Allies launched a counter offensive against a German Army demoralized by it's lack of success. By using the tactics of surprise, air power and massed tank attacks the Allies drove eight miles into the German lines and inflicted a defeat which the German Commander, Erich von Ludendorff called 'a black day for the German army'. It was the beginning of the end and the German army started to fight its way home.

By 29th August, the British army had retaken Bullecourt where Private Johnson from Blithfield had been killed at the start of the German Spring

Offensive on 21st March. Also recaptured were the Somme battlefields of 1916, also lost to the Germans during their March Offensive. The Allies had the upper hand and were to retain it.

A breakdown in the German High Command at the end of September and the increasing unrest of the German people, resulted in Germany wishing to seek an armistice. The armistice was signed at 5am on 11th November and at 11am the guns on the Western Front fell silent. The war was over at last.

Although the war was over and the armistice had been signed, the prophecy made by the British Foreign Secretary, Sir Edward Grey at the outbreak of the war in 1914, was to be realised....

' The lamps are going out all over Europe; we shall not see them lit again in our lifetime'. The armistice had merely lit a pilot light.

The conditions imposed on Germany by the terms of the armistice were onerous and some thought excessive. Germany, after all, had not been defeated unconditionally on the battlefield and many in Germany realised this, as did some on the Allied side who warned that Germany would seek to exploit this situation. Indeed, Marshal Foch, the Allied commander warned that within 20 years war would again erupt in Europe. He was inaccurate by just a few months.

Over the next decade, a certain Adolf Hitler played on this humiliation as he saw it. He obtained power in Germany and led it into the Second World War which claimed the life of another young man from Blithfield and another Bagot who had come to fight from a far off country.

Effectively there has been one World War in two parts.

Could it be, that even at the end of this conflict, it was not until the end of Communism and the freedom brought to the countries of Eastern Europe in 1992, that the lamps in Europe were fully lit again?

LEADING SEAMAN FRANCIS KENNETH FELL

Great Britain declared war on Germany on 3rd September 1939, after her diplomatic efforts to curb Adolph Hitler's territorial ambitions failed.

Leading Seaman Fell died on the 19th August 1942 aged 21. He was the son of George and Catherine Fell of Admaston.

The D Day landings of 1944 and the Allies campaign to help rid Europe of Nazism is well known. Perhaps a little less well known is the Dieppe Raid some two years earlier in 1942.

This was a large scale operation against the enemy-held port of Dieppe on the northern French coast in which 6,000 mainly British and Canadian soldiers, the RAF and the Royal Navy took part. They attacked on a front of 11 miles and although some key objectives were taken, the Germans quickly re-grouped and the operation ended in complete failure.

Over 1,000 soldiers were killed and 2,000 taken prisoner.

The Royal Navy lost 75 sailors and 206 were wounded. A total of 269 were listed as missing and Leading Seaman Fell was one of those sailors. One destroyer and 33 landing craft were sunk.

At the time this exercise was officially known as 'a reconnaissance in force' but it has since been recognised as one to test the possibility of whether an enemy held port could be successfully taken and held in order to make an invasion of mainland Europe possible.

This operation was in fact a pre-cursor to D Day.

From the lessons learnt, planners were able to re-direct their efforts to find a more effective strategy. It was realised on that June day in 1944 when the "compliment" for William the Conqueror's invasion of 1066 was repaid in that return trip across the English Channel to Normandy, but in this case to liberate rather than to conquer.

The realisation a port could not be taken, and also that to supply the allied armies with munitions, fuel and food was crucial if mainland Europe was to be successfully invaded led to two floating harbours, code named 'Mulberry', being floated across the English Channel. These were anchored down to successfully serve as the ports required soon after D Day.

This one explanation for the action sufficed for many years after the end of the war, not only for the general public, but also for those servicemen who took part.

It has only been very recently made known that part of the reality behind the planning of the operation was a far more clandestine affair, making the primary reason for it unclear.[1]

---

1 See Other Histories - The Dieppe Raid - An enigma? p.306

Plymouth Naval Memorial stands on The Hoe overlooking Plymouth Sound. On it are engraved the names of 7,000 navy personnel of the First World War and Leading Seaman Fell has his name engraved among 17,000 of the Second World War who were lost or buried at sea.

'ADOLPH HITLER' PAYS A VISIT TO THE PARISH OF BLITHFIELD.

Hitler's here! Hitler's here"! the cry went up from some members of the Blithfield Home Guard as they were enjoying some liquid sustenance one dark night in The Gate Inn, which stood just over the Blithfield parish boundary in Lea Heath. [1]

In August 1940, just a few weeks before Hitler's Luftwaffe had been denied mastery over the skies in the Battle of Britain by the R.A.F. and twelve months after the war began, Germany began it's bombing blitz on British cities. Over the next months these intensified, and during December 1940 German bombers flew frequently over Staffordshire, the unmistakeable drone of their engines identifying them from aircraft of the R.A.F. The county did not have targets sufficiently important to them for specific attention, but their ultimate destinations did.

Liverpool was the most heavily bombed city after London during the Second World War and suffered over 4,000 killed during the blitz on it. Manchester suffered too, both cities providing tempting targets for the bombers by way of Liverpool's docks and Manchester's armaments factories.

Two of the most devastating raids occurred during what are remembered as the Christmas Blitz, when on three consecutive nights, 20-22 December 1940, Liverpool was attacked, and on the nights of 22-23 December, Manchester had it's turn when 684 people were killed and over 2,000 injured. In most cases the German bombers began their flights of destruction from airfields in France and Belgium and their flight paths took them over the English countryside towards their urban targets.

On the night of 23rd December 1940, Blithfield became a victim of the blitz when three bombs and a number of incendiaries fell on the parish.

The Uttoxeter Civil Defence Area, which included many of the surrounding villages of the town, including Blithfield, kept a record of war related incidents. It's entry for that night state.....*23rd December 3 H.E (1 U.X.B.)* [2] *and 20 Incendiary Bombs (Magnesium type) at Blithfield. No casualties. Some damage to windows in Church and Rectory &c.*

---

1 With Blithfield having no public house within its boundary, this pub, which changed its name to The Wicket before being recently converted into a private dwelling, was the nearest hostelry for Blithfield folk. Harold Martin is the grandson of the publican, (who also was the village blacksmith) and remembers the night well.

2 H.E. - High Explosive. U.X.B. - Unexploded Bomb.

The bombs fell in a line up to and across the road leading to the church and exploded outside the church yard boundary wall. The last bomb fell inside the church yard and buried itself feet away from the north wall of the church and failed to explode! Consequently the church was spared severe damage.

One of the windows in the North Aisle of Blithfield Church commemorates the event on that December night. One of its panels depicts the coats of arms of the three British armed services and that of the Merchant Navy surrounding the black cross of Germany. The window was installed by Nancy, Lady Bagot in 1965 and is by Goddard and Gibbs of London.

On the previous night one bomb fell and exploded harmlessly, near Rookery Farm, Bromley Hurst.

During 1940, a total of 56 bombs fell in the Uttoxeter area and only 9 failed to explode. 77 incendiary devices were also dropped.

None of these bombs resulted in death or serious injury, although on 29th August, one house in Uttoxeter was badly damaged with three slight casualties when six bombs fell in New Road. In the first incident on 30th June, nineteen bombs fell in a line from Abbots Bromley to Loxley with a sheep being the only casualty.

In total darkness, German aircraft were guided to their targets by radio beams, but they were never-the-less prone to navigational errors and adverse weather conditions. This led heavily loaded 'planes being in danger of running low on fuel over enemy territory. Additionally, mechanical faults and damage to aircraft caused by British anti-aircraft guns and night fighters increased the danger, particularly on their journey home.

These were the main reasons why these bombs were jettisoned, rather than dropped intentionally on intended targets, and of course, there would be no point in returning to the safety of their airfields with a bomb laden aircraft. However, there were, around the time of the Blithfield incident, soldiers of the Welch Regiment camped in the grounds of Blithfield Hall.

There was also one incident which baffled Uttoxeter Civil Defence investigators -

18th August PARACHUTES dropped in district- no trace of containers or man found. One of the war's mysteries.

The last bombs fell in the Uttoxeter area on 3rd June 1941.

MN

Remembering 1940.

The lower sections of one of the windows in the north aisle of Blithfield Church replaced following bomb damage in the Second World War.

The left panel shows the black German Cross surrounded by the Coats of Arms of the British armed services and that of the Merchant Navy.

On the right is the Coat of Arms of the Knights of the Garter with its Latin motto "honi soit qui mal y pense" (evil to him who evil thinks)

Flying Officer
EDWARD CHRISTOPHER BAGOT R.A.A.F

Edward Christopher Bagot, RAAF

Edward Bagot was not of Blithfield parish, this county or country. He was from the Australian branch of the Bagot family and lived in Adelaide, South Australia.

As was the case in the First World War, many people from Dominions and countries of the British Empire volunteered to fight for the 'home country' in the second conflict.

He is included here as his memory is preserved by way of the memorial plaque placed high on the south wall of the chancel in Blithfield Church by his parents. No doubt their reason for this was not only the family connection to Blithfield parish, but that their son was based at Hixon , in the neighbouring parish, and Edward paid regular visits to Blithfield during his service training there.

On 12th May 1943 he wrote home to his parents describing his experience when he first visited Blithfield Hall...

Tonight I am sitting in a hotel in Stafford. Today has been the most astounding day I've ever experienced. Lord Bagot [1] wrote asking me to go and see him when I got leave, so yesterday I rang him and consequently have spent today at Blithfield...Blithfield could come straight out of a book about someone going to a haunted castle that has been asleep for seventy years- as it has been...An old servant came and took me in, up the now used back stairs to the one sitting room used by Lord Bagot. He lives in three rooms out of eighty-two and is a lonely, but charming, old man...He took me all over the house, which must be one of the most complete museums in existence...The whole country reeks of mystery, there are no large towns or bus routes within a 10-mile radius of Blithfield, hence the place is still primitive. From time immemorial the Bagots have been there and the dark Needwood Forest with

1 Gerald, 5th Lord Bagot.

it's glorious oaks and strange goats have cast this air of mystery '.

Hixon was home to 30 Operational Training Unit, Bomber Command, during the Second World War.
Hixon OTU was formed on the newly built airfield at Hixon on 28th June 1942 and along with OTU Lichfield was the only other to be formed in the county.
Accommodation at the airfield was provided for nearly 2,400 officers and 445 WAAF's and the main aircraft type based there were at least 30 Vickers Wellington bombers. These aircraft were used to train pilots and navigators for night-bomber crews and the nearby Bagot's Park was used as a practice bombing range.

The main thrust of the training regime involved two flying exercises.
Firstly, the so called 'Bullseye' training exercises gave trainee pilots and navigators experience of long distance formation flying over relatively safe territory. These exercises were usually carried out over the Irish Sea.
Secondly, once the necessary experience had been achieved, aircrews were then sent on leaflet dropping raids over France.
Aircrews were also instructed in bomb aiming techniques and air to air firing training in order to prepare them for front line bombing operations over enemy territory.

As the air bombing campaign intensified, OTU's from all over the country were expected to make up the aircraft numbers for the ever increasing large scale bombing operations over Germany.
Hixon OTU's first outing on a large scale operation came on 13/14th September 1942 over Bremen. Hixon despatched four Wellington bombers on the raid which consisted of a total of 446 aircraft. All four of Hixon's aircraft returned safely, although two found the need to land at other airfields due to technical difficulties.

Two nights later, Hixon sent another four aircraft when Essen was attacked by Bomber Command and again all the Wellingtons returned safely. In these raids, the Hixon aircraft were lucky. In the first raid a total of 21 aircraft were lost and in the second 39 did not return, OTU aircraft being the main casualties. It is not known if Edward Bagot was involved in any of these operations.
Hixon OTU was the training establishment for aircrew from the Royal Australian Air Force and the Royal Canadian Air Force, who both provided vital additional personnel for the Allies air war.

Being training establishments, these units suffered high losses throughout the war and Hixon was no exception. It was said by airmen who had been posted to OTU's after a tour of bombing operations, that their lives were in less danger 10,000 feet over Germany.

Thirteen Wellington bombers at Hixon, Bomber Command OTU
being re-fuelled in preparation for a mission in early 1944.

They are of the type in which F.O. Edward Bagot would have
completed his training at Hixon.

Pilot and navigator inexperience, technical difficulties, the weather- and of course, enemy action- played their part in the high losses of aircrew and aircraft.

Hixon's first fatal accident took place on 31st October 1942 after a practise bombing exercise when all the crew were lost after crashing near the airfield at Amerton. Thereafter there were another six aircraft and aircrew lost in crashes in the vicinity of Hixon airfield.

It was after its return from a Bullseye mission in the early morning of Wednesday 7th July 1943, that one of the six Wellington bombers which took part, came down on Blithfield parish. It crashed after losing control in cloud on the farmland of Newbuildings Farm, a short distance from the Gate pub. All six crew perished. Young Harold Martin was awakened by the explosion and bright flash through his bedroom window.

The following Saturday, the eight year old walked to the crash site with his aunt where there was a large crater and little evidence of any wreckage. However, the lad was soon attracted to something lying on the ground and he picked it up. It was an airman's glove. Inside it, was a hand.
Harold maintains another aircraft came down on Newbuildings land- 'the 15 acre' - but this sounds as if it was more likely to have been a crash landing in which the crew escaped serious injury.

RAAF aircrews seem to have been particularly vulnerable in these losses, that said however, without any knowledge of the proportion of their pilots in training at Hixon.

Of course, there were many other losses of aircraft from Hixon, some with their crews being lost without trace after they had crashed in the Irish Sea. During the war, Bomber Command lost a total of over 55,000 aircrew.

Edward Bagot escaped all these calamities and eventually graduated as a Flying Officer and joined the Pathfinder Force of Bomber Command [1], one of the most demanding roles in the RAF.

Flying Officer Bagot was listed as missing from Air Operations over Brunswick, Germany on 14th January 1944. He was aged 22 and an only child.

---

1 See Other Histories - The Pathfinder Force of Bomber Command. p.308

CARYL ERNEST, 6th LORD BAGOT - the last Lord at Blithfield- and NANCY, LADY BAGOT

William, the 4th Lord Bagot, was the last in the direct male line of the family, which stretched back nearly 900 years, to occupy Blithfield Hall. He died, without a son and heir, in 1932.

Tenants of William 4th Lord Bagot and others, attend his funeral at Blithfield Church in 1932. Included are John Shipley- from a farming family of some 300 years standing in the parish-, Thomas Deakin and Charlie Kent, his son-in-law, who served his country in the First World War.

Nearly 150 years of political, social and economic change, and two world wars in England saw to it that by the middle of the 20th century, many landed aristocratic families in the country were facing severe financial difficulties. So much so that during the 1930's, 40's and 50's many country houses came under the wreckers ball and it came to Australian, Nancy Spicer, to ensure the same fate did not come to Blithfield Hall.

The rapidly changing economic landscape of the country, declining land rents, family tragedy and the changing aspirations of British people all played their part in this process and the Bagot family was by no means immune from any of these consequences. A new tax regime designed to pay for the new 'Welfare State' in Britain after the Second World War was also to fall heavily on the shoulders of aristocratic families.

Caryl Ernest – 6th Lord Bagot

Heir to Blithfield, Caryl Ernest Bagot moved to Paris after leaving school where he learned to speak fluent French, subsequently moving to Calcutta to work where he met Margaret McMenemy who he married in 1911. Moving back to England, during the First World War, he joined the Irish Guards and served as a Lieutenant in the their Second Battalion. He was wounded in action in September 1917, when in charge of a patrol on a reconnoitre mission, after a platoon had been reported missing. Mr Bagot's wife died in 1937.

The following year, Mr Bagot met Nancy Spicer and they married in 1940, he 63 and she only 21 years old.

Blithfield Hall had not been home to a family since the beginning of the First World War and during the Second World War it was home to Gerald, the Fifth Lord Bagot [1], a bachelor and race horse enthusiast. He was a second cousin of William the 4th Lord. Consequently with few of the rooms occupied and with little maintenance having been undertaken, the building was in very poor condition [2].

Gerald died in 1946 aged 81, but not before agreeing to sell the Hall and most of the Blithfield estate to the South Staffordshire Water Company who wished to construct a reservoir in the nearby Blithe valley.[3] It seemed the 600 year long history of Bagot's at Blithfield was about to come to an end.

Australian, Nancy, Lady Bagot.

She married the Sixth Lord in 1940

---

1 On his accession to the barony, Gerald could not be traced. He was eventually found training race horses in Paris. Earlier he had lived in the Arizona Desert where his nearest neighbour was, he claimed, an outlaw. He had also spent time in Argentina where he trained polo ponies.

2 In 1939, Nancy Spicer and her husband to be, paid their first visit to Blithfield Hall and were greeted by Gerald who took them up to his apartment of two rooms where they noticed that he had attached pictures of race horses onto the 18th century wood block painted Chinese wallpaper with drawing pins.

3 See - Blithfield Reservoir p.218

On becoming the 6th Lord Bagot, Caryl and his wife, who were then living in London, paid a chance visit to the Hall in 1945. It had already been sold, and Lady Bagot, in similar fashion to her fellow Australian, Edward Bagot, fell under its historic spell.

Consequently, Lord and Lady Bagot asked the Bagot Trustees to re-purchase the Hall, together with 30 acres of surrounding grounds including the rectory, from the Water Company, which they did. So on the 2nd March 1946, the huge task began of bringing the Hall back from the brink of a very uncertain future, and Lord and Lady Bagot eventually made the Hall their home.

In 1956, the Hall was opened to the public and as well as the attraction of the Hall itself, Lady Bagot included a toy exhibition and display of Bagot historic costumes. Latterly, the added attraction of helicopter flights was introduced, which for a five minute ride at a guinea (21 shillings) a time, gave visitors aerial views of the Hall and surrounding area.

However, with Lord Bagot's advancing age and succession issues in mind, it was decided to auction the Hall and Estate, and in 1959 Lady Bagot purchased it from the Bagot Estate trustees for £12,000.[1]

Lord Bagot died on 5th August 1961 leaving his wife and their adopted daughter, Cara.

At it's peak the Hall was attracting 30,000 visitors per year but eventually it became clear that even this was not a long term solution to provide income for Blithfield Hall's upkeep. Consequently, in 1980 Lady Bagot made the decision to convert the Hall into four private residences[2] and also to renovate the rectory which had been ravaged by fire in 1961. By 1988 the work had been completed and the homes eventually occupied.

Just after the death of her Australian mother in 1979, Lady Bagot, while reading through family papers left to her, made a surprise discovery.

Among them was the death certificate of her maternal great great grandfather, John Ford, detailing his death at Bathurst, New South Wales in Australia, one of the oldest settled districts in that country, and it also stated he had been born in Staffordshire.

Subsequent research discovered he had been baptised at St Mary's Church in Stafford in 1790.

The surprise was compounded when it was found that his name appeared in an account written in a newspaper of a trial held at Stafford Assizes on 24th July 1817 at which he had been accused of stealing a mare.

---

1 This figure equates to around £265,000 today

2 History repeated itself when Lady Bagot sued the builder- Mr Wright- for his delay in completing the conversions. In 1398, Sir John Bagot, who built the original hall, sued his builder (Robert Stanlowe - wright) for "work so negligent that it had fallen into ruins".

Lord and Lady Bagot outside the main entrance at Blithfield Hall in August 1959.

Below, Ladies of the parish who acted as guides and helpers when the Hall was open to the public. They are pictured with Lord Bagot and his agent, Major John O'Neil, on the left. Soon after, the Hall was put up for auction. It was sold to Lady Bagot for £12,000 on 18th September 1959

Criminal penalties in that period were severe and, as a result, the prison system was overwhelmed. Prison conditions were primitive, overcrowded, punishments harsh and disease rife, particularly on board the prison hulks, decommissioned Royal Navy ships moored in various English harbours.
A man could be hung for many offences including petty theft of 5 shillings (25 pence), and in one case for impersonating a pensioner. Many a jury however acquitted offenders rather than see them hang. This was not always the case and horse and sheep stealing were notoriously and severely dealt with.

Although his accuser did not appear, John Ford pleaded not guilty and no evidence to the contrary was produced, he was sentenced to be hanged.
Subsequently, however, his sentence was commuted to transportation...*to the eastern coast of New Wales... for the whole term of his natural life.*
Ironically, many of the 'good and lawful men' involved in handing down Ford's sentence were landed aristocrats who would have been well acquainted with the Bagot's of Blithfield of the day and whose descendants were to become well acquainted with the Lord and Lady Bagot of Blithfield 200 years later.

Many of the sentences passed down in criminal trials were dubious to say the least as indicated by John Ford's case, and included people who were totally innocent of any wrong-doing. Given different situations and opportunities, some would have easily bettered themselves and become upstanding citizens and John Ford proved to be one of these.

On 13th November 1817, prior to his transportation, John Ford was detained in the prison hulk 'Retribution' which was moored at Woolwich. He was aged 27. He was subsequently taken aboard the convict ship Neptune which, along with 169 other men, set sail for Australia on 20th December 1817. In this, the convict passengers were fortunate in that the ships crew included Surgeon Superintendent Thomas Reid who was a prison reformer. He saw to it that his charges were well looked after during the four and a half month voyage.[1] The Neptune dropped anchor at Port Jackson, New South Wales on 5th May 1818.

No sooner had John Ford's feet touched Australian soil, he took advantage of the clean slate he had been offered, for in 1819 he was an overseer for road works, and in 1821 had received a Conditional Pardon. Later in that year he became principal overseer on a farm, receiving a salary of £25 per year and then an overseer on an estate.

He subsequently progressed, and on his death through his entrepreneurial flair, he had amassed a fortune of £14,000 and an estate of 3,000 acres.

So in 1939, when the then Nancy Spicer first visited Blithfield with her

---

1 See Other Histories - The Transportation of Criminals and the Convict Ships. p.309

husband to be, she had no idea she was returning to the county of her ancestors and where she was to spend the rest of her life.

To Nancy, Lady Bagot, Blithfield Hall proved to be her life's work when she determined, with the support of her husband, to ensure it's survival during the 20th century and beyond. As well as three separately named properties, the north wing of the house still retains the name of Blithfield Hall where the Bagot name continues. Latterly, Lady Bagot took up residence in a ground floor flat where she lived until her death on 27th February 2014 aged 94. She is buried alongside her husband at St Leonard's Church, literally just over the wall from the home she fell in love with 70 years earlier.

Blithfield Hall is now, in 2018, 620 years since Sir John Bagot built it, the home of Charlie Bagot-Jewitt and his family. He is the great nephew of Caryl, 6th Lord Bagot.

Shaun Bagot is now the 10th Lord and lives in London.

BLITHFIELD HALL 2016

Converted into four private residences in 1980, one, 'Blithfield Hall', has been home to Charlie Bagot-Jewitt and his family since 2004. This view to the south-east, shows Blithfield Reservoir in the background.

For nearly 700 years, it has been home to the Bagot's of Blithfield.

BLITHFIELD RESERVOIR

As motorists drive along the B5013, Rugeley to Abbots Bromley road and their vehicles sweep down from the crest of the hill in Admaston, they are faced with the most striking geographical feature in Blithfield parish.

Blithfield Reservoir is the largest area of water in Staffordshire and covers 790 acres at top water level. It is 2.4 miles long, has an average width of 0.5 of a mile, the maximum depth is 48 feet and the average depth is 18 feet. It has a capacity of 4 billion gallons and the gross yield of water is 16 million gallons per day.

Some years prior to the beginning of the Second World War, the South Staffordshire Waterworks Company began to realise that the existing water supply was not going to be sufficient to serve the increasing demand from both domestic and industrial users.

In 1939, the company obtained an Act of Parliament for the River Blithe Scheme which sought to impede the flow of the River Blithe and to construct Blithfield Reservoir as well as the ancillary work required, which included the necessary road diversions. The outbreak of war that year delayed the work although the two 33 inch mains which were to take water from the new reservoir to the Seedy Mill pumping station near Lichfield, had been laid in 1938.

Before construction of the reservoir began, it was necessary to purchase the land required which amounted to some 2,350 acres. 1,585 acres of this was bought from Gerald, 5th Lord Bagot which also included Blithfield Hall the ancestral seat of the Bagot Family. [1]

In order to control farming operations, which ran the risk of pollution, farms on the perimeter of the new reservoir, amounting to some 1,100 acres, were also purchased.

The catchment area for the reservoir is 27,000 acres and extends northwards for 17 miles upstream. Consequently, an agreement was sought from the authorities of the industrialised and heavily populated areas north of Creswell in order to divert sewage from the Blithe valley and into the River Tean. Of the 16 million gallon yield per day estimated to be produced by the reservoir, 5 million gallons was required to be discharged into the River Blithe below the reservoir embankment (dam) as river compensation water.

Work began on the dam in autumn 1947, by sinking a cut off trench some 3,250 feet long across the wide flat valley and at an average depth of 80 feet below ground level so as to reach the impermeable marl. Prior to excavating the trench, interlocking steel piling was driven down into the

---

1 See - Caryl Ernest 6th Lord Bagot and Nancy, Lady Bagot. p.211

BLITHFIELD RESERVOIR

SITE PLAN

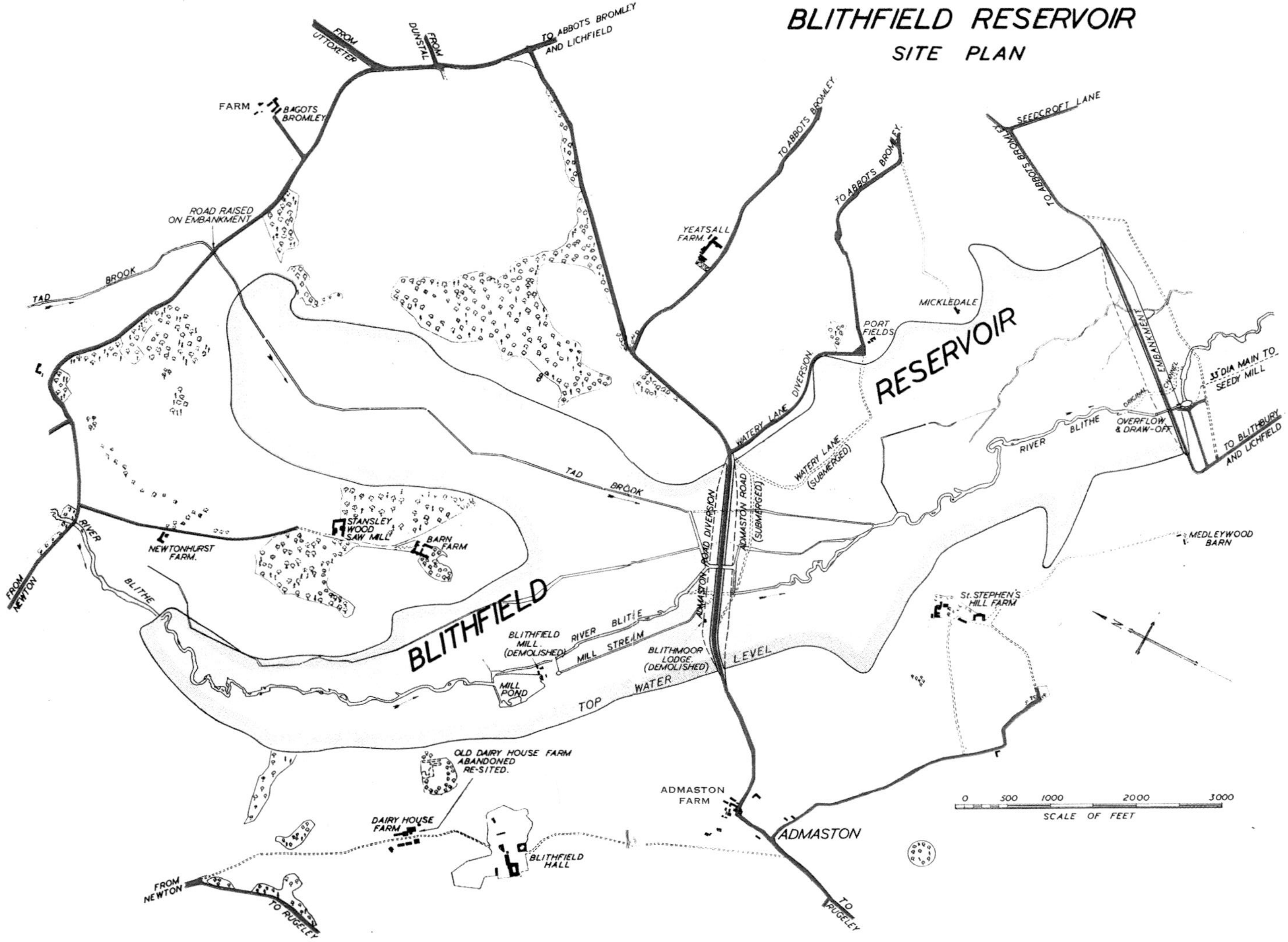

FROM UTTOXETER
FROM DUNSTAL
TO ABBOTS BROMLEY AND LICHFIELD
FARM
BAGOTS BROMLEY
TO ABBOTS BROMLEY
TO ABBOTS BROMLEY
SEEDCROFT LANE
TO ABBOTS BROMLEY
ROAD RAISED ON EMBANKMENT
TAD BROOK
YEATSALL FARM.
MICKLEDALE
PORT FIELDS
RESERVOIR
EMBANKMENT
33" DIA MAIN TO SEEDY MILL
TO BLITHBURY AND LICHFIELD
OVERFLOW & DRAW-OFF
RIVER BLITHE
WATERY LANE DIVERSION
WATERY LANE (SUBMERGED)
ADMASTON ROAD (SUBMERGED)
ADMASTON ROAD DIVERSION
TAD BROOK
MEDLEYWOOD BARN
STANSLEY WOOD SAW MILL
BARN FARM
NEWTONHURST FARM.
RIVER
FROM NEWTON
BLITHE
BLITHFIELD
BLITHFIELD MILL. (DEMOLISHED)
RIVER BLITHE
MILL STREAM
BLITHMOOR LODGE. (DEMOLISHED)
MILL POND
TOP WATER LEVEL
St. STEPHEN'S HILL FARM
OLD DAIRY HOUSE FARM ABANDONED RE-SITED.
DAIRY HOUSE FARM
BLITHFIELD HALL
ADMASTON FARM
ADMASTON
0 500 1000 2000 3000
SCALE OF FEET
FROM NEWTON
TO RUGELEY
TO RUGELEY

The Kitty Fisher Bridge, Stansley Wood , supposedly named after a girl who jumped from it and drowned.

Blithmoor Lodge (above) along with Blithfield Mill were among only three buildings demolished to make way for Blithfield Reservoir.

ground until it reached the marl in order to form the sides of the trench. This provided a safe and secure environment for the trench to be excavated preventing the passage of large amounts of ground water entering it. This was a major hazard and as excavation proceeded, it was necessary to pump a maximum of 2 million gallons of water per day from various sections of the trench. Part of the trench near the river was left unopened until it was possible to divert the river over a completed section of the trench.

The trench was then filled with concrete up to ground level in order to prevent passage of water under the embankment. This concrete barrier varied in width from 6 feet to 10 feet and in depth from 46 feet to 108 feet. Above this, a puddled clay core wall was built up to form a water- tight barrier along the centre of the embankment and terminated about 5 feet above top water level. At ground level the core wall is 16 feet wide at the base tapering to 6 feet. The outer slopes of the embankment consist of some 546,000 cubic yards of sand and gravel. The upstream face was clad with concrete panels 14 feet square and 12 inches thick which were cast on site. A wave break was installed along the top of this protective sheeting. The downstream slopes were soiled and grass seeded.

Concreting operations being carried out between the interlocking steel piling of the cut-off trench which forms the lower part of the core of the dam. The workforce consisted mainly of Irish labourers and de-mobilised servicemen of the Polish Re-Settlement Corps

Another major task was to divert the existing highway from Rugeley to Abbots Bromley and construct the causeway and five-span reinforced concrete bridge to carry the new road. This was built up to a height of 35 feet and length of 900 yards with sand and gravel excavated from the site and clad in the same way as the upstream face of the reservoir embankment in order to protect it against wave action. Another road to be submerged by the reservoir, the aptly named Watery Lane, was replaced by a new concrete road along the north-eastern shore and below the new causeway.

BLITHFIELD RESERVOIR.

TYPICAL SECTION OF EMBANKMENT

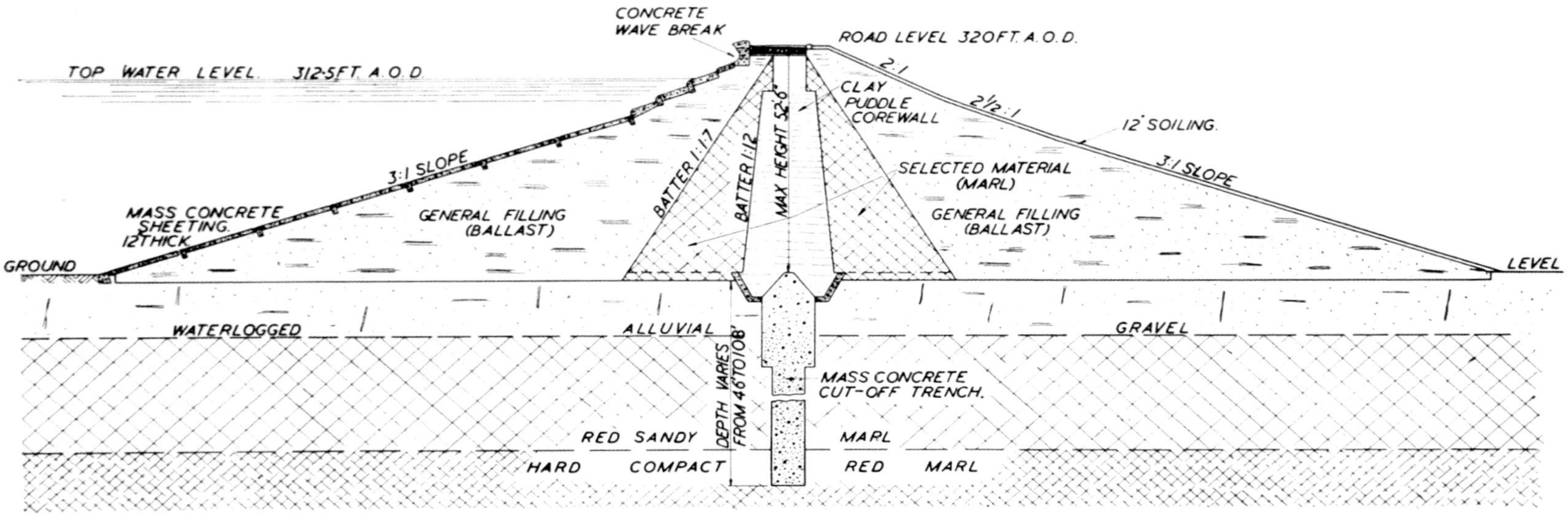

CONCRETE WAVE BREAK
ROAD LEVEL 320FT. A.O.D.
TOP WATER LEVEL 312·5FT. A.O.D.
2:1
2½:1
CLAY PUDDLE COREWALL
12" SOILING.
3:1 SLOPE
3:1 SLOPE
BATTER 1:1.7
BATTER 1:12
MAX HEIGHT 52'6"
SELECTED MATERIAL (MARL)
MASS CONCRETE SHEETING. 12"THICK
GENERAL FILLING (BALLAST)
GENERAL FILLING (BALLAST)
GROUND
LEVEL
WATERLOGGED
ALLUVIAL
GRAVEL
DEPTH VARIES FROM 46' TO 108'
MASS CONCRETE CUT-OFF TRENCH.
RED SANDY
MARL
HARD
COMPACT
RED
MARL

NOT TO SCALE.

A.O.D - Above Ordnace Datum - The height taken relative to the average sea level at Newlyn, Cornwall by land surveyors.

The bulk of the building materials, including the clay used for sealing the embankment and the sand and gravel for the concrete, was obtained from the reservoir basin, the gravel being screened and washed and crushed on site.

Before the reservoir could be filled, an area of 55 acres of woodland and scrub was cleared which involved felling approximately 11,000 trees of various sizes and removing 7 miles of hedgerow. The only buildings submerged were Blithfield Mill and the thatched Blithmoor Lodge. Being too close to the reservoir, Dairy House Farm had to be abandoned and resited nearby. It was also necessary to plough up a considerable area of pasture in order to reduce the amount of organic matter.

Most of the 20 cranes used during construction were steam driven, with nearly 100 lorries, 14 bulldozers, 14 Dragline excavators, 18 tractors and scrapers and 24 pumps of varying sizes, making up the plant used for the project. A total of 112,390 cubic yards of concrete, 27,000 tons of cement and 1,765 tons of steel were used for the Reservoir and Road Diversions.

The maximum labour force employed during construction work was 495 men and a camp capable of housing 130 men was built on site which was largely occupied by Irish labour. About one third of the total labour force

An aerial photograph, towards Admaston, showing work on the causeway. It shows the old Rugeley to Abbots Bromley road and the River Blithe, Tad Brook and Kitty Fisher Brook having been diverted into the central channel under the bridge and then back to follow their original courses.

Work progressing on the causeway and bridge

The project nears completion as the water begins to build up behind the dam was drawn from men of the Polish Re-Settlement Corps,[1] who were billeted in a camp a few miles away from the site. In addition, coaches ran daily from the Potteries, Lichfield, Rugeley and Cannock area to bring other men to the construction site.

After completion of the overflow or spillway, the discharge tunnel and the valve control house, the construction was largely finished by June 1952.

Despite a gale blowing down a marquee the night before, on 27th October 1953, the centenary year of the South Staffordshire Water Company, the Reservoir was opened by Queen Elizabeth the Queen Mother. More than 8000 people came to the event from all over the Midlands and among them were several hundred girls from the School of St Mary and St Anne in Abbots Bromley who *"enthusiastically waved their red banded straw hats in loyal enthusiasm"*.

The Queen Mother described the project as " *of being of the highest social importance"*. She added *" When considering a great undertaking such as this we may sometimes think with sadness of the green fields that are lost to us. Few, however can doubt that the benefits which will flow from the Blithfield Reservoir will justify the change in the valley through which the Blithe has for so long wound unchecked. The water that will now be husbanded will minister the needs of nearly one million people spread not only over south and mid Staffordshire but as far away as Derbyshire, Worcestershire and Warwickshire". A 100 years ago the only water available in the districts to which the new supply will be available came from stagnant canals and even from coal pits.* [2] *When we recall the harshness of life in those days we may, I think rejoice that blessings will flow in abundance and purity from these great waters...I have much pleasure in declaring Blithfield Reservoir open.*

After the ceremony she was entertained to lunch at Blithfield Hall by Lord and Lady Bagot along with dignitaries from the water company and county.

In 1962, a severe storm saw huge waves on the reservoir which not only blew over the causeway but also over the dam which had no top wall along its length which would have prevented the water from soaking the far grass bank. Soon becoming waterlogged, the ground began to slip downwards

---

1 The Polish Re-Settlement Corps was formed in 1946 after Polish servicemen, who had served with the Allies against Nazi Germany during the Second World War, were demobilised from active service from the British armed services. The Communist occupation of Poland and the Allies subsequent recognition of the newly installed Communist government there meant that the Polish government in exile ceased to be recognised. Consequently many Polish personnel in Britain were reluctant to return home to a communist regime. They were given a choice in which they could emigrate to Commonwealth, or other countries, return home to Poland or settle in Britain, which many chose to do despite a campaign by trade unions to turn public opinion against them. The trade unions saw the foreign workers as being a threat to 'British' jobs.

2 See Other Histories - Clean Water Please p.311

Queen Elizabeth, the Queen Mother taking her leave of Lord and Lady Bagot after they had entertained her to lunch at Blithfield Hall.

Water being blown over the dam during the storm in February 1962

forming large cracks. The storm also managed to dislodge some of the heavy concrete flagstones which face the water side of the dam. Sandbags had to be hastily placed to block these holes in order to prevent serious damage to the dam wall.

After the storm, a wall was built along the top of the dam so as to deflect water back into the reservoir in the event of another storm and the concrete facing to the water side of the dam were replaced.

The severe droughts of 1976 and 1995 alerted the water company that measures were necessary in order to maintain the water levels in the reservoir. Consequently, in the late 1990's, a pipeline was laid to the reservoir from where the River Blithe enters the River Trent at Nethertown. The fact that there is ample water here to avoid affecting the compensation flow of the River Blithe, enables water to be pumped back into the reservoir where it enters at the south eastern edge of the causeway, and at times of low water levels this can be seen in operation.

As well as the River Blithe, the Tad Brook and Kitty Fisher Brook flow into the reservoir, the latter aledgedly acquiring its name from a girl of that name who jumped from the bridge which crossed it, and drowned. In previous drought conditions it was possible to see the remains of this, as well as those of Blithfield Mill.

Since it opened in 1953, the reservoir has become an important amenity to those who enjoy the outdoor pursuits of angling, sailing and birdwatching and recently a series of Blithfield Reservoir Walks have been opened up by South Staffs Water. These facilities draw people from far and wide in order the enjoy the countryside in Blithfield and to wile away their leisure time.

The River Blithe flowing south into Blithfield Reservoir.
The smaller Kitty Fisher Brook can be seen to the left .

Blithfield Reservoir in 1994. Hot air balloon flights were popular in the late 1990's and early 2000's particularly with those who received them as gifts for special occasions.

The reservoir is one of the most important bird habitats in Staffordshire where many migrating wild fowl overwinter and many rare birds have been observed. In 2016, during their observations and studies, ornithologists managed to include Blithfield in the British Trust of Ornithologists record book when they confirmed a Goldcrest, Britain's smallest bird, to be the longest living bird of that species recorded in Britain. They attribute this to the warmer winters being experienced throughout the country.

In 1996, the water company opened an education centre which drew in school children so they could learn about the countryside. To some children, particularly those from urban areas, the visits were a revelation. One child saw a cow and wondered what it was while a small boy was terrified of walking through the woods "because of all the wild animals".

In July 2003, the 50th anniversary of the opening of Blithfield Reservoir by the Queen Mother, royalty were again made welcome at the Hall when H.R.H. The Earl of Wessex visited and planted a tree to commemorate the occasion.

The severe droughts of 1976 and 1995 revealed the remains of Blithfield Mill, with the mill pond and sluice gates (top) and the mill pond wall, and remains of tree stumps (bottom). It is unlikely these low water levels in the reservoir will be repeated for now, at times of low rainfall, water is pumped back into the reservoir from where the River Blithe enters the River Trent at Nethertown. The low water levels in 1995 depicted here, coincided with a record demand of water of 450 megalitres (125 million gallons) from the South Staffs Water supply system.

the 21st Century

A THOUSAND YEARS OF FARMING - THE MAINSTAY OF BLITHFIELD'S ECONOMY.

For nearly one thousand years, Blithfield folk have tended and tilled the pastures and fields of the parish and kept a careful eye on the weather, on which farming success depends to ensure the best crops and produce possible in order to feed their families and the wider community. This is one factor which is as true today as it was in 1086 and the farming methods carried out then changed very little for the next 800 years. Manual toil, with the assistance from oxen and horses was the norm until the 19th century when machines – steam engines, threshing machines and seed drills – began to appear on British farms, although it was a little later when farmers in Blithfield took advantage of them.

In 1086, King William went to great pains to record the taxes he could expect to receive from the farmers of the period, in what is now the parish of Blithfield, and came up with the result of 60 shillings; 20 shillings from the manor of Blithfield and another forty from the manor of Newton.
When comparing these values to other local manors,[1] it seems Blithfield's farmers could compete well, and then, as now, the fertility of the soil was crucial to a good return at harvest time. Lichfield valued at £15 and Cannock at 20 shillings clearly indicate this. Lichfield commands some of the best arable soils in Staffordshire and the Domesday Book day lists it having land for 73 ploughs (i.e. land in cultivation). Cannock on the other hand is listed having land for 15 ploughs and a high density of woodland, as it has now being on the edge of Cannock Chase with its relatively poor stony soil. Additionally Cannock is situated at a higher elevation and therefore at a slight climatic disadvantage.

Much is made in Domesday of ploughs and plough teams in all areas of England indicating that arable farming was a pre-eminent activity over that of pastoral agriculture and animal husbandry, although it cannot be the case that these activities were not in themselves unimportant. Among all agricultural produce, grain would have been the easiest to trade and store in times of surplus whereas meat, milk and vegetables, being prone to spoilage in store and transport, would have been consumed locally. By the middle of the 11th century, oats were being grown more widely in order to feed the expanding population of horses which in turn led to increased trade and larger towns.

Most of the tools used by Anglo-Saxon farmers are still recognisable today. The scythe and the sickle particularly, were strikingly similar to today's product. The primitive plough, which utilised a vertical coulter

1 See Blithfield at the time of the Domesday Book p.2

with an iron tip to cut the soil before being turned by a wooden mouldboard, are still the most recognisable and essential features on today's machines, and the harrow which then, as now is still basically a frame sporting downward facing spikes in order to till the ground. In both cases however they are now made of steel rather than wood and are very much larger.

The farming cycle has not changed to any large degree, dependent as it is on the seasons, with ploughing and sowing in January, hay-making in June and July, harvesting in August and winnowing in November and December, although the latter is achieved today in one operation with the combine harvester. Agrarian innovations, particularly since the middle of the 20th century, have introduced new strains of crops, agrochemicals, larger and more powerful machines and farming methods which enable today's farmers to depend a little less on the vagueries of the weather and seasons.

In the Middle Ages, land was tilled according to the 'strip' system of cultivation where narrow strips of land were ploughed, tilled and sown with adjacent strips being alternately left fallow. This system was in use up to the 19th century, when enclosure of land was introduced, which has resulted in the familiar patchwork fields and hedges seen today. It has been calculated that the area of land under cultivation in 1086 was broadly similar to that in the late 19th century, although its distribution is somewhat different due to increased urbanisation and successful drainage of marsh land, particularly in the Fens.

After the Norman Conquest in 1066, land throughout England was distributed among the close retainers of King William who had supported him in his conquest of the country and in most cases, the previous Anglo-Saxon landholders were dispossessed. However, this privilege had to be paid for by way of the new landholders supporting the king with knights in times of war or by in lieu cash payments. The slaves, bordars, cottars and villains described in the first chapter of this book formed the base of the hierarchical pyramid and they paid rents, in cash or food to their respective lords. This system of land ownership and social order became known as the feudal system.

In 1348, a catastrophe hit England. The bubonic plague, the Black Death or Great Pestilence as it was known at the time, is estimated to have killed nearly half the country's population, reducing it from around 4 million to around 2 million.

There is no doubt that the parish of Blithfield was affected by it, for as has been mentioned, some of the family de Blithfield were thought to have been victims. In the belfry of Blithfield Church, the board on the wall listing the rectors of the parish, the fateful date of 1349 appears against the name of Thomas de Leys.

In 1351 after the worst of the plague had passed, labour was in short supply and peasants were able to demand higher wages for their services. With reduced prices for most commodities, landowners were losing money and sought to lease out land to more enterprising peasants who in turn could then lend money on to other ambitious individuals. Their good fortune was short lived however for king and parliament later ruled that wages should return to pre- plague rates. The social upheaval which followed began the gradual decline of the feudal system in England. Prices fell dramatically. A horse which cost 40 shillings before the plague could be bought for 6s. 8d, a fat ox for 4 shillings and a cow for just one shilling and a fat sheep sixpence. However, wheat increased in price to 1 shilling a quarter [1] up from 6 pence because of a shortage of labour to grow and reap the crop. Much arable land was consequently turned to pasture and sheep. England's fame abroad for the production of excellent wool steadily increased trade so that by the early 16th century, vast fortunes were being made in the product.

In 1362, the Bagot family married itself into the story of Blithfield with Ralph Bagot's marriage to sole heiress of the Blithfield estate, Elizabeth de Blithfield. Consequently all rent from it in the parish, and beyond, helped to ensure the wealth and influence of the Bagot family into the 20th century.

Additionally, over time, land from the descendants of the original landholder of the manor of Newton, the de Weston's, who also held land in the manor of Weston-under Lizard in 1086, was sold to the Bagot family so that by the end of the 18th century the Bagot's held the majority of land in the parish.

During the Civil Wars rent from the Bagot land of Sir Hervey Bagot, by now amounting to over 2,000 acres in mid Staffordshire, was sequestrated and passed onto the parliamentary regime of Oliver Cromwell after his triumph in the war against the Royalist forces of King Charles l. After the restoration of the monarchy in 1660, normality was restored to the Bagot family when their rents were returned but they had nonetheless suffered heavy losses.

By the early to mid 19th century new innovations in agriculture, which had been taking place during the previous century, would have been beginning to influence farming in Blithfield.

Charles ' Turnip' Townsend introduced the four crop rotation system, which included turnips and clover for the first time, which improved land fertility. Robert Bakewell's innovations in selective animal breeding, which involved crossing different breeds of cattle and sheep, improved meat, milk and wool production. Along with Jethro Tull's invention of the seed drill in

1 A measure of weight – 28 pounds

1701, Andrew Miekle's threshing machine of 1786 and Patrick Bell's reaping machine of 1828, all these innovations helped the process of the agricultural revolution which overturned age old techniques and practices. Additionally, enclosure of common land, which had been used by smallholders for centuries to bolster their meagre incomes, bought about larger farm units, economies of scale, improved efficiency and higher production. Even the invention of the humble cylindrical clay drain pipe played a significant part as, during the 19th century, many millions were laid in order to drain the land more efficiently.

In 1860, William, 3rd Lord Bagot sought to improve the facilities on his Blithfield and other estates following a report produced for him by agricultural expert Andrew Thompson. It advised him of ways to do this by taking advantage of the new agricultural techniques and building innovations of the time.

In 1846, following the general decline in wheat prices over the previous fifty years due to the repeal of the corn laws, it was realised that farmers would find difficulty in providing themselves with a living in the future should the, by now, outdated agricultural practices be continued. Land enclosure in particular, which had seen rapid expansion, required a new approach to land management.

Consequently, legislators introduced a series of Land Improvement Acts which enabled estate and land owners to borrow money for agricultural improvement and pay this back over a number of years.

Thompson's report shows that Staffordshire landowners on 26 estates borrowed £176,918 between the years 1850-60 for under-draining and the improvement of farm buildings under the scheme.

The following extract is from the report to Lord Bagot from Andrew Thompson dated 30th October 1860:-

In accordance with the instructions which I had the honour to receive from you, I duly made the necessary inspections of the different farms and lands which his lordship is desirous of improving by means of a loan of £23,000 under the provisions of this Act - £12,200 at Blithfield and £10,800 at Pool Park. (Lord Bagot's estate in north Wales). *The work is proposed to be exacted throughout with the best materials and in a satisfactory manner and with this outlay his lordship will have got the buildings on his Staffordshire estate very nearly all improved and in good tenant-able repair*

The report stated that the Staffordshire estate...*comprises 10,961 acres of which – occupied farms and lands 8,115 acres, mansion, gardens, pleasure ground and home farm 707 acres, wood and plantations, nursery grounds 2,138 acres...of this extent 213 acres have been excluded as I understand...* (it has)... *been sold. The actual rental of extent let to tenants is £11,298 19s. 0d. but this amount is considerably under the revenue of the estate, the land in hand and the woods being in fair paying order...His lordship is, however, very poor and though anxious to improve his estates cannot really afford to pay much himself...*

The report estimates drainage on the Staffordshire estate to cost...*£6,000, farm roads £200 and farm buildings £6,000.*

Drainage. *It is calculated that... 3000 acres require draining. Unfortunately within a very recent period an erroneous system of drainage has been adopted viz. shallow drains taken across the natural fall of the land and although the occupiers have within the last 30 years buried a large quantity of tiles and pipes supplied by their landlord, very little benefit is now derived from the effects of such drainage and in fact...it would have been better if the work had never been done, as shallow drains out of order only serve to hold stagnant water, which sours the land.*

...It is proposed to ex spend the sum of £6000...(and)...preference will be given to the occupiers who are most eager to have their land drained and are willing to pay a fair percentage on the outlay, but I will observe that in this respect I found the tenants, who are on the whole a most respectable class of occupiers most anxious to have their land drained on the deep permanent system...the drains will be placed 4 feet deep and generally from 8 to 12 yards apart... then minor drains being laid with pipes of 2 inches in the bore...

Messrs Girdwood who are to superintend the works hope that...the cost will be £5 13s. 6d per acre.

Buildings. *Although a good deal has been done in the erection of new buildings, I found homesteads on several farms in a very dilapidated and worn out state.*

Of the £6000 allocated for farm buildings, Thompson proposes the following - *£3,675 allocated for -*

New set of buildings and dwelling house	*£2900*
2 pairs labourers cottages	*600*
5% for contingencies	*175*
	£3,675

New homestead *– Newbuildings farm, Blithfield.*

It is proposed to lay out a new farm of 355 acres in the township of Newton and parish of Blithfield and to erect on a convenient site near the centre of the farm a dwelling house and suitable buildings at the specified cost of £2900. At present the lands of which this farm is to consist are divided into two farms for which the buildings are inconveniently placed at some distance from the land in the village of Newton and are for the most part in a very dilapidated state. On one of these farms of 211 acres, the farmhouse, occupied by Mr Edward Burgess (who is to be the tenant of the new farm) is a ruinous old brick and thatched place with the bedrooms in the roof. This house is not even fit for labourers and cannot be converted into cottages.

The buildings which consist of brick and boarded walls and thatched roofs, are likewise in a ruinous state and not half sufficiently commodious for the land.
The farmhouse of the other farm proposed to be added is capable of being converted into 2 cottages, which is intended, but the buildings, excepting a small stable in fair order, are very old and inconvenient. There is therefore a good case for...the new homestead, which according to the drawings...prepared by Messrs John and James Girdwood [1] *has all the advantages of modern improvements and conveniences.*
There is one essential point however in which I think is deficient and that is the accommodation for cows. Upon a dairy farm of 300 acres it is common for 50 cows to be kept and there is only accommodation for 40.[2] *There should be additional tying for another 10 cows especially as the extent of pasture and meadow exceeds by 57 acres the quantity in tillage. Estimate for these buildings including 5% for continences is £3045 appears sufficient for the farm including accommodation for 50 cows. The company's yearly charge at the rate of £6 12s. 4d. per cent for 25 years will amount to £201 9s. 6d. or 11s. ¾d. per acre.*

Newbuildings Farm, Newton, built by William, 3rd Lord Bagot in 1862 at a cost of £2,900. It is pictured here in 2004

It was unusual for entirely new farmsteads to be included in the improvement schemes. The Staffordshire report only included the establishment of four others in the county, including Lord Bagot's new farm.

Thompson's report goes on to describe his plan for the two pairs of labourers cottages planned for the Bagot estate at a cost of £600: -

It is proposed to erect two pairs of cottages... one at Yeatshall [3] *the other erected in Blithfield township at a convenient situation for the home farm or any of the tenants. These cottages have each three bedrooms and are in other aspects conveniently arranged. In the township of Blithfield, containing 1,413 acres, there are only seven cottages occupied by farm labourers which shows that some new ones are much wanted. The sum applied for these cottages is £600 or £150 each to which is added 5% for contingencies. This addition should not be allowed as the maximum charge for each cottage should not exceed £150.*

1 Employed by Lord Bagot.
2 The same farm today has 110 milking cows.
3 Situated opposite Yeatsall Lane on the B5013 road, half a mile from the reservoir causeway.

The cottages in Blithfield were eventually built in the middle of Newton. Previously known as the Dairy Cottages, they were agricultural labourers homes attached to Dairy House Farm, the home farm to Blithfield Hall. They have recently been converted into one luxury private residence as have those at Yeatsall.

In another report to Lord Bagot dated 30th September 1861, further improvements were proposed for Oakfields Farm on the Bagot estate in Blithfield. For the sum of £115 a brew-house and offices were to be added to the farmhouse. The farm is reported as being of 245 acres and states that...*additional buildings are much wanted but have not yet been decided on. The proposed brew-house, or more properly cheese making apartment, was very necessary, the cheese hitherto been made in the kitchen where the food was cooked...*

...His lordship is most anxious to improve his estates but unfortunately he is not in a position to spare much out of his income, though he is most willing to put existing buildings which are to stand in tenant-able repair...

In March 1862 Andrew Thompson makes a report on progress of the improvements on Lord Bagot's Blithfield estate in which he refers to an inspection when he...*examined the new homestead which is in progress in Newton. I found the buildings partly roofed in and the farmhouse commenced.* He comments on the *...bricks which are being made on the spot and the doubtful quality of some being too soft.* He is assured however that *...Mr James Girdwood would carefully select bricks and discard those unsuitable...*otherwise Thompson is satisfied that...*the materials are of good quality and the work is well executed.*

In November 1862 he reports on additions being made to Newton Farm, occupied by Mr Shipley, where new buildings were to be erected.

He reports that... *This farm consists of 243 acres of which only 48 are in tillage, the remainder being all in pasture. The farm house is a good sized house in excellent order and so are all the other buildings...these buildings were erected 20 years since...the only old building is the barn which being in a very dilapidated state is proposed to be pulled down...The new buildings to be a barn, a root house with hay loft over...*

Another report for Lord Bagot in 1864 proposes further additions to Oakfield Farm, occupied by Mrs Holland: -... *a dairy, a cow house for ten cows, calf house and piggeries... at a cost of £300. There are 30 milch cows kept. The company's yearly charge on the outlay of £300 would be £21 5s. 3d. or 1s 7d. per acre and I have no doubt that the farm for letting will be increased in value...in consequence of the outlay.*

Andrew Thompson's report also mentions additions and improvements to Admaston Farm in Blithfield parish, which he reports is in good repair. Other farms improved on Lord Bagot's Blithfield estate were at Dunstall,

Heatley, Bagot's Bromley, Blithbury and Forge Farm in Abbots Bromley.

By 1866, of the 22 farms on Lord Bagot's Blithfield estate described in Andrew Thompson's report as having defective farm buildings, half had been subject to varying degrees of improvement. These had replaced old, ruinous, worn out or sometimes collapsed buildings which Thompson described as *some of the worst I have seen...* and was surprised...*that the occupiers should have been able to carry on so long with them.*
He concludes:-...*His lordship is anxious to finish the work but has not decided whether to take out a further loan or do it by other means...*

At the start of the 20th century, fissures began to appear in the centuries old traditions of land ownership in the parish. After the First World War, social attitudes in Britain had changed and together with tragedy and domestic difficulties within the Bagot family, the ever increasing tax burden placed upon the land owning aristocracy and other wealthy individuals, matters came to a head in 1933. It had been 100 years since William, 2nd Lord Bagot took out his £100,000 loan and it is assumed this had not been completely paid off, so along with the other inescapable realities the following result was inevitable.

William, 4th Lord Bagot had died in 1932 and in September the following year an advertisement appeared in a national newspaper which announced:-

By Direction of the Trustees of the Rt. Hon. Lord Bagot.

INVESTORS, FARMERS & SPECULATORS, be on your mettle!
THE BLITHFIELD, FIELD AND LEIGH ESTATES,
lying between UTTOXETER and RUGELEY
THE WHOLE LET TO SOUND TENANTRY. 6,982 ACRES. INCOME £9645.
SOME OF THE BEST MIXED FARMS IN THE MIDLANDS,
NUMEROUS SMALL HOLDINGS, ACCOMODATION LANDS AND
PORTIONS OF 8 VILLAGES...

The greater part of the Bagot estate had been offered for sale. It was the end of an era and gave tenants the opportunity to buy the farms and homes which in some cases had been rented by members of their families for generations.
The sale would be offering *freehold, residential, agricultural and sporting estates* which comprised *37 first class dairy and mixed farms, 17 smallholdings and accommodation lands and 52 cottages.* The estate included *portions of the villages of Newton and Dapple Heath* in Blithfield parish, and neighbouring *Heatley Green, Abbots Bromley and Colton,* and

those of *Field, Middleton Green and Leigh* near to Uttoxeter.

Additionally, the remaining portions of the Bagot estate in North Wales, Pool Park, - *'twixt Ruthin and Denbigh,* - was offered for sale, amounting to *802 acres* and also included *farms, small holdings, cottages, and The Crown Inn, Llanfihangel...* This sale was conducted from the Castle Hotel, Ruthin on the 26th September 1933, the main part of the estate having been sold in 1928.

On Thursday, 21st September, 1933 at 11 o'clock prompt in the Town Hall at Rugeley, the auctioneers hammer finally came down on what was probably the largest sale Staffordshire had seen, certainly in that year. The proceeds of both sales amounting to £157,278 which today would equate to nearly £10.5 million. A payment of nearly 24% of this amount went toward paying the death duties of William, 4th Lord Bagot.

This, however was only the first major sale which was to affect the loss of the Bagot family's estate, including Blithfield Hall, their home for over 600 years.

A few years later in 1939, the fate of the Bagot estate was all but sealed when The South Staffordshire Waterworks Company submitted plans for the construction of a new reservoir in the Blithe valley. They required 270 acres from the Trustees of the Bagot Estate out of its total remaining acreage of 4,029. Although some of the farms surrounding the new reservoir would not be totally affected by the plan, a 1938 report sent to Gerald, 5th Lord Bagot, and his heir Mr Caryl Bagot, advised that these should also be sold to the company as the rental income from them would be greatly reduced. It also recommended the...'*Mansion', in view of its material detriment... and the extreme improbability...ever being required as a residence...* be sold. In total, the report stated, this would add up to 1,612 acres which it concluded should be sold to the Waterworks Company. Additionally, it was recommended that Bagot's Park and Bagot's Wood amounting to some 1,762 acres should be eventually sold as it would prove to be *'a heavy burden to the estate'* as nearly 20 miles of fencing needed to be maintained. This would leave only 655 acres of tenanted land which the report suggested should also be eventually sold.

The report valued the land due to the water company at £30,800 (£1.93m) or £19 per acre (£1191) and the remaining farms and adjoining land at £20,000. (£1.25m)[1]

The report suggested that should its recommendations be accepted and the sale price of £50,800 (£3.2m) achieved, on investment at 3%, £1,778 (£73,900) per year would be produced and after tax at a rate of 5 shillings (0.25p) in the £, an income of £1,333 (£83,600) would be provided. This would be an increase of £603 (£37,800) on the figure currently earned, the

1 The figures in brackets represent those adjusted to 2017 values.

report stated.
With this in mind, Lord Bagot's keenness to sell and a wish to avoid a compulsory purchase by the water company, Lord Bagot and his Trustees agreed to an offer of £70,000 (£4.4m) by South Staffordshire Waterworks, which included Blithfield Hall and its grounds, the report citing that... *the opportunity of improving materially the financial position of the Settled Estate should not be lost.*

An indication as to the prevailing values and costs in 1938, can be gleaned from the following statement of estimated annual income and expenditure expected for the Blithfield Settled Estates for the year 1939, as appended to the report sent to Lord Bagot: -

INCOME				
Rents as from Lady day next	2370	(148,599)		
Rents from Sporting	163	(10,220)		
Ley Stock in Bagot's Park	37	(2,319)		
EXPENDITURE				
Income Tax			405	(25393)
Land Tax			81	(5078)
Tithe			170	(10659)
Rates			130	(8151)
Fire Insurance			68	(4263)
Estate Wages			490	(30713)
Garden Wages			204	(12790)
Materials for Repairs			135	(8464)
Workmen's Insurance			7	(438)
Agent's Salary			150	(9405)
Sundries			20	(1254)
			1860	(116,608)
ESTIMATED SURPLUS			730	(44530)
	2590	(161138)	2590	(161138)

The sale of Blithfield Hall to the water company involved Lord Bagot needing to sell its contents. That day came on Monday, 24th September 1945, and over three days the vast majority of -*THE REMAINING VALUABLE Contents of this Residence*- were sold.

Included were items of Chippendale furniture, Persian, Wilton and Axminster carpets, 17th and 18th century silver, Old English and Oriental china, paintings by, or attributed to Reynolds, Kneller, Hoppner, and J.M Wright, together with a library of some 3000 volumes.

Although the Hall was sold, as we have read, Caryl 6th Lord Bagot and his wife Nancy, Lady Bagot purchased the Hall and thirty acres of the surrounding ground back from the water company. Thereafter, Lady Bagot was keen to reunite some of the Hall contents, particularly the paintings of Bagot ancestors, to, as she saw it, their rightful home. By advising auction houses of her intention, she was able to achieve prior notice of any sale which contained these items and was successful on a number of occasions in her goal. They remain in the Hall at this present time.

Even after this second trauma, a portion of the estate remained, and the coup de gras was delivered on Wednesday, 19th September, 1962 when that part which had been owned by the Bagot family for nearly 1000 years was offered for sale -

By Direction of the Special Personal Representatives of the Late Sixth Lord Bagot...The Remaining Portion of the Blithfield Estate, Abbots Bromley, Staffordshire..., was offered for sale.

As well as three farms, two smallholdings and three cottages, the main portion of this sale included Bagot's Park and Bagot's Wood which in all totalled 2,369 acres, with a gross rental value of £2,053.

Of the trees in Bagot's Park at the time of the sale, it was stated that only the trunk of the Beggar's Oak remained and that the... *Squitch Oak, reputed to be over a thousand years old has a girth in excess of 40 feet and is still an example of the trees which were so well known in the Midlands. Another famous tree which is still standing, is the "Walking Stick," a tree with 75 feet of clean vertical trunk...*

Most of the trees in Bagot's Park had been cleared away in 1933 following the death of William, 4th Lord Bagot.

The sale catalogue states that... *The area of land in Bagot's Park is worthy of note. At present it is rough parkland let at a low rent to agricultural tenants, but the land is capable of great improvement in condition and consequently in rent. It is comparatively rare for such a large block of land to come on the market in Staffordshire, so the parkland could well prove to be an extremely valuable long term investment.*

And so it was. A Staffordshire farming company took advantage of the possibilities and after all the standing trees, including the remains of the Beggar's Oak, were cleared, it set to and ploughed up the land and proceeded in the profitable cultivation of cereal crops. This was assisted with the lucrative addition of a government policy which provided subsidies for most agricultural produce.

Its glory days over, the Beggars Oak in Bagot's Park pictured in 1959, a few years before the park was sold, finally cleared of all trees and ploughed up.

At the time of the sale, Bagot's Wood, the large wooded area adjacent to Bagot's Park, was subject to a lease with the Forestry Commission which was carried over when the farming company also purchased this property.

Needless to say, all the farms which William 3rd Lord Bagot had improved nearly 100 years before were sold, in some cases to existing tenants. Oakfields Farm was sold to sitting tenant Mr George Hampson in the final sale. In the first sale Manor Farm and Newton Farm, in Newton were also sold, respectively to the tenants, Mr John Shipley and his cousin, also John Shipley, a family who can trace their ancestry back in the parish some 300 years. At the present time, descendants of all these families continue to occupy and farm these holdings. Some of old families have moved away from the farming life, through bereavement or circumstance, but continue to take an active part in parish proceedings.

One activity which seems to have endured for at least 1000 years is that of farm contracting where farmers, and as is the case today, specialised businesses, hire out access assets to others so that they can minimise costs. In the Domesday Book, entries show that plough lands sometimes do not equal the number of plough teams. The entry for Blithfield shows this to be equal – two plough teams and two plough lands. Scholars believe that in cases of excesses of plough teams, these would be contracted out to other manors who had a deficiency.

In the 20th century, one family who took advantage of this activity early on, particularly during the 1930's and 1940's, was that of the Coopers who farmed at Drointon in the neighbouring parish of Stowe-by-Chartley. Farmers in the locality, including those in Blithfield, were able to avail themselves of new, and then revolutionary machines in order to complete their harvesting tasks without their need to invest in specialist machinery. Arthur Henry Cooper had farmed in Blithfield for some 30 years, renting from the Bagot family, where, at Newbuildings Farm in 1927, he hosted the Uttoxeter Ploughing Match at which local farmers pit their ploughing and hedge laying skills against one another. He moved to his new farm in 1933 after the first Bagot Estate sale. In 1941, Mr John Shipley hosted the event at Manor Farm, Newton. The ploughing match was held again at Newbuildings Farm in 1955 and also in 1980 when the Woodward family farmed there. The following year, it was held on Mr George Hampson's Oakfields Farm, Admaston.

'Bluebird', the last working shire horse in Blithfield parish.

Two parish children take advantage of his gentle nature under the watchful eye of the farmers son at Newbuildings Farm in 1959

In 1945, three sons of Mr Cooper formed a new business at Drointon next to the home farm and invented an automatic draw-bar for tractors, which is still an indispensable item fitted on the vast majority of tractors manufactured today.

Eric Leslie Cooper was born in Blithfield, as was his wife, and they spent all their married life living here. During the latter half of the 20th century, they started and built up a successful farm machinery sales business at Drointon.

This was a time of plenty for the British farmer. The depression in agriculture which had lasted 70 years had come to an end but not necessarily because of favourable market conditions or abundant harvests.

After the end of the Second World War, communist Russia and the capitalist countries of the United States and Western Europe were increasingly at loggerheads,

Above: Harvesting under way on Mr John Shipley's Manor Farm, Newton in 1925. Mr Shipley is loading stooks of corn which will be threshed of their grain later in the year. Combine harvesters had not yet made an appearance on the farms of Blithfield.
Below: In 1934, this was the scene in the neighbouring parish at Drointon where a steam engine drives a stationary baler, baling hay for the Cooper family. This machinery was contracted out to farmers in Blithfield. The small boy watching the work is Eric Cooper.

and the threat of a nuclear war was real as tensions waxed and waned during ' The Cold War ' period.
With the deprivations of the Second World War still a potent memory, policy makers throughout Europe wished to ensure ample supplies of food would be available in the event of another world conflict.
Consequently, farmers throughout Europe were subsidised to produce food, which was placed in vast storage facilities as an insurance measure in case of war. These were to be soon dubbed as being 'butter mountains and wine lakes' by sceptics and those who opposed the policy.
Ancillary businesses to that of farming were able to capitalise on this policy and Eric Cooper's company was no exception. However, competition among manufacturers of farm equipment was keen and they were all anxious to ensure a share of farmers' cash. Eric Cooper's business held franchises of large multi-national tractor and machinery manufacturers, including that of local excavator maker, J.C.B. of Rocester near Uttoxeter.
In order to maximise sales of their products, from time to time manufacturers introduced sales incentives to their dealers and if a particular sales target was reached, sales staff would benefit by way of various prizes.
One prize Eric Cooper's business was able to take advantage of was a trip to New York on the British cruise liner Queen Elizabeth II. After a few days stay in that city, passengers would fly back to England on a 'Jumbo' jet aircraft at a stately speed of around 500 m.p.h. However, at this time it was possible to make the journey a good deal faster, and in style. Instead of the return trip taking around six hours, it could take only three for the journey from New York to London. Being aware of this and being outside the remit of the prize, it was arranged that on paying the difference in cost, Eric and his wife Lucy, would return on the supersonic airliner Concorde.[1] On the occasion of Lucy Cooper's funeral in Blithfield Church on 6th June 2012, the rector was prompted to say during her eulogy that, *'Lucy could easily claim to be the fastest woman this parish is ever likely to see for some time, as she and Eric came home on Concorde at 1400 mph!.'*
Eric Cooper died on 18th August 1992.

One of the windows damaged by the bombs dropped near Blithfield Church in 1940 was that in the east wall of the north aisle. The new window to replace it was installed in the year 2000 by Edith Lucy Cooper in memory of her husband.

With the collapse of Communism in the U.S.S.R and Eastern Europe in

1 To date, the only supersonic airliner to have seen passenger service. The product of an Anglo-French collaboration, it flew successfully and latterly, profitably, for 40 years. The British Airways London to New York service was very successful and popular with business people and celebrities. Concorde was withdrawn from service in 2002.

Rejoice in the
Lord Always

The window in Blithfield Church installed
in the year 2000 in memory of Eric Cooper

1989, agricultural policy changed again to reflect the needs of the market. Although agricultural subsidies were not withdrawn, they were angled to encourage environmental issues which were becoming an increasing concern in Britain and internationally. Farmers in Blithfield and countrywide, are now conducting their businesses at the mercy of world markets and as in 1086, while not in the literal sense, endure famines and feasts when prices fluctuate as markets wax and wane. Indeed, dairy farmers would today sometimes be at odds with Mary Bagot when in the 1820's she wrote- *The farmers grow rich on their dairy farms...* - and their...*'milch cows...*[1]. A rationalisation of the dairy industry over the last twenty years has seen many dairy farms in Blithfield- and countrywide- diversify into more profitable areas of agricultural activity.
In order to save on the high cost of farm labour and gain efficiency, dairy

1 The common name of the period for dairy cows and a term used to indicate any enterprise which is deemed to be a source of easy profit.

farmers are increasingly turning to robot milking machines. Arable farmers too are needing to achieve the economies of scale by increasing their land holdings, either by purchase or rent. They are also utilising ever larger and expensive tractors and machinery in order to make best use of the labour available to them, usually that of family members.

In 1086 the priority for the peasant farmer was to pay rent to his Lord who owned the land, and of course to feed his family. Nearly 1,000 years later this has not materially changed for, although most farmers own their land, for some, the priority is to cover their bank overdrafts as they endeavour to pay the high costs involved in 21st century farming.

As the Book of Proverbs reminds us, ...*the poor man is the rich man's slave, borrow money and you are the lenders slave.* Slaves then, slaves now!

However, at the present time, high land values at upwards of £9,000 per acre and government subsidies act as sufficient security for banks to provide ample loans.

Today, if government policy is implemented -post Britain's exit from the European Union- British farmers can look forward to further encouragement as far as care for the environment and wildlife is concerned. This, however, against the backdrop of ever more mouths to feed, in Britain and the world.

To combat this conundrum, it is promised technology will come to the rescue. Driverless tractors, small flying drones to monitor and administer smaller amounts of chemicals to growing crops and the contentious issue of genetically modified crops are all vying for position in order to revolutionise the farming industry over coming years. However, the weather is one phenomenon mankind has not yet been able to control.

Blithfield's farmers will no doubt be anxious to play their part.

TWO HARVESTING SCENES SEPARATED BY NEARLY 1,000 YEARS.

Above – Anglo-Saxons at work with tools still recognisable today. The man on the left sharpens his scythe with a whetstone which he has dipped into the bucket of water at his feet. In some parts of the country this was a scene familiar into the early 20th century.

Below – Harvesting underway in Blithfield in 2014. A combine harvester discharges its bounty into a trailer being drawn alongside, while the farmers family look on.

St. LEONARD'S CHURCH
in the 19th, 20th & 21st CENTURIES

In the middle of the 19th century, St Leonard's Church was subject to more additional building and work on the fabric, the first since the clerestory was added in the 16th century. Another period which saw significant restoration to the fabric of the Church and addition of amenities to it was during the latter half of the 20th century.

During these times, work included the following:-

A mortuary chapel was built in 1829-30 by the second Lord Bagot on the north side of the chancel. It has since always been used as a vestry and is supposed to have replaced a smaller one on the same spot.

A new south porch was built to a design by the architect G.E. Street about 1860 and replaced a wooden porch which formerly stood there. This in turn replaced the entrance to the Church through a door in the west wall of the tower in 1678.

The chancel roof was restored in 1851 with oak from Bagot's Park and from a design by Augustus Welby Pugin from what was supposed to have been the original 13th century roof. This had been substituted with a flat panelled roof in the latter part of the17th century.

In the nave, the flooring was replaced in 1853 with tiles by Minton. These are considered unique because of their embossed design. They were copied from medieval tiles found in the Church which are said to have had a similar pattern. The floor was restored in 1964, with new cast iron gratings by Mr and Mrs Eric Cooper of Newton.

The fine oak roof was put up about 1853 as an exact copy of the original but with more carved bosses at the junctions of the beams. These were embellished with gilding by Nancy, Lady Bagot in 1966.

A new pulpit, designed by Pugin, was installed in 1846 replacing a 17th century oaken one which was converted into a chest and now serves as a cupboard for prayer and hymn books at the west end of the south aisle.

In the tower, two bells were a gift from the Duke of Westminster on 19th January 1878 at the coming of age of William, fourth Lord Bagot and a new bell was installed as a gift from parishioners on the occasion of Queen Victoria's Jubilee in 1887. In 1952, a report by bell founders John Taylor of Loughborough stated that the bells and their frame 'were in a poor way'. They were subsequently re-hung by the children and grandchildren of ex rector, the Rev. D.S. Murray. On the recommendation of Taylor's, a new floor was installed by Mr and Mrs A.H. Cooper on the occasion of their Golden Wedding in 1957, this in order to provide a guide for the bell ropes.

The clerestory glass in the south wall was installed in the middle of the 19th century. Victorian glass in the clerestory's north wall and south wall of the south aisle was replaced in the 1960's by Lady Bagot and is by Goddard and Gibbs of London.

As a keen organist himself, Rector, Reverend A. Stanley Towlson oversaw the installation of a new organ in 1965, which replaced an instrument of 1865 vintage. It was brought into use on Whit Sunday 1965 after a fund raising campaign to raise the £3,500 cost. (£65,000 by 2017 prices). It has proved to be well worth the expense, for annual organ concerts during the first decades of the 21st century have raised money in order to benefit the maintenance of the Grade 1 listed Church.

During the 1960's the Rev. Towlson also oversaw and organised significant stonework repairs to the Church.

The east window in the chancel was installed in 1964 by Nancy, Lady Bagot in memory of her husband Caryl Ernest, sixth Lord Bagot and is also by Goddard and Gibbs. It replaced a window of 1856 installed in memory of Richard Bagot, alternately Rector of St Leonard's Church Blithfield, Bishop of Oxford and Bishop of Bath and Wells.

Some windows in the north wall of the clerestory and in the north aisle were damaged by bombs exploding near to the Church during the Second World War. Most of these were replaced by Lady Bagot in the 1960's and are again by Goddard and Gibbs.

The window in the east wall of the north aisle was replaced by parishioner Mrs Lucy Cooper in the year 2000, and is in memory of her husband Eric.

In 2002 the old Victorian heating system was replaced and in 2016 the churchyard boundary wall was re-built and renovated by courtesy and generosity of a parishioner.

In 2018, a son of Mr and Mrs Cooper, Neville, introduced twenty-first century technology into the bell-chamber of the Church. Both a parishioner and bell-ringer, he has installed a digitally controlled carillon[1] which enables the bells to be rung remotely and in any sequence at the touch of a computer button.

It is notable, certainly in the case of St. Leonard's Church, that the welfare of the fabric of the building seems to coincide with that of the general and relative wealth of the country. The addition of the clerestory by Sir Lewis Bagot was at a time when Henry VIII set the country on a new trajectory by rejecting Catholicism in favour of Protestantism, which has been argued was the catalyst for England to become the great world power 300 years later.

The 19th century was another period when that power peaked and wealth to the country was brought about by the Industrial Revolution. From the

1 Carillon - a set of bells sounded through a keyboard or mechanically.

1960's to the present day, it has generally been a time of economic optimism. It can be safely said that most parish churches are in better condition now, in the early part of the 21st century, than at any time since the Victorian period. This has coincided with a country that is one of the most prosperous in the world.

However, the existence of local parish churches being central to parish life is by no means secure, their role having been gradually eroded from that position over the last fifty years or so. There have, during this time, been many diversions available to most people which take up their leisure time.

Many village communities are no longer static. The old families, who saw a cohesive and largely self contained life within them, having died out and their relatives moved on.

While the rural economy in Blithfield is still dominated by farming the land, increased mechanisation has ensured that far fewer people are employed than in times past. This has been a significant factor over the last fifty years in encouraging young people of farming families to seek other, and more lucrative opportunities away from their place of birth. Farm owners, tenants and farm labourers had hitherto been the mainstay of parish life, and its church, and their sons and daughters moved in to take their places.

Only a generation ago, for the most part, the church entirely relied on contributions from these people in order to maintain it. They also gave their time and talents, and regularly worshipped there.

This was possible due to the relatively low costs incurred in such an undertaking.

Those who have been moving in from urban environments have tended to be retired people, but also include young professionals who perhaps do not feel the same sense of 'belonging' as those who have been born and brought up in their parish. This perhaps reduces the need to contribute accordingly. Full and well paid employment, together with generous retirement provision over the last two generations has seen to it that those who wish to seek a rural place to see out their remaining years have increased the cost of properties, which has also prevented young people from settling in English villages.

The increasing age of many church congregations, the lack of younger people unable or unwilling to follow on, increasing costs and bureaucracy involved in church governance, means that challenging times lie ahead.

In order to meet these costs, fund raising social events, both inside the church and elsewhere, help to offset some of these difficulties.

In 2018, as Britain embarks on another landmark period in her history with her exit from the European Union, it will be for posterity to determine whether this will encourage or deter the generosity of those who wish to

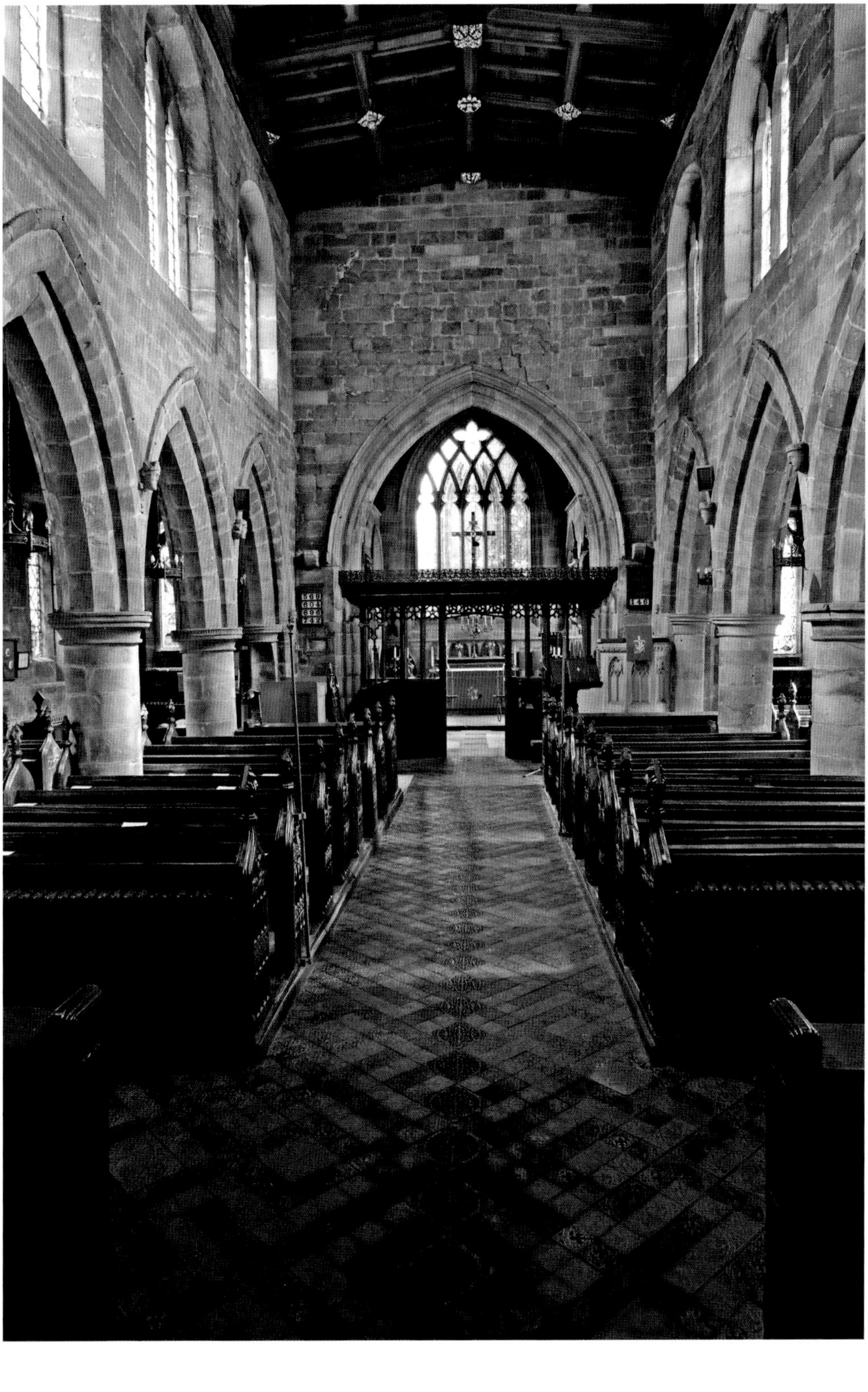

see the churches of England survive, not only as the historic buildings they are, but essentially as places of worship, which in itself is threatened by the indifference of many to the traditional practise of Christian religion in this country.

However, to re-quote two people who have been mentioned, and featured, in this book, William Cowper -*'God moves in a mysterious way, His wonders to perform'*- and the anchorite and mystic, Julian of Norwich- *'All shall be well...'*

A wedding at St. Leonard's Church, Blithfield.

2018

TALES FROM THE MEMORY BANK

As a schoolboy, Harold Martin[1] remembers an encounter with the 6th Lord Bagot around the year 1947.

By this time, the school at Admaston had closed and parish children were being educated at the Church School in Colton. On his way home from school one afternoon with his friends, they took a fancy to scrumping some of his Lordship's Siberian crab apples and young Harold, and one of his chums, Ivan Cooper duly climbed the tree. Suddenly, Lord Bagot appeared and the rest of the lads ran off, leaving the two hapless chums to face the ire of his Lordship. Looking up into the tree and pointing his stick, he called out, " I know you two; young Cooper from Dapple Heath and young Martin from the Gate Inn", and then proceeded on his way. However the lads had not escaped retribution.

The next day, at school, they were both called to face the class by the Headmaster, Mr Broughton, who demanded to know what they had been up to on their way home from school the previous afternoon.

"Nothing, Sir" came their joint and meek response, all the time knowing that punishment was about to be dispensed. It surely was, by way of two sharp strokes of the cane across their outstretched palms.

This was not the only incident in which young people of the parish had incurred the wrath of their elders.

While attending a family funeral in the north of the county, Eric Cooper met up with his cousin, Ivan, who had moved away from Blithfield many years before. He was keen to hear of the place of his childhood and asked the whereabouts of a certain resident he had cause to remember to his cost.

He went on to recall that when carol singing and visiting her farm, the singers received their hosts 'Christmas Greetings ' by way of the full contents of a chamber pot which descended on them from an upstairs window.

---

1 Harold Martin, now aged 83, has a keen memory of the past. He was born at the Gate Inn, and he now lives only a few yards away from the now private house. He has never lived in Blithfield parish but has always considered himself of it. A countryman through and through, he worked on the same farm for over 60 years, a service which was duly recognised when he received an award from the Staffordshire and Birmingham Agricultural Society in 2009. It was, he was reminded at the ceremony, a feat that was unlikely to be repeated. He continues to be occupied by keeping hens which supply free-range eggs which he sells to local people and entertaining those who care to listen to his memories of times past.

One mystery which was not satisfactorily resolved to a previous generation of parish residents, was the identity of a strange character who came to live in Blithfield for a short while in an early year of the Second World War.

Known only as 'the Count', he was thought to have been of Polish, or some other eastern European extraction. He resided at the old Dairy House farm, the Home Farm of Blithfield Hall.

The Blithfield rumour-mill convinced itself he was a fifth columnist.[1]

A more plausible explanation was that he was an aristocratic acquaintance of Lord Bagot and had perhaps fled his home in Europe after the Nazis had invaded his country.

Apparently he disappeared as quickly as he had arrived, which no doubt was the reason for parishioner's suspicions.

Some years after the end of the Second World War one regular customer of the Gate Inn was local character and farm worker Bill Green, who used to walk to the pub every evening in his hob-nailed boots. One summer night, a parishioner was busy painting his driveway gates when Mr Green went on his way. At closing time, after drinking his money's worth, he stumbled back home to see that the parishioner had finished painting the gates but had not had time to paint the gate posts. Mr Green stopped, looked at the paint work and not noticing the decorator, tottered on the spot for a moment or two and announced; ' I dunner reckon much to a mon who peents his geets but dunner peent his pocises', and then wobbled off on his way home to his long suffering wife.

On another occasion he was accosted when standing in the middle of the public road while relieving himself of some of his excess consumption. He merely looked up, moved to the side of the road and carried on.

Despite drinking large quantities of beer, chewing twist [2] and eating chocolate, Mr. Green, retired and lived into his nineties.

Harold Martin's uncle, Joe Martin, kept the blacksmith's forge at Admaston. It has long since been made into an attractive home.

As a keen young lad interested in goings-on, Harold would visit his uncle to keep an eye on how things were done.

On one occasion, farmer customer Mr Hampson was at the forge and in playful fashion, picked the lad up and placed him in the coke[3] barrel. This frightened young Harold.

It was not long though, before Mr Hampson received his comeuppance!

---

1 A spy or traitor.

2 Twisted tobacco

3 Fuel for the forge

Some time later, there was Harold in a cultivated field of Mr Hampson, while his uncle was repairing Mr Hampson's seed drill.
A component had come adrift from the large steel spoked wheel of the simple implement and it was necessary for the blacksmith to make another, which he had and was in the field to fit it.
As it was necessary to remove the wheel to be able to do so, Mr Hampson used his manpower to lift the machine while Joe fitted the part. Alas, it was slightly to big and required filing to the correct size.
While this was being done and Mr Hampson was engaged, both hands occupied ensuring the relatively light weight seed drill was kept from damage while the wheel was re-fitted, the mischievous lad saw his chance.
He filled the farmers wellington boots with soil!

Harold Martin

Harold Martin remembers his mother cycling to nearby Rugeley for provisions soon after the parish bombing incident in 1940. He was riding with her, sitting in a child seat mounted on the bike. His mother was curious of objects lying in a field next to the road and went to investigate.
She picked one up. It was one of the incendiary bombs which had, fortunately, gone off.
He also recalls being out with parishioner, Harry Lane, who during the war was in the Home Guard. Suddenly a low flying German bomber appeared with Mr. Lane shouting frustratingly, 'If I had my rifle I could bring him down! ' Apparently, the imposter flew off to cause some havoc in Rugeley.

Harry Lane was the parish lengthman[1] for many years. He lived with his three sisters, Nellie, Lizzie and Mary at Vaughans Lane Farm in Newton.

In the 1950's, the organisers of a village Christmas Whist Drive all agreed the proceeds should be divided between all the old folk of Blithfield parish

1 Length-men were employed to maintain the highway drains and keep the roadside verges mown of grass.

and publicised the fact in the local newspaper.
Some weeks later, one elderly resident of the parish mused upon the offer during a mealtime with his family and added that he had seen none of the money he had expected. Being, as he was, in his late eighties he quickly added ' I reckon they think I onner ode enough'.

Although an activity now seriously frowned upon, many years ago another pastime for some young folk of the parish was bird nesting. Even so, the youngsters knew the importance of only taking one egg from the nest.
One exception to the rule was the Moor Hen or Water Hen. These birds can lay up to twelve eggs, and they are delicious with bacon for breakfast, so any opportunity was taken to relieve nests found of only two or three eggs. Being a 'watery parish', with the River Blithe and the reservoir, there was plenty of opportunity to seek them out.
One Saturday afternoon three parish youngsters thought to scout through the shallows of the reservoir where Moor Hens nest in the reeds.
Suddenly one of the lads disappeared up to his neck in water, although the water he had been walking through was only a few inches deep. He had stepped into a sink-hole from which a tree had been removed when the reservoir was constructed.[1]
He was promptly extracted, but what to do? Certainly not to expect him to go home with his soaking wet clothes. Rather, dry them out, return home and say nothing of the incident.
The trio promptly repaired to the old Dairy House Farm which was only a short distance away and now a ruin, after being abandoned due to the construction of the reservoir.
Unfortunately, time was not on the side of the youngsters. Despite the lads' clothes not being thoroughly dry, at 8.30pm. way past tea time, they all returned home to a sound telling off by their parents to whom all the afternoons happenings had to be revealed.

It was after a funeral at Blithfield Church in the 1970's that one elderly lady's embarrassment was covered remarkably well, even though she herself became uncovered!
After the service and committal she was walking up the church path with her daughter and fellow mourners. Suddenly, an essential item of the elder lady's underwear fell to the ground. An initial look of astonishment from her daughter was immediately followed by the command, 'Step out and move on!'...

---

1 The reservoir perimeter areas are now strictly out of bounds to the general public.

REFLECTIONS

As the ink in the writers pen begins to run dry, there is time to reflect on this history.
It has travelled through nearly 1,000 years of change and shown the roles that some of the inhabitants of this small parish in the middle of England have played in our country's history.

In 1848, the Reverend Francis Edward Paget wrote of these changes after having concentrated his thoughts while alone in the church at Blithfield. With particular reference to it, and its congregations down the ages, he wrote...

"There is one venerable and dearly loved fabric which I now seldom see, but into which, whenever I am able to revisit it, I never fail to enter and linger alone amid its aisles to hold communion with the unseen world around me. ...How great have been the vicissitudes of human things since Saxon Hereman raised the first rude oratory on this site! Many indeed have been these changes, yet, whether they who assert or those who deny the spiritual supremacy of the Papacy were administering here, these old grey walls have had the same calming and soothing influence upon successive generations... And yet a briefer space than these eight hundred years will suffice to tell of the effects of chance and change...yet when I look on these grey walls I remember I am but sharing the emotions of whole races of Christian pilgrims gone before"

Now, near the end of the second decade of the 21st century, we too can reflect on these chances and changes since Francis Paget wrote those words some 170 years ago, which have brought change which he would have not have dreamt possible.

Two of the radical changes featured in this book which changed England and ultimately, the world, took place nearly three hundred years apart and both are now being mimicked simultaneously by present day events.

Historically, they involved one Blithfield resident - Richard Bagot directly. The other, Mary Bagot, was alarmed by the consequences and prospects of the changes she was witnessing as the Industrial Revolution gathered pace.

Just as Henry VIII cut England adrift from Europe 500 years ago, - the consequences of which are still being felt in the country today, - the United Kingdom is again divorcing itself from the European Union after a marriage of nearly 50 years. Voters in the Br(itish)exit referendum of 2016 cited interference from the continent by its imposition of unwanted laws and excessive immigration for their decision. Ironically it is the Irish border, between the Protestant north and the Catholic south, which at the moment is proving to be a major obstacle in the 'divorce' negotiations between the U.K. and the E.U.

Alongside this, another Industrial Revolution is not only affecting the United Kingdom but the developed world which again, as in the 19th century will introduce new technologies and innovations which threaten social upheaval into the bargain. Developments being promised such as robots, artificial intelligence, genetic modification of crops, gene therapy, driverless cars etc. and perhaps even the way the country is governed are sure to affect the lives of everyone, even those of Blithfield folk, as historical events have done in the past.

The Rev Francis Paget makes direct reference to the role of the church in his writing and also Blithfield Church, which in one form or another has been the focal point for the residents of the parish for nearly 1,000 years.
By 1086, Christianity had gained a strong foothold in England and churches were springing up in towns and villages throughout the land, where they are still a familiar feature.

In the early days of Christianity, fewer but larger Minster churches served the relatively low number of followers of the new faith and priests would travel out from these to minister to those in need.
Today, this seems to be a process which is being repeated. The decline of the role of the church in the lives of many people over the last fifty years or so, has seen church congregations decline, church incomes suffer and subsequently a reduction in the number of clergy. Today, one priest aided by junior and part time ministers may serve up to five parishes or more as is now the case for the parish of Blithfield. Emissaries sent out today by the State in order to compile a new Domesday Book would not find a resident priest in Blithfield for there has not been one for over 70 years since the

last Lord Bagot was in residence at Blithfield Hall. Congregations of the Church are now being served by clergy from the larger parishes of Abbots Bromley, Colton, Colwich and Great Haywood.
Coincidentally, over this period, Great Britain has seen a large increase in the immigration of people of other races and creeds who will no doubt add their own dimensions to the spiritual make up of this country in the future.

It will not be too long before the second Elizabethan Age comes to an end. It is one which has seen the country transformed beyond the imaginings of those born during the start of the record breaking 64 year reign of Her Majesty, Queen Elizabeth II.
King Charles III will inherit a monarchy which will be a far cry from the autocratic ideas of King Charles I which helped give rise to division in England, civil war and much heartache for Sir Hervey Bagot and his family.
Ironically, today it seems to be members of the Royal family who are trying to highlight the plight of the under privileged in their support for charitable causes of many kinds.

The coming years and decades will seek to record whether these related events will see another rise in the fortunes of Great Britain or whether the country will be obliged to defer further to the economic power and politics of others which it has done since the years when men from Blithfield fought for King and Country in two world wars.

Whatever challenges and delights lie ahead through these *'chances and changes'*, some from the parish of Blithfield will still wish *'to hold communion with the unseen world around them'* in the church here.
Many former residents of the parish, after leaving it in life for various reasons, are not averse to returning to it in death. Here they seem to be echoing the words of Francis Paget, when after leaving the parish of his childhood and making periodic return visits, he wrote:

...There I have seen kinsfolk and acquaintance committed to the dust in sure and certain hope; there, are some sleeping whom I have loved as I never can love again; there, when my own work is done, I would gladly lay my bones beside their bones, and not part in death with those from whom in life I was nor divided...

In Blithfield, over many centuries, the two water mills which ground wheat for the parish's farmers have long since disappeared, but the parish is contributing to the welfare of the country after a new windmill, or to be more accurate a wind turbine, was erected in 2014. Only a stones throw away from where Mary Queen of Scots passed by on her way to her fate at Fotheringhay in 1586, the turbine stands 75 meters high and generates 500 kilowatts of electricity, enough to power 500 homes.

A short distance away from where, in the 12th century, Hereman de la Bolde was summoned to face his water ordeal, a solar array gathers sunlight which produces electricity for the farmer who now occupies his home. Both these initiatives are contributions in the transformation of Britain's dependence on fossil fuels which have powered our economy for over 200 years.

Journeys to warmer climes, once the preserve of Mary Bagot and the Lords' Bagot of the late 18th to mid 20th century, are now possible for many who are in some cases, able to spend many months away from their homeland living in their retreat homes in Spain and France. Mary Bagot journeyed for many weeks when she travelled to Malta, while Eric and Lucy Cooper flew 3,000 miles across the Atlantic Ocean in three hours.

Time can only tell of the effects these future changes will have.
Perhaps someone a thousand years hence will write of them and of the role played in them by some people from Blithfield.

They may just start their account — Time has been kind to the parish of Blithfield...

THE VILLAGE OF NEWTON IN BLITHFIELD PARISH

THE VILLAGE OF ADMASTON IN BLITHFIELD PARISH

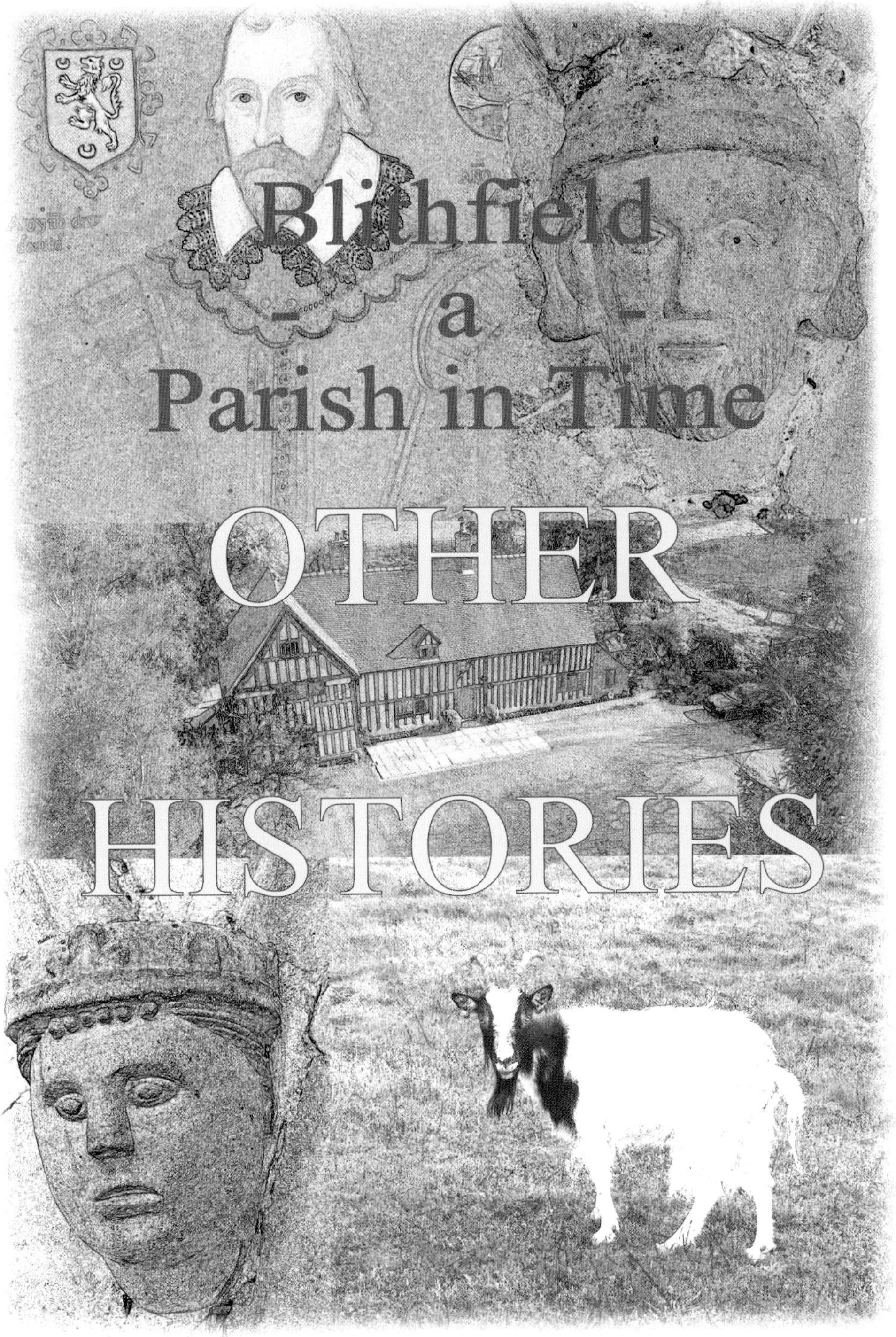
Blithfield
- a -
Parish in Time
OTHER
HISTORIES

DESERTED MEDIEVAL VILLAGES

At Booth, in the parish of Blithfield, is what is known as a D.M.V. or deserted medieval village. It is part of a listed site which includes a moat, and under a separate listing of Grade ll* is the 15th century privately owned farm house. They are scheduled as ancient monuments of national importance and are protected by law. Many restrictions govern them and any disturbance or interference is considered a criminal offence.

There are known to be around 6,000 moated sites in England which surrounded an island or islands on which dwellings or churches stood. Some of these islands are known to have been used for horticulture. Only scant evidence of most moats remain as some have been partially filled in or exist only as depressions in the ground which are seasonally filled with water. Both of these aptly describe the site at Booth.

In the majority of cases, moats were purely status symbols around high status residences and served no practical defensive purpose. Moated sites were popularly built between 1250 and 1350 and are concentrated mainly in the Midlands and eastern parts of England.

The high diversity of size and form of moated sites gives an opportunity to study the distribution of wealth and status throughout the countryside and many will preserve artefacts and organic remains which will help this task.

The site at Booth is a rare example in Staffordshire of a moated site together with that of a D.M.V. which has not been unduly disturbed by past development. It is known to contain remains of a number of house plots and property boundaries as well as shallow dry ponds, a waterlogged pond and ditches and other concealed features which could still remain under the soil. Surviving particularly well is the 25m by 15m earthwork which is thought to be that of the oratory. In 1368, Richard de la Bolde was granted a license by the Bishop of Lichfield to build an oratory [1] which was still depicted on 17th century maps along with a bridge across the moat.

The reasons these villages disappeared vary, from changes in land use; economical viability; enclosure and depopulation- the latter being a prime reason during the years of the Black Death, (1349- 1350).

Of the medieval village which existed at Blithfield, there is no trace, its site most likely having been covered by centuries of on-going building and additions to Blithfield Hall.

In medieval England the villages would consist of a small group of houses, gardens, yards, a manor house, village green and church in much the same way as they do today. They also provided some form of administrative function to the parish as well as providing for the spiritual needs of the local community.

1 A private medieval chapel

The 15th century privately owned farmhouse at Booth.
Aside from the church, it is the oldest building in Blithfield parish.
It is on the site of a Deserted Medieval Village which is, along with the house, Grade II (star) listed by Historic England.
Below is the 17th century Vaughan's Lane Farm, the only thatched house remaining in Newton. It sits alongside the lane of that name, an ancient road which led to Stafford.

Newton Farm

HENRY III 1207-1272

The bronze effigy of Henry III
in Westminster Abbey

Henry III (the fourth monarch of the Plantagenet royal house) was crowned in Gloucester on 28th October 1216 at only nine years of age. He succeeded his father King John who signed the Magna Carta in July 1215.

The 13th century was a turbulent period which saw feuds between the king and his barons, challenges to his throne and violent unrest between the English, Welsh and Scots.
Henry was not a monarch of any military prowess and won no glory on the battlefield.
He was a pious man who found art and architecture more to his liking. During his reign learning flourished, particularly at Oxford, where there was an inspirational pursuit of knowledge.

On 6th July 1245, Henry laid the foundation stone to begin the complete re-building of Westminster Abbey at his own expense. This was his most notable achievement.

It was completed in 1269 and on 13th October that year, Henry, with his brother and sons, carried the coffin of St Edward the Confessor, (Henry's personal patron saint) from the old abbey to it's new resting place behind the altar of the new abbey.
The original abbey had been built 200 years before by the Saxon king Edward, the only English monarch to be canonized.

It was probably because of his dislike of confrontation, military matters and certainly his misjudged European ambitions, that contributed to another notable event during Henry's reign.
It was his barons' grievances and his willingness to bow to their demands which led to the beginnings of the English parliament. (From the French, 'parle` - meaning to talk).
For the first time, in 1254, parliament called on two knights [1] from each of the English shires, to vote on taxation for the defence of Gascony in France, which was then under the English Crown. Previously, policy was agreed between the monarch of the day, his close retainers and powerful members

[1] William Bagot of 'Bromely Bagot' was one who represented Staffordshire in the Parliament of 1258.

of the clergy. There were also further curbs on royal power in the Provisions of Oxford in June 1258 which led to the beginnings of the House of Commons.

Henry III died, at 65 years old on 16th November 1272 after a 56 year reign-until then the longest in English history.

He was buried, fittingly, in Westminster Abbey and it was his original intention that all future monarchs be buried there. However, his heart was taken to Fontrevault Abbey in Anjou France, the ancestral home of the Plantagenets and the place where Richard the Lionheart and Henry II lie buried.

During the 13th century, 200 years after the Norman Conquest and the gradual loss of French lands by the English crown, a true English national identity was beginning to be forged. Many of the ruling class, being of Norman French descent, were feeling themselves to be more English than French. It was not long before English replaced French and became the language of the royal court and aristocracy at large. Consequently it can be concluded that from the changes brought about in the 1200's, the century Blithfield Church was built, the England we know today was in embryonic form.

ELEANOR OF PROVENCE 1223 -1291

Queen Eleanor's carving in Blithfield Church

The stone figure at the hood moulding of the pillar of the south arcade in Blithfield Church is thought to be that of Eleanor of Provence who married Henry III, at Canterbury on 14th January 1236.

She was only 12 years old to his 28 and she had never seen him or set foot on English soil until her wedding day. Six days later, she was crowned Queen at a lavish ceremony at Westminster, which provided a 1000 strong procession and a rich banquet to which almost every nobleman and priest in the land attended.

The marriage was designed to further Henry's continental ambitions which later attempted, were thawted by the barons' unwillingness to accept the huge cost they entailed.

Eleanor was very well connected. She was sister-in-law to the king of France, Louis IX and her family were from the southern Provence and Savoy regions of that country.

Stone carving of Eleanor of Provence in Westminster Abbey

Throughout their 36 year marriage they were devoted to each other and had five children. The eldest, Edward, succeeded his father as Edward I and his daughter Margaret, became queen of Scotland [1].

Both King and Queen shared a strong loyalty to their respective blood relatives, which led to the Queen appointing some of them to high positions in England. This earned her a great deal of unpopularity among the barons and English people who mistrusted foreigners.

This, of course, was not achieved without the support of the king. After all, even though she was queen, she needed the goodwill of her husband and had to be

1 Some irony here as Edward I, known as Long-shanks on account of his height, became infamous in his battles with the Scots earning him another nickname - 'hammer of the Scots'

careful not to displease him.
Henry also showered privileges, titles and land on his penniless French half brothers- again to the anger of the barons- causing him to eventually expel them at the barons' insistence.

For her part, being well educated, a leader in fashion, ambitious and strong willed, Eleanor never ceased to stand by the king in his difficulties and was fiercely ambitious for her children.
That she was trusted by the king there is no doubt for she acted as regent, with the king's brothers' counsel, when Henry was in France for 10 months in 1253/4. She shared the king's piety and was distraught when Henry died in 1272.

She became Queen Dowager and survived the king by twenty years, the last fourteen of which were spent in the nunnery at Amesbury, in Wilshire, where she died in 1291.

THE 'ARCHITECT '

The architect of St Leonard's Church? as seen in the nave

In his book, "Notes on the Early History of Blithfield," published in 1919, former rector of St Leonard's, The Revd. Murray [1] records that the stone carving pictured is thought to be that of '*a layman, the architect of the church?'* Today, we would record him as being the master mason, as architects, as we know them today, were unknown in the middle ages.

The concepts of modern construction such as structural engineering, loading calculations and architectural design were also unknown to the builders of the period.

It fell to the master mason, a highly skilled craftsmen, to oversee all the tasks used to build not only the humble parish church, but the awe inspiring cathedrals which were being built or re-built, all over the country, and Europe in the 12th,13th and 14th centuries.

He would have risen to his position by spending many years in his trade and learning from experience and from that of his mentor.

All the stone cutting, carving and laying was carried out under his supervision.

To the casual eye it can seem amazing that such buildings were completed without the aid of modern techniques and machinery.

However, all the designs and methods were based purely on the understanding of proportion, the geometry of the square, rectangle and circle and calculations that were familiar to the ancient Greeks.

Treadmill cranes, pulleys and ropes were used to lift stone into place. Wooden scaffolding, supported on beams inserted into 'put log' holes in the walls, provided platforms from which to work at higher levels. These are still visible today in some castles and cathedrals.

Soaring, elegant arches were achieved by inserting timber frames or

1 The Rev Douglas Stuart Murray was the great-grandfather of the present Duke of Atholl, Bruce Murray- 12th Duke.

centring. The walls were then built around them and the arch 'key stone' inserted at the pinnacle to lock the structure. The centring was then taken away.

Consequently, armed with only a compass, set square, measuring stick or rope and plumb line, the master mason had all he needed to complete his monumental projects.

This is not to say that mistakes were not made with these methods. In order to advance their profession, and because they lacked the mathematical skills to calculate structural loadings, it was necessary to apply the trial and error technique. This resulted in occasional disaster because, in most cases, the loads exerted on the lower structures were too great to support the towers and spires as they rose ever higher as time passed.

The Lantern at Ely Cathedral

Famously, the crossing tower of Ely cathedral collapsed in1322 destroying part of the choir. It was re-built- not to it's detriment- and replaced with the magnificent lantern tower we see today. Ely is a World Heritage Site.

One of the scissor arches at the east end of the nave at Wells

At Wells cathedral the foundations were not sufficient to support the tower at the crossing and so the solution of the medieval masons was to include the ingenious 'scissor' arches, 100 years after the Cathedral was begun in1180.

Another disaster occurred at Lincoln when the spire came down during a severe storm in 1549. Obviously this cannot be attributed entirely to the miscalculations of the architect. At the time however, Lincoln's spire was the tallest structure in the world. It was not re-built.

The keen eyed will notice a building error in Blithfield Church.

The pillar supporting the wall of the north arcade at the western end of the church is not centred.

There is speculation that this is due to this part of the church being rebuilt after some kind of structural failure of the tower in the 16th century. Architects believe the buttresses on the outside of the tower, as well as other features, date from this period. Why it was not centred is not known, but now after 500 years, the structure is still sound, as can be seen.

To the medieval peasant, these buildings, particularly the cathedrals, would have been truly awe-inspiring- they still are today. Living as they did in their flimsy timber houses and with very few- if any- stone buildings in their town, they would have seen the cathedrals as the builders intended - the representation of heaven on earth and worthy to be called the House of God.

THE ANCHORITES

An anchorite was a man, or woman, who was determined to follow the most extreme practise of religious observance. After an elaborate ceremony, which included being given the last rites, they would take up permanent residence in an anchorites cell. This was a small room built onto a church and usually on it's north wall, a position which denied the occupant the light of the sun or any warmth from it. Additionally, once the recluse was inside, the doorway was built up. However, three small openings in the wall were provided. Through one, food was passed and waste removed, another enabled communication with visitors and the third was a 'squint', included in the wall of the church in order the anchorite would be able to observe the proceedings of church services. Denying themselves all worldly comforts, its distractions and the company of others enabled a life of continual prayer and contemplation in an effort to achieve the ultimate goal of spiritual enlightenment.

The anchorites would have had private means in order to be supported in their chosen lifestyle. Consequently they were able to draw on the help of one or two servants who brought their food, removed waste and attended to visitors who came to seek the anchorite's counsel.

The anchorite tradition had its beginnings in the 11th century and reached the height of its popularity in the 13th century, the period when St Leonard's church at Blithfield was built. During the Reformation in the 16th century many anchorites were turned out of their cells, which began the decline of the practise.

Probably the most famous anchorite, or in this case anchoress, was Julian of Norwich who despite the name, was a woman, as many were. She was born in 1342 and little is known of her. Even her real name is not known or the date of her death. After a series of religious revelations, she became an anchoress at the church of St Julian in Norwich where, in 1395, she wrote The Revelations of Divine Love [1] describing her revelations. It is considered a classic of the spiritual life and the first book to be written in English by a woman.

She died c.1416 and her cell was pulled down during the reformation. The old church was all but destroyed during the Second World War, but has since been rebuilt along with a shrine to the medieval mystic.

---

1 "All shall be well, and all shall be well and all manner of thing shall be well."
"He said not 'Thou shalt not be tempested, thou shalt not be travailed, thou shalt not be dis-eased'; but he said, 'Thou shalt not be overcome".
"God made it, God loves it, God keeps it".
From- The Revelations of Divine Love by Julian of Norwich

BAGOT'S PARK and the BAGOT GOATS

Bagot's Park was part of the extensive estate of the Bagot family, and had been since at least the 12th century, well before they made their home at Blithfield. It covered nearly 1,000 acres and was famous throughout the county for its well stocked stand of oak trees. It is in the parish of Abbots Bromley, four miles from Blithfield and was part of the manor of Bagot's Bromley.

In 1813, William Pitt wrote of the Park and surrounding woodlands in his General View of the Agriculture in the County of Stafford....

...The first and best timbered estate is that of Lord Bagot in the neighbourhood of Abbots Bromley. The woods extend over many hundred acres, and almost wholly consist of oak, the ripest, finest and best that I ever saw; and I believe I run no risk of exceeding the bounds of truth, if I say, the best in the kingdom. A very large quantity of oak in these woods is now quite ripe, and some decaying. Many of the oaks carry timber to the length of 60 and 70 feet; and in Bagot's Park there are many hundreds of very extraordinary bulk, containing from 200 to 400 feet of timber in each. Much of the timber is of considerable antiquity, and mentioned by Dr. Plot as full grown timber in 1686...I was informed upon the spot, that for these woods £100,000 have been offered, and that his Lordship has half as much timber in Denbighshire, total value £150,000 which at the three per cents at the present price would purchase an income...of more than 6000 guineas per annum...

The most famous arboreal inhabitant of the park was the Beggars Oak, which in 1823 stood at over 60 feet high, while the branches spread 50 feet in every direction to cover an area of nearly 8,000 square feet.

Legend has it that it received its name when a lord of the house refused alms to a poor man sheltering under it. The beggar's curse was that the first born of the family would not thrive.

J.G. Strutt, in 1822 maintains the name derives '*...from the accommodation it is so calculated to afford in it's ample canopy 'star proof ' and in its moss grown roots, the weary mendicant who may have been tempted to seek the shade of its branches for repose or shelter'.*

Other famous trees were the Squitch Oak and Lord Bagot's Walking Stick which stood for seventy feet before its first branch. Most of these famous oaks were cleared from the park in 1933 and sold in order to settle death duties after the death of William 4th Lord Bagot, although The Beggars Oak and Lord Bagot's Walking Stick then still in full leaf, were given temporary reprieve from the woodsman's axe.

The Beggars Oak in Bagot's Park, pictured in the early 20th century- note the timber props under the boughs.

On 1st November 1933, a national newspaper reported:
The last of the Needwood Forest, beneath who's oaks John o' Gaunt hunted wolf and the wild boar, has been sold out of the Bagot estate to pay to the Crown in death duties, vaster gifts than it bestowed 800 years ago – and the noble trees are already under the axe.
The trees will soon be gone. Will the goats go? That is the question asked by the country folk of Rugeley and Abbots Bromley. The herd bestowed on the Bagot family by William the Conqueror has dwindled within memory, from 200 to 60, and the legend runs; "when the goats die out, the Bagot will be gone".

Over the centuries deer and the Bagot goats roamed the park, the latter having done so since being acquired by Sir John Bagot 600 years ago. They remained in the park until 1962 when the Seventh Lord Bagot decided to sell them, and Bagot's Park itself.
The majority were obtained by the Bagot family of Levens[1] in Cumbria, while fifteen remained at Blithfield until 1977 when they were given by Nancy, Lady Bagot to the Rare Breeds Survival Trust.

1 Descended from Sir Charles Bagot.

Bagot's Park in 1933, showing trees being cleared and the Bagot Goats.

The Beggars Oak, below left, and Lord Bagot's Walking Stick -standing 70 feet without a branch- were spared the axe until 1962. Also below, felling a tree - hard work!

In 1987, the Bagot Goats Breeders Group was formed in order to save the goats from extinction. In 2007, the goats were considered to be on the critical list for that fate but now numbers are increasing thanks to the goats being kept at many different locations, including at nearby Shugborough Park Farm and Baginton, Warwickshire at the former home of Sir William Bagot in the 14th century. With their ability to graze in rough scrubland, they are useful for conservation grazing schemes.

Bagot's Park was sold to a local farming company in 1965, the trees cleared away and the land ploughed for cereal crops. Bagot's Wood however, which surrounds the park, is still there and now is leased from the landowner by the Forestry Commission.

One of the Bagot goats at the former home of Sir William Bagot in Baginton, Warwickshire.

BAGOT'S PARK - A HIVE OF INDUSTRIAL ACTIVITY

Bagot's Park and the surrounding area became the early crucible of industries that in later times would become significant parts of the national economy.

Recent discoveries and archaeological evidence in Bagot's Park suggest that it played an important role in glass production during the medieval period and that glass was being produced there between about 1300 and 1615, with production peaking in the 15th century.

In 1349, Edward III ordered the purchase of glass from Staffordshire for St Stephens Chapel in Westminster Palace and a Staffordshire man, John Glasewryth was hired by a famous glass maker from Sussex, indicating that the county was, even then, noted for the manufacture of glass.

It is thought that, in all probability, Glasewryth came from either Rugeley, Wolseley or Abbots Bromley, then some of the most well known centres of glass production in Staffordshire. It is reasonable to assume the glass installed into the tower windows at Blithfield church was made locally, for it dates c 1325 [1]. In 1418 an order was placed with John Glasman of Rugeley for a quantity of plain glass which was to be installed in York Minster.

Glass making in Bagot's Park is documented in 1508 being carried out by Thomas Hervy during the time of Sir Lewis Bagot,

In 1588, Richard Bagot and Ambrose Henzey, a glass maker from Lorraine in France, entered into an agreement to erect a 'glasshouse' in the Park. Bagot was to pay £40 for the raw materials and provide wood from the Park and to provide convenient lodging at a reasonable rent for Henzey's workmen.

Henzey was to reimburse Bagot within one year either in cash or glass at 8 shillings per case.

The glasshouse was still existing in 1615 when Jacob Henzey was the 'chief workman'

That year a Royal Proclamation forbade the use of wood in glass furnaces. The ban imposed, in an early conservation measure,... *for increase of tymber and fyrewood in forest parkes, Chases, mannors and tenancies for future ages...*

By this time Walter Bagot had been continuing his father's business and was keen to carry on in spite of the ban, and he petitioned the King for

---

[1] This glass is now deteriorating irreversibly due to high levels of magnesium present in the glass when it was made.

permission.
He wished to be 'allowed to work the timber which had already been felled because the sale of the wood otherwise was impossible. Permission to carry on the work would enable him to support his many children'[1].
However, it was not long before glass making ceased in Bagot's Park.

After the Park was sold from the Bagot Estate in 1965, the clearance of timber and the ploughing up of the land revealed evidence of glass slag at various locations. A total of 15 sites have been identified since and it has been found that the main product was Crown window glass with at least one furnace being built in brick and stone with a clay dome and evidence of a timber and tile roof.

Locations of glass furnaces survive today by way of local place names: Glasshouse Farm (at nearby Marchington), Glass Lane at Bromley Hurst and Glasshouse Coppice.

Another product which was being produced locally was iron.
In 1588, in his role of Steward of the Queen's Estates in Staffordshire, Richard Bagot was inundated with letters from Ministers pressing him to favour Fulke Greville, the first Lord Brooke [2], who requested a grant of all the Lands, Woods and Iron Works which had lately belonged to Lord Paget of Beaudesert. The lease included all the wood and trees in Cannock Forest, as it was then known, and all those in Haywood Park. Greville eventually achieved his wish and then requested assistance with water from the River Blithe for his Iron Works at the Forge at Abbots Bromley. A channel was dug which conveyed water to the forge where Forge Farm now stands. This forge was in use at least as early as 1561 and in 1588 it produced 96 tons of pig iron.
In addition to the Abbots Bromley forge, Greville had obtained forges in the Rugeley area and, by the time his lease expired in 1623, Cannock Chase had been denuded of trees due to the many Iron Works in the Rugeley area which needed charcoal as fuel. The normal practise of coppicing had, due to lack of regulation, been neglected thereby preventing a sustainable supply of wood for the furnaces. It was around this time that coal became to be increasingly used throughout England as an alternative fuel to wood and charcoal.

Greville's lease was passed on to Thomas Chetwynd and the Bromley Forge was still in use in 1680 although by 1750 it had been abandoned. The iron produced was sold to ironmongers in Birmingham.

---

1 He had eleven children

2 Fulke Greville 1st Baron Brooke was a poet, dramatist and statesman. He became Chancellor of the Exchequer under James I in 1614 and was granted Warwick Castle in 1604. He was murdered in 1628 by a disgruntled servant.

FRIENDS AT WAR.

Colonel William Salesbury (pronounced as in Salisbury) and Sir Thomas Middleton[1] were two friends who found themselves enemies as a result of the allegiances the Civil War forced the people of England to make.
Salesbury was a staunch royalist who owned a vast estate near Ruthin, north Wales, while Middleton sided with the Parliamentarians.

They found themselves opposed to each other literally as well as ideologically when Middleton was sent to Wrexham in North Wales in order to capture the castle at Denbigh where Salesbury was Governor and defender for King Charles l.
William Salesbury's allegiance to the Royalist cause was such that he fortified and provisioned Denbigh Castle from his own purse.[2]

In 1643, an effort began to persuade Colonel Salesbury to surrender the castle to Middleton's Parliamentary forces without bloodshed. Consequently, and no doubt bearing in mind their former friendship, Middleton, and another as will be seen, found the need to write many letters [3] and to show much patience in Colonel Salesbury's determination not to do so.
His letters begin-

Letter from Sir Thomas Middleton to the Governour of Denbigh Castle. - November 14, 1643. - att Wrexham.

The former friendship, and familiarity, which hath passed betwixt us, doth not onely invite, but also engage mee to use all possible means, not only to continue, but alsoe to increase the same, which on my parte being done and offered, however things fall out hereafter, I am excusable before God and the world. It hath pleased God, by reasons of all the distractions of the times, for the present to put us in a way of opposition one to the other; the cause being

1 Sir Thomas Middleton's family were from Chirk Castle, North Wales.

2 It would appear that the royalist garrison at Lichfield commanded by Colonel Richard Bagot, was not so fortunate with its finances. It was continually in want of money and provisions. One lady who had fled Ireland with her valuables intending to travel to London, took refuge in the Lichfield garrison on her way, where Colonel Bagot relieved her of these to the value of £2,000. An application to the king for their return did not produce any result.

3 The letters are transcribed using the original text and spelling. Prior to Dr. Samuel Johnson's Dictionary of the English Language of 1755, there was no defined standard in English spelling.

well understood,... Sir, through all opposition God hath brought mee with considerable force to Wrexham; able both to defend myself, and offend my foes;... This power by God's grace I will labor to put to execution, and this is the intente of my coming into these parts. Sir, I understand that for the present you are in armes in Denbigh Castle, and Governor thereof;...and therefore I doe hereby invite you, and desire God you may embrace it, that you would...lay down your armes, and deliver up that castle to mee,...which if you shall doe, you shall not onely be protected in person and estate, by mee and my power, but alsoe you shall approve yourself, as formerly you have been, A PATRIOT, and preserver of your country, a lover of religion, and an instrument of the public good;... and so desire God to direct you, and remayne,

Your ould and true friend and kinsman

THO: MIDDLETON.

Colonel Salesbury replies -

Answer to Sir Tho: Middleton's Letter, or Summons.

In Nominie Jesu.

Sir, I desire not to live longer than I approve myself true to my King and country, a true lover of the Protestant religion, and that I yealde chearful and hearty obedience to my King and Parliament;...But to be playne; to betraye soe great a trust as the keeping of Denbigh Castle,...I will never account him my friend that should move mee to it. But I cannot say you doe so, for I shall with all pleasure and willingness, yeald it up as you desire (that is) when I am commanded by my King, and Parliament. And for the discharge of that trust...and for noe other cause, I have armed myselfe, and those armes,... I shall beare, and use for the service of my King and countrey and not to use violence and oppression; this is my answer to you...and would bee your true friend as far as truth and loyalty would give him leave.

WIILIAM SALESBURY.

Denbigh Castle, this 15th gbris 1643

In 1645 command of the Parliamentary army besieging the castle passed to Sir Thomas Mytton. This was because a recent law, passed in Parliament, forbade any M.P. from holding an army command. Sir Thomas Middleton chose to retain his position as an M.P and relinquish his army post. [1]
This did not, however, bring to an end the efforts to encourage Colonel

[1] Sir Thomas later became disillusioned with the Parliamentary cause and supported the return of Charles II. In 1659, he helped lead the failed Royalist uprising in Cheshire, when Sir Hervey Bagot was arrested and detained by the Parliamentarians and only released on a surety of £2,000.

Salesbury to give up his castle and letters sally to and fro between Salesbury and his new adversary.
It would appear that Mytton too was a friend of Salesbury's. It seems in earlier and happier times they enjoyed a game of tennis together.
The letters continue:-

General Mytton to Colonel Salesbury.

Ruthin, 7th Aprilis, 1646.

Sir, I have here inclosed a list of those that are brought prisoners hither; how many are thyne I doe not yet know; but I am heartily sorry things doe grow soe high between us, and so are your friends at London. Sir, I besseich you remember your countrey, your selfe, and your posterity, and goe no futher this way...If you please to make use of me, as an instrument to make your peace with Parliament, rest assured you shall engage the best endeavours of him, that will shew himself to be,

Your ould friend, and humble servant
THOS: MYTTON.

Credit me, the king hath noe army left him in the field, in any place of the Kingdome.

Colonel Salesbury in Answer.

Worthy Sir... I have bin, and am dayly robbed, and spoiled contrary to the law of God, and this kingdom, for noe other offence that I know, but for loyalty to our King. The Parliament (if I may soe call it) I have noe way offended, unless in being loyall to my King...and...for the keeping of this place, his Majesties own house; which (without regard of my own life, lands or postirity,) with God's assistance, I will endeavour to make good for him, to my last gaspe, soe I rest, your poore kinsman, and ould play fellow, to serve you.

WILLIAM SALESBURY.
Denbigh Castle, this 8th of April, 1646.

I take the King's own person for sufficient armey; and what armeys alsoe in England should of right be his. Upon my credit, noe more of this place but one man killed, and that (as they say) after quarter given; one others pate cutt slightly. Too much security hath lost many a fayre game at Tennis, as you know; and soe fared it with our men last day.

General Mytton replies by way of his 'Summons' in which he reminds Colonel Salesbury of *the losse of christian blood* in the war *and the worke of reformation...in great measure perfected in most parts of the kingdome...* and that...*having no hopes of reliefe....I doe... hereby sumon you, to deliver into my hands the castle of Denbigh... upon Monday next, by nine of the clocke in the morninge; assuring you that you may have better conditions both for yourselfe and the rest of the castle with you, if you refuse not my first summons...if you doe refuse it...the whoall charge of this siege may, for the saving of this poore exhausted countrey from ruyne, bee mantayned out of your, and there estates, which will certenly be prosecuted by him, who rather desires to bee unto you...your ould friend and servant,*

THOS: MYTTON

Denbigh Town, 17th Apr:1646

I expect your answere by nine of the clocke too-morrow morning.

Colonel Salesbury's Answere.
In Nomine Jesu.
18th Aprilis, 1646

I am sorry to see the ruine of my in'ocent native countrey...and sensible of the effusion of christian blood...and in answere to your summons, I will say no more, then, that with God's assistance, I doe resolve to make good this place, till I receive OUR KING'S COMAND, AND WARRANT of my discharge; to whome, under God wee are all tyed by common allegiance...
Your ould friend and servant
WILLIAM SALESBURY.

Colonel Salesbury then received a communication from a representative selection of townspeople of Denbigh entitled 'The Bumkins Petition' extracts of which read:-

Gentlemen, Wee on the behalfe ourselves and our poore and wasted countrey, are enjoyned (by as many of the inhabitants therof, as are met here this day,) to present unto you our deplorable condition. Having such stronge confidence in your publike affec'on towards us, that wee cannot believe you delight in our ruine; it is a common and true saying, that the preservation of the people is the supreame law;...If by detayning this Castle from the Parliament's possession, you engadge the forces that are against you to lye on us...you recede from those principles that supreame rule points at...
The petition goes on to remind Colonel Salesbury that the of garrisons in

other parts of the country have surrendered and that...*it is the earnest expectation of our deare native countrey, that you will noe longer occasion the continuance of these heavy, and insupportable pressures upon us...If your countreys present sufferings, and approaching ruine, be not by you prevented...you will give unto many thousand innocent and helplesse people cause to have you in bitter remembrance, as long as your name or interest in this countrey shall remayne amongst us; excuse our playness with you, w'ch proceeds from the weight and smart of our grievances; and take our desires into your deepe and serious consideration...*
The effect of this I hartyly wish it may take; for the avoyding of spilling christian blood, and the ruyne of many poor, and rich, by continuance of a seage for reducement of that Castle.

SYMON THELWALL

The petition is also signed by another forty seven people.

Colonel Salesbury begins his reply:-

Cosin Thelwall. and the rest of the subscribers to the letter sent to this Castle the 8th of this instant May. How I became interested in this place and command is very well knowne to the best of you... and he goes on to remind them that the Castle has been supplied and garrisoned at his own expense, and that...*since the scope of your desires proceed from your private interests, give me leave to take equall care of my loyalty and reputation...And to conclude with your bitter pill; I will not deny, but as the most savory meate tastes bitter to a distempered pallate, so my faythfullness to his Majesties service may seeme bitter to those that are redy to fall from there allegiance, which if you, and others had not done, this countrey and other parts of the kingdome, had not bin in this misserable condition they are now in; neyther had there bin any occasion of this kind of entercourse beetweene you and your kindsman,*

And the King's loyall subject

WILLIAM SALESBURY

On 24th June, Colonel Salesbury received a second summons from General Mytton in similar vein to his first, reminding him that Canarvon and Beaumaris castles had surrendered to Parliamentary forces as had the whole island of Anglesey. He again asks Salesbury to deliver up the castle and gives a deadline for his reply. In his next letter to General Mytton however, Colonel Salesbury counters him with demands of his own:-

...What the castle and towne of Carnarvon, the castle of Beawmarish, with the

whole Island of Anglisea have done, doth noething concern mee; that must lye upon there accompt who were therein entrusted by our King...As for the ruine of this...countrey, I am hartily sorry, that soe noble a gentleman, soe generally beeloved, as yourselfe, of soe ancient, and soe worthey a stocke, should be made the prime actor therein....but for further prevention of the loses of innocent Christian blood...doe you withdraw your forces from before this Castle and countrey; I shall give you good assurance, that this garrison shall neyther bee hurtful nor burthensome to the countrey; desiring your consent, that I may send twoe gentlemen to our King...to bee assured of his pleasure; till when, with God's leave, I shall cherefully runne the extreamest hassards of warr...lastly for your summons, when I see the auctority you have from our King, and his Parliament, commanding mee to deliver this place into your hands, I shall with God's helpe return you a speedy, honest, and playne answere, till then,

Your well-wishing Servant

WILLIAM SALESBURY.

What ruine shall befall this countrey, I refer it to the supreme Judge from whome noe secritts are hid, so I rest, and soe I am, There is a God that judgeth the earthe.

The answer from General Mytton on 30th August 1646 takes no regard of Colonel Salesbury's demand and Mytton again writes for a reply by...*to-morrow morning between 8 and 9 of the clocke,* to which Colonel Salesbury replies:-

In my answer to your second summons I desired your consent to send a gentlemen or two to our King, to knowe his pleasure; but I received noe answer from you as yeat;...

WILLIAM SALESBURY

General Mytton's reply:-

Sir... wherein you desire to send to the King; I doe assure you, above three months since I received command from the Parliament, not to suffer any, upon any pretence whatsoever to goe unto the King, which I exactly performed...and is not in my power to grant you...,

- and then it seems General Mytton takes action to try and force Colonel Salesbury into submission for he writes to the general -

Sir, The coming of more forces to besiege this place will noe way move my resolution;...which...can never be done, before my King receave and accompt of my proceedings...and since I must beeleeve your hands are tyed up...that I must apply myself to other means in that particular for my satisfaction; which will take up sometime; and if I must quit the place, I professe, I rather you had the honor of it, then any other person in England...tho' give me leave to tell you, that the addition of a new force, bee the consequence what it will, will but add to my honor, which is all I have left to care for.

I remayne, your servant
WILLIAM SALESBURY.

Ult. Augti 1646

By way of applying himself to other means for his satisfaction Colonel Salesbury writes directly to the King, presumably clandestinely, as he writes:-

In Nomine Jesu.

May it please your Majesty,

I have presumed to make my humble address to you by this gentleman, Mr Eubull Thelwall,[1] *to let your Majestie understand, that this Castle hath been now for severall months byne closly besieged; what matter of action hath in that time happen'd I humbly refere your Majestie to his relation, wherein I beseech your Majesty to give him creddit, praying for your Majesties health and happines, I remayne,*

Your Majesties loyall subject,
WILLIAM SALESBURY.

The King duly replies as follows:-

Newcastle, the 13th of September

Coronell Salesbury,

I hartley thank you for your loyall constancie, and assure you, that whensoever it shall please God to enable me to show my thankfullness to my friends, I will particularly remember you. As for your answer, I refer you to these messengers, to whom I have clearly declared my mynde; commend me to all my friends, so I rest,

Your most assured friend,
CHARLES R

After a siege by the Parliamentary forces of nearly six months, Colonel Salesbury at last receives the command he has been waiting for when the King Charles I writes:-

1 William Salesbury's son-in-law.

To our trusty, and well – beloved Colonell William Salesbury,
Governour of the Castle of Denbigh, in Wales.

CHARLES. R.

Whereas, Wee have resolved to comply with the desires of our Parliament, in every thing which may bee for the good of our subjects... wee have thought fitt...our intentions of sittling a happy and firm peace, to authorise you upon honorable conditions, to quit, and surrender the Castle of Denbigh, entrusted to you by us, and to disband all the forces under your commands; for which your soe doeing this shall bee your warrant, Given at Newcastle, [1] *the 14th of September, 1646.*

On 26th October 1646, Colonel Salesbury finally surrendered to General Mytton who granted him the 'honours of war' when the Parliamentary musketeers lit their matches at both ends as the Royalist garrison marched out of the castle.

Denbigh castle was the last to be surrendered to Parliamentary forces during the first Civil War and Colonel Salesbury escaped with his honour intact. The castle defences were never breeched. It was recorded that the defenders held out against their adversaries *with hearts as hard as the very foundations of the castle, being an unpiercable rock.*

On the eve of his execution, the King remembered Colonel Salesbury sending him his cap of crimson satin embroidered with gold and silver thread a replica of which is in the possession of the Bagot-Jewitt family at Blithfield.

Along with his contemporary, Sir Hervey Bagot, William Salesbury suffered heavy financial penalties during the Cromwell years. However, at the Restoration of the Monarchy in 1660, he received an annual payment of £800 from Charles II but died that same year aged 80.

1 After the Parliamentarians prevailed at the Battle of Naseby in which Colonel Richard Bagot was killed, the Royalist cause was all but lost and Charles I allied himself with the Scots with a view to prolong his struggle from north of the border. The Scots took him to Newcastle-on-Tyne on 9th May 1646. The Royalists finally surrendered at Oxford on 24th June. However, the second Civil War soon followed, with battles against the Scots and Irish and famously, the Battle of Worcester in 1651 when Charles II, being defeated, fled the country. After taking refuge at Boscobel House in Shropshire and hiding in an oak tree there, he was helped on his journey to exile in France by Jane Lane, niece of Sir Hervey Bagot and grand-daughter of Walter Bagot.

AÑO DONI 1632
ÆTAT: 52

Colonel William Salesbury

It is thought that William Salesbury was a privateer in the West Indies in his earlier years and that the depiction of the ship in the picture refers to this. The Salesbury's family motto is "What God wills will come to pass"

A replica of the cap given to Colonel Salesbury by King Charles on the eve of his execution.

H.M.S. BELLEROPHON

H.M.S. Bellerophon was one of the most famous ships to have sailed in the Royal Navy.

She was a 74- gun third-rate ship of the line and was launched in 1786. She had a crew of 550 and was nicknamed 'Billy Ruffian' (the crew had difficulty with pronouncing Bellerophon).

It took 2,000 oak trees (50acres) to build her as well as 100 tons of iron bolts and 10,000 square yards of canvas. For her battles she was provisioned with 80 tons of shot and 20 tons of gunpowder. Her final cost came to over £38,000 which would relate to £5.7 million at present day prices.

She served during the French Revolutionary and Napoleonic Wars in the early 19th century and took part in some of the most famous battles fought for our country.

France declared war on Britain after the success of the French Revolution of 1789. In June 1793, Bellerophon fought in the battle known as the Glorious First of June against the French fleet off the Atlantic coast near Brest. The victory saw the British sailors capture almost a third of the enemy fleet.

In 1798, Bellerophon joined the Mediterranean Fleet and was detached to reinforce Rear Admiral Horatio Nelson's fleet taking part in the decisive defeat of the French at the Battle of the Nile. Five French ships were sunk with the loss of 4,000 men. The British escaped almost unscathed.

Bellerophon at Trafalgar(centre) surrounded by enemy ships at the Battle of Trafalgar

When a short peace treaty with the French ended, Bellerophon again joined battle in 1805.

On the 21st October, with the fleet again under Horatio Nelson, she engaged the Franco-Spanish fleet at the Battle of Trafalgar.

She sustained much damage and heavy casualties, including the death of her captain. Nelson too, was killed by a French sniper.

But as every school boy used to know, the British won the day and the most famous sea battle in British history.

After emergency repairs in Gibraltar, Bellerophon received the honour of escorting HMS Victory, Nelson's flagship, with his body aboard [1], back to England.

After Napoleon Bonaparte's defeat at the Battle of Waterloo on 18th June 1815, he arrived in Rochefort, France on 2nd July.
Wishing to travel to America he found British ships blockading the port.
Being pressured by the French to leave their soil or be imprisoned, Napoleon elected to surrender to the British and to seek political asylum after they had denied him passage to America. Napoleon was therefore invited to board HMS Bellerophon and did so. Crossing the deck, he approached the Captain and offered his surrender with the words, ' I am come to throw myself on the protection of your Prince and your laws'.
With Napoleon in custody, the Napoleonic Wars were finally over and he was transported to Plymouth. As one military historian wrote, ' *in the ship that had dogged his steps for 20 years'.* It was her last sea-going service.

HMS Bellerophon in Plymouth Sound in August 1815 with Napoleon on board. Sightseers are in small boats eager to catch a glimpse of him when he came out on deck, usually at around 6pm each day.

Napoleon contemplates his future aboard HMS Bellerophon

Still aboard Bellerophon in Plymouth Harbour, on 31st July Napoleon was told that he would be taken forthwith to the remote island of St Helena in the south Atlantic and to exile.
The Bellerophon was not considered sufficiently sea worthy to complete the hazardous journey and so Napoleon was transferred to HMS Northumberland for the voyage. Napoleon died of cancer on St Helena on 5th May 1821.

Later in 1815, Bellerophon was paid off and converted into a prison ship. It was during this period that the penal system began to impose sentences on criminals of deportation to the British Colonies, principally Australia, in order to relieve pressure on the prison system in this country.

With the name Bellerophon being transferred to another ship, she was renamed Captivity. After the last convicts left in 1836 she was sold and broken up, a rather ignominious end to her illustrious career.

---

1 Nelson's body was preserved in brandy for the voyage.

NEEDWOOD FOREST

Needwood Forest lies adjacent to Bagot's Park to the east, and although only remnants of it remain, it is still designated as such on to-day's maps. It was ancient woodland, and was estimated to have covered an area of over 15 square miles in 1813 when William Pitt recorded it in a survey for Staffordshire on behalf of the Board of Agriculture, a time when the population of the country was expanding rapidly. Pitt concurred with Mary Bagot when he described it in the chapter of the survey headed "Waste and Unimproved Lands"....

Needwood Forest is a most interesting spot. Here near ten thousand acres of one of the finest soils of the kingdom lie in a state of nature, wild and romantic! beautiful in the eye of the fox-hunter and sportsman...

Although, he goes on -
But, considering the state of population, and consumption of landed produce, its continuance in its present state is certainly indefensible upon any sound principles of general policy. Here the warblers of the wood chant their mellifluent notes, and the herds of deer range at will over the plain, or through the thicket...The woodcock, the snipe, the pheasant, and the partridge, abound with profusion; but all too often disturbed by their tyrant master, man. The natural disposition of this extensive forest comprehends a great and beautiful variety of aspect. Gradual eminences and easy vales, with meandering rills, and now and then a more abrupt swell, form the general feature of the forest: a fit subject for any degree of improvement by human art and industry...

In reply to a letter from Sir William Bagot, M.P. for the county of Stafford, in which he must have written of his concern for the impending fate of the forest when it was being debated in Parliament, his wife's brother, John St. John MP, writes as follows:-

...Believe me when I affirm to you that my partiality for poor old Needwood is such that every stroke of the ax in that sacred grove woud fetch a sigh from the bottom of my heart...Money for appropriation of the forest would go to the king and take popularity out of the measure... Let all those who revere the love, the present inhabitants of Blithfield and all those who have partaken of the sports of Needwood and the Hospitality of Blithfield unite and then its rights and Royalties shall remain untouched by the hand of power... If I can be

of any use consistent with the Duty of my Office you may depend on me...

Honrable

J St. John

Dec. 19 1779.

William Pitt's agricultural survey goes on in his argument to conclude:-

This forest, in an improved state, might be rendered one of the most delightful spots in the kingdom, it's form and aspect comprehending such a great and beautiful variety: and the staple of its soil being equal to the fullest crops of the most valuable grain, or to the fatting of stock of the first quality. The sportsman could have little reason to complain, if his liberal allowance of 1000 acres, as here proposed, should be suffered to remain woodland, and this in the wildest and romantic part where the natural aspect tends to the protection of the favourite objects of his amusement... This forest is stocked with deer, horned cattle, and horses; but no sheep are suffered to feed on it. The supposed stock may be, about 3000 deer, and 3000 of all the other kinds in summer; but much fewer in winter. The keeping of the 3000 horses and horned cattle, charges at 12s per head for the summering, amounts to...about 4s per acre, upon the whole extent of the forest is all the advantage...the public derive from this tract; the deer not being managed in any system for public advantage, or for the supply of subsistence and employment of the bulk of mankind... 220 acres I will suppose be occupied by the lodges, and other small enclosures. This is already in an improved state; 8000 acres will then remain for improvement. The moment that these shall have been enclosed, and buildings for occupation erected on them, they will be worth, for a term, as many guineas per annum, and would be improved to a higher value...

Despite all the concern and lobbying over the issue an Act of Parliament decided the fate of Needwood Forest as William Pitt noted -

Needwood-forest. Since drawing up the former account, an Act of Parliament has passed, and been acted upon; for the enclosure of this fine tract of land. Part of the holly and oak timber have been sold and cleared off, the deer have been destroyed, the necessary roads have been laid out and formed, part of the Duchy of Lancaster share has been enclosed, and some progress made in filling up the timber plantations; some progress is also made in the subdivision and enclosure of other parts of the forest, but none in the improvement of cultivation...

Since that time, the 'improved' forest area has been used as intended, for the production of agricultural produce, but in 1987 a proposal was put forward to create a National Forest in England.

Mainly due to its sparse cover of woodland at only 6% and its central location, an area of 200 square miles was designated for the new National Forest, which takes in that of the ancient forests of Needwood in the west to Charnwood in the east.

With dependency on British agriculture being able to feed the country's population no longer a pressing issue, environmental concerns over mankind's detrimental effect on the climate and the need for recreational diversions for the British public, the forest aims to increase woodland cover by a third of the total area, to some 66 square miles. The forest also takes in areas which had been sites for coal mines, another industry which declined in the late 20th century for economic and environmental reasons.

The proposal received strong public and government support and up until 2012, some 8 million trees had been planted.

As a matter of interest to the reader, William Pitt also outlines his idea on the improvement of Cannock Chase under the same chapter heading as that of Needwood Forest:-[1]

Cannock-heath is the most extensive waste in the county, but its extent cannot easily be determined with accuracy; I estimate it at about 40 square miles, or upwards of 25,000 acres: Large tracts of land on the north and west parts of this waste, consist of a good light soil, adapted to the turnip and barley culture; the east and south parts are a colder gravelly soil in many places covered with heath to a large extent; yet I have no doubt but the whole may be bought into cultivation; and that some of our enclosed land now under cultivation, is not at all of a superior quality to this waste.

This generally was the situation until after the First World War when the Forestry Commission took advantage of the 'gravelly soil' in order to grow a large area of conifers for the timber industry which still continues. Another important aspect of its use at the present time is for recreational pastimes.

1 The word Forest - now used to describe a large area of trees was, in earlier times a term in law to denote an area where it was unlawful to hunt or kill animals without the consent of the owner. Similarly the word Chase, in this context, describes as area of unenclosed hunting ground.

THE GURKHAS

In Blithfield Church to the right of and above the west door is the memorial plaque to Hervey and Humphrey Bagot. It reads as follows:-

SACRED TO THE MEMORY OF
CAPTAIN HERVEY BAGOT RN
THIRD SURVIVING SON OF THE LATE
REV^{D} WALTER BAGOT RECTOR OF THIS PARISH AND MARY HIS SECOND WIFE
WHO, AFTER TEN YEARS OF ACTIVE AND DISTINGUISHED SERVICE
DIED IN LONDON ON THE 18TH JANUARY 1816
IN THE 23RD YEAR OF HIS AGE
AND IS INTERRED AT FULHAM, MIDDLESEX

ALSO LIEUT. HUMPHREY BAGOT, HIS NEXT BROTHER
OF THE 19TH NATIVE INFANTRY OF THE BENGAL ESTABLISHMENT
WHO DIED ON THE 16TH APRIL 1815
OF WOUNDS RECEIVED THE PRECEEDING DAY
IN A SUCCESSFUL ATTACK UPON THE GOORKAH ARMY
ON THE HEIGHTS OF MALOWN,
IN THE COUNTRY OF NEPAUL, EAST INDIES
IN THE 22ND YEAR OF HIS AGE.

It is well known that Gurkha soldiers from Nepal have served alongside their British counterparts in many of Britain's conflicts for many years. They have their own units within the British Army which are based in this country, although Nepal is neither a British Dependent Territory or a member of the British Commonwealth.

How was it then, that a young man from Blithfield was killed while fighting these fearless warriors and was buried somewhere in that mountainous country over 200 years ago?

The 19th century was a time when there were many opportunities for young men, particularly those from upper class families, who were able to take advantage of positions offered by the ever expanding and increasingly far flung British Empire.

As well as the diplomatic service, the armed services absorbed many young men eager to do their bit for the defence and expansion of the Empire in far off lands.

Initially, Britain's influence and later expansion in India, was through the East India Company, a trading organisation given a Royal Charter by Elizabeth I in 1600 in order to compete with the Dutch East India Company who were already trading successfully in India and the Spice Islands. Even by today's mega-corporation standards, these two organisations eventually became the largest companies the world has ever seen.[1]

By 1602, the Honourable East India Company, to give its full title, had set up their first trading post in India and over time the Company brought in increasing revenue for England, and itself, through its two way trade of produce between England and the sub-continent. Not least of these was tea, initially imported from China, which in the late 17th century started the very English custom of drinking tea[2], which in turn kick started the pottery industry in its production of fine china for which Staffordshire became world famous.

The flag of the East India Company in 1801. It has been argued that it inspired the Stars and Stripes.

Over the next century, the Company became increasingly powerful and influential in India and was able to expand its trading territories there utilising its three private armies, the Bengal Army being one. The 19th Native Infantry in which Lt. Humphrey Bagot fought was just one battalion of the Bengal Army which consisted mainly of sepoys- Indian native soldier- who were commanded by British officers.

Robert Clive[3] from neighbouring Shropshire, was one of the most successful of those men employed by the company in achieving this goal of expansion.

For their part, the British government were satisfied with the advantages this trade and economic benefit was bringing to this country, but in 1772 financial difficulties and other irregularities in the East India Company saw to it that the government began to check and control its activities. In 1784 the company lost its role as the ruling power in India and the British

1 The Dutch East India Company was twice as large as the largest company in 2018.

2 In Blithfield, during middle of the 18th century, tea was regarded an expensive treat in the household of Sir Walter Wagstaffe Bagot. He rarely allowed it to his daughters!

3 Clive of India rose from being a clerk in the East India company at aged 18, to the position of Governor of its possessions in India at the age of 32 in 1758. Being both a great soldier and administrator, he tried to reform the company and tackle corruption which aroused hatreds. He was exonerated after a parliamentary inquiry into his conduct. After a period of depression, he took his own life in 1774.

government began direct rule and appointed India's first governor general,[1] although the E.I.C. retained its trade monopoly, and its armies.

Clive of India's campaign had expanded Britain's influence and control in India to the border of Nepal, when the country was wishing to expand its own territory. The East India Company was anxious to gain access to the trade possibilities with Tibet and could not do so without annexing Nepal which the Gurkha people of that country would not allow. Consequently in 1814, and in response to Gurkha raids into British controlled territory, the British and the Gurkhas went to war.

The British soon found the mountain men to be formidable and brave opponents, but after many costly battles the British prevailed, and a peace treaty was signed in March 1816.

The Anglo-Nepalese, or Gurkha War ended with mutual respect between the combatants, and indeed during the war itself, Gurkha deserters were being persuaded to join the army of the East India Company as irregulars. So impressed was the British Commander with the new recruits, that in April 1815, the very month Lt. Bagot died, a battalion was formed which later became the 1st King George's Own Gurkha Rifles. This, and other units of Gurkha soldiers, served with the British Indian Army until India gained independence from Britain in 1947, when four Gurkha regiments were transferred to the British Army.

The Gurkhas have served with distinction in the British Army in most of the conflicts in which they have been involved. Today, there are six Gurkha units serving within the British Army.

The Bagot family's involvement with the Gurkhas did not end with Lt. Humphrey Bagot's death. Ironically, Colonel Alexander Bagot commanded a Gurkha regiment during the Indian Mutiny in 1847. In 2001 a contingent of Gurkha soldiers even joined the congregation in Blithfield Church for the funeral service of Heanage Charles, 9th Lord Bagot who had been a Major with the 6th Gurkha Rifles.

The 200th anniversary of the Gurkha's association with the British Army was celebrated in 2015.

There appear to be no records detailing the exploits of Captain Hervey Bagot.

---

1 A position offered to Sir Charles Bagot of Blithfield in 1828,which he declined due to health worries.

THE BATTLE OF THE SOMME - 1916

The Battle of the Somme began on 1st July 1916 and ended some five months later on 18th November 1916.
At the end of the first day the British casualties totalled 57,000 including 19,000 killed. It was the greatest loss, in a single day, in the British Army's history. At the end of the battle the British casualties totalled 420,000, Second Lieutenant Edward Bagot being just one.
The French casualties were 200,000 and the Germans 400,000 and during this time the allied front advanced a maximum of only 7 miles.

The First World War was the first to be fought on an industrial scale and at its start, army tactics had not yet advanced sufficiently to counter the stalemate caused by the use of large quantities of devastating mechanised weapons which led to the inevitability of trench warfare.
But this was soon to change. In order to counter the ineffectiveness of initial artillery bombardments and soldiers leaving the relative safety of their trenches to attack the enemy only to be scythed down by their machine guns, in 1916, during the Somme battle, the 'creeping barrage' was first used.
Soldiers would leave their trenches with an artillery barrage advancing as they advanced and just ahead of them. This had the effect of preventing the enemy machine gunners from unleashing their deadly fusillades.

It was also on the Somme where a highly secret new weapon was introduced.
On 15th September 1916 the first tanks[1] made their first appearance on the battlefield at the Battle of Flours Courclette.
They had been shipped out from England under a veil of secrecy and officially were known as "Machine Gun Corps, Heavy Section". Until the eve of the advance very few in the British Army had even heard of them.
Weighing 28 tons and only able to to travel at a top speed of 1/2 mph, they were highly prone to breakdowns and while they were effective at deflecting rifle and machine gun fire they were no defence against artillery. They were also defeated by mud, which was a perennial presence on the battlefields of France.
As an indication of their unreliability, 49 tanks (all the army possessed) were assembled on the 11th September in readiness for their first battle. Seventeen tanks failed to reach the front line and another 7 failed to work at zero hour. So only 25 tanks rolled into No Man's Land that 15th day of

---

1 The name 'tank' derives from the need for secrecy, and this code name was given under the guise of water tanks.

A Mark 1 'Male' tank with grenade deflector, on the Somme battlefield in September 1916

September 1916. Winston Churchill, who championed their development, complained "my poor 'land battleships' have been let off prematurely on a petty scale". It had been argued that more tanks would have been far more effective but Field Marshall Douglas Haig decided to proceed into battle with those available. There was no radio contact with the crew; carrier pigeons were used instead. Their appearance however, took the Germans by complete surprise and instilled some terror with the cries going up of 'the devil is coming, the devil is coming' and some of them fleeing.
Again however, tactics faltered when the tanks' effectiveness was not fully exploited as the infantry failed to follow up the gains the tanks had made.

What was probably one of the very first reports filed on their use was made by Lieutenant Bagot's Brigade C.O. when he wrote on the 15th September -

'...attacking from Ginchy with, today, the new so called TANKS otherwise known as Caterpillars or Crabs. There are two models, male and female.
Male has two 6 pounder guns, female several machine guns, both types heavily armoured, said to move over any ground or any trench...'

Another new weapon introduced in the Battle of the Somme, this time on the German side, was the use of 'liquid fire' from what was called the flammenwerfer or flame projector, (flame thrower). This was designed to melt the barbed wire entanglements but was also effective as another terror weapon.

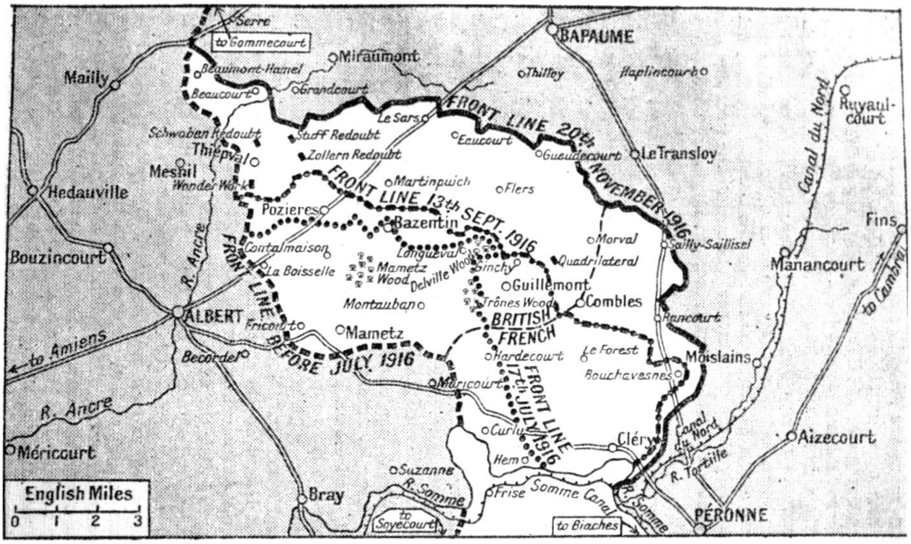
Serre
to Gommecourt
BAPAUME
Miraumont
Beaumont-Hamel
Grandcourt
Thilloy
Haplincourt
Mailly
Beaucourt
Ruyaulcourt
Canal du Nord
Le Sars
FRONT LINE 20th NOVEMBER 1916
Schwaben Redoubt
Stuff Redoubt
Eaucourt
Thiepval
Zollern Redoubt
Gueudecourt
Le Transloy
Mesnil
Wonder Work
Martinpuich
Flers
FRONT LINE 13th SEPT. 1916
Hedauville
Pozieres
Bazentin
Fins
Morval
Sailly-Saillisel
Bouzincourt
Contalmaison
Longueval
Quadrilateral
Manancourt
R. Ancre
La Boisselle
Mametz Wood
Delville Wood
Ginchy
Guillemont
to Cambrai
Montauban
Trônes Wood
Combles
ALBERT
FRONT LINE BEFORE JULY 1916
Fricourt
BRITISH
FRENCH
Rancourt
Mametz
to Amiens
Becordel
Hardecourt
Le Forest
Moislains
Maricourt
Bouchavesnes
FRONT LINE 17th JULY 1916
R. Ancre
Méricourt
Curlu
Cléry
Canal du Nord
Aizecourt
Hem
R. Tortille
Suzanne
R. Somme
English Miles
0 1 2 3
Bray
Frise
Somme Canal
to Soyecourt
to Biaches
R. Somme
PÉRONNE

Map of the Somme battlefield July-November 1916. Ginchy, where Edward Bagot was killed, is in the centre of the map

THE
ROYAL FLYING CORPS

The Royal Flying Corps was formed on 13th May 1912. It was part of the British Army, who had recognised the role aircraft could play in supporting it during time of war. The RFC was split into the Military Wing and Naval Wing, and by, 1914 the Naval Wing was put under direct control of the Royal Navy and The Royal Naval Air Service was founded.

Only 11years had passed since the first powered flight by the Wright Brothers and early aircraft were crude and not capable of aerial combat, but they were effective at directing artillery fire and photo reconnaissance, particularly after wireless communication with the ground was perfected in May 1915. By 1918 photographs could be taken from 15,000 feet.

At the start of the First World War the RFC only consisted of 113 aeroplanes and 5 squadrons, one observation Balloon squadron and 4 aeroplane squadrons. (RFC No. 2 and 3 squadrons were the first fixed- wing squadrons in the world)

The RFC first saw action on 19th August 1914 and received praise from the Commander of the British Expeditionary Force, Sir John French, when it warned, via it's aerial reconnaissance, of an impending German attack on an exposed French position during the First Battle of the Marne.

Early pilots carried revolvers and rifles for use against the enemy 'planes they encountered and bombs were carried by aircrew and dropped by hand from the open cockpit. However, all through the war, the development of aeroplanes continued apace and paved the way for them to be used in effective aerial combat and bombing missions against enemy strategic positions

Initially, casualties were largely due to accidents although when full aerial combat commenced losses were as high as 1 in 4 killed, a similar proportion to infantry losses in the trenches. Throughout the war, parachutes were not available to the RFC's powered aircraft pilots although they had been in use by balloonists from 1915.

In 1915, the Germans began to bomb civilian targets in Britain with their Gotha bombers and Zeppelin airships leading to the RFC being called to counter this threat. It is recorded that a Zeppelin flew over Abbots Bromley, and possibly Blithfield, when it proceeded to drop bombs on Burton-on-Trent in 1917.

The RFC was to have played a vital role during the first day of the Battle of the Somme in order to report on the effectiveness of the initial seven day British artillery bombardment against enemy trenches, but low cloud prevented this resulting in the catastrophic losses of British infantry when they attacked on the assumption that enemy positions had been destroyed. However, a total of 800 aircraft were lost and 252 aircrew killed during the Somme battles between July and November 1916.

A BE 2c of No 2 Squadron prepares to start off on a reconnaissance mission in Summer 1915, Hesdigneul, France

By now however, the rapid expansion of the RFC began to strain their recruitment and training regimes, as well as the supply of aircraft.

In 1917, British 'planes began to match their German counterparts in terms of performance and armament when the Sopwith Camel and Bristol Fighter were introduced. They were able to turn the tide of initial German superiority which in that year had become known as 'the Fokker Scourge', after the famous German Fokker fighter aircraft which had taken a heavy toll of RFC 'planes.

In response to a report by South African General Jan Smuts, on 1st August 1918 the RFC and RNAS were amalgamated to form a new service, the Royal Air Force which had equal standing with the Army and Royal Navy and came under the control of the new Air Ministry.

At the end of the conflict the RAF had grown into an organisation with a total of 22,000 aircraft and 290,000 personnel but had seen 9,378 aircrew killed and
7,245 wounded. A total of just under 7,000 tons of bombs had been dropped and 11 VC's awarded.

TRENCH ART OF THE FIRST WORLD WAR

It can be easy to think that a soldier's life during war time is fully taken up with acts of derring-do, bravery and generally trying to make life as uncomfortable as possible for his opponent. While this can be true some of the time, it certainly is not the case all of the time.

Not all enlisted soldiers are asked to fight and some can spend their time in reserve battalions without even seeing any battles at all, or even the front line. Fighting soldiers were relieved, sometimes for long periods, before they were called to the front line again. Inevitably, this meant soldiers with a certain amount of time on their hands, and some of those with an artistic bent took these opportunities to produce what has since become known as Trench Art.

Raw material was plentiful for this activity from the detritus of war. Shell cases, bullets, even aluminium from crashed Zeppelin airships were the materials mainly utilised.

This was transformed by servicemen - and others - into vases, letter openers, cigarette cases and lighters, snuff boxes, aeroplanes, tanks, candlesticks, jewellery and a myriad of other items. These would have served as souvenirs for the servicemen's families and friends on - hopefully - their return to England.

Charlie Kent [1] was one of these servicemen who had the advantage over some in that he, being in the Army Service Corps, would have had access to more sophisticated tools than most. This would have been possible as he was responsible for the maintenance of army equipment.

Some of the results of his work are shown in the photographs.

In common with many servicemen, Charlie Kent spoke little of his experiences of the war on his return home. In one story which did emerge, he told of being visited by a senior officer who, on inspecting his handiwork, pointed to several items and announced, 'Kent, I shall have these' and promptly departed with them.

Driver Kent said they were the best of those he had produced.

Not all trench art was produced by individual soldiers. Both during and after the war, enterprising civilian individuals and small firms well behind the front lines produced items for sale to war correspondents and others who had cause to visit, and sold their wares as souvenirs and mementos. In fact it was the case that the majority of items were made in this way.

---

1 Driver Charles Frederick Kent was the author's grandfather.

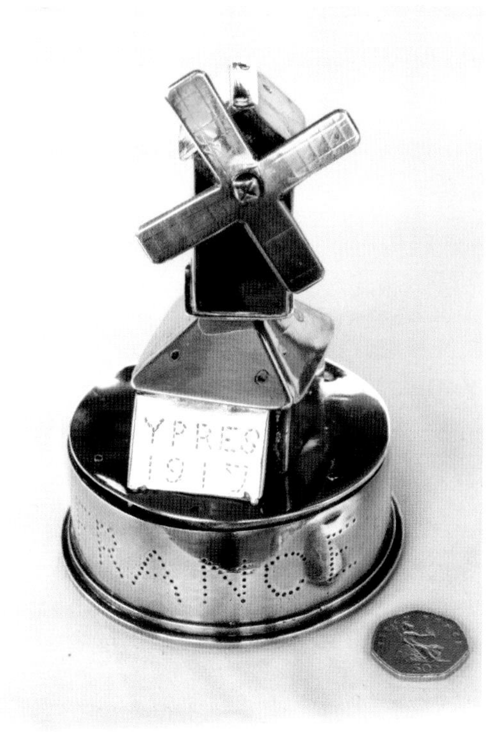
YPRES
1917
FRANCE

'TRENCH ART'

items made by

Driver Charlie Kent, A.S.C.

during the

First World War

WINDMILL

This was made when Driver Kent was stationed near Ypres in Belgium during the Third Battle of Ypres (Passchendaele) in August 1917

It is made of brass and wood, the base being from a 6 pounder shell case

TANK

made from brass shell and bullet cases, copper and wood.

ASC

SHAMROCK PLAQUE

made from oak, tunic fabric and buttons, cap and uniform insignia with brass bullet case stand.

Driver Kent spent time training in Ireland and his A.S.C. Company was attached to the British Army's 16th Division which was made up of many Irish regiments

THE DIEPPE RAID - AN ENIGMA?

The military disaster that was the Dieppe Raid, has long been debated among historians as to the reason for it.

In 1942, the war was not proceeding well for the Allies. Great Britain was in no position to mount an all out assault on fortress Europe on her own account. The United States was barely out of the starting blocks concerning any military assistance they could provide, after joining the conflict only eight months earlier. The German army was running rampant in Russia and were looking invincible there, to the point where the Russian leader, Stalin was repeatedly calling for a second front in the west in order to relieve his desperate situation.

It was obvious to top commanders that sooner or later, an assault on 'Fortress Europe', from Britain, would be necessary in order to defeat Nazi Germany.

The supreme and very successful efforts by British Intelligence in breaking the German 'Enigma' codes at Bletchley Park during the war are well known.

From early on, British codebreakers were able to determine German military intentions by intercepting their radio transmissions and deciphering the messages to provide allied armed forces with priceless information so that counter measures could be taken.

With Britain relying on half its food and all its oil being imported, one of the most major threats facing this country was the 'U boat menace'.

Prime Minister Winston Churchill said this was the part of German military strategy that worried him the most. German submarines were initially very successful at intercepting Allied merchant shipping in the Atlantic and sinking hundreds of thousands of tons of valuable and vital supplies.

Codebreakers at Bletchley had succeeded in breaking the German Naval Enigma codes which gave the authorities the ability to steer convoys away from the U boat packs which prowled the Atlantic shipping lanes.

In February 1941 however, the success of the British led the Germans to suspect that their codes had been broken and they introduced another level of complexity into their cyphers which 'blacked out ' the British.

British Intelligence realised the urgent need for action to relieve this situation which allowed the German Navy free reign to wreak havoc in the Atlantic. The stakes could not have been higher.

In September 1940 when the U boat attacks began to gather pace, Admiral Godfrey, the Director of Naval Intelligence, assured the codebreakers at Bletchley that he '*was setting up an organisation to arrange 'pinches'... and I think the solution will be found...(by) talent in your department and mine who can think up cunning schemes'.*

His 'cunning scheme' in this case was to involve British Commandos in a raid on German Naval headquarters in Dieppe in order to 'pinch' material which would have been of valuable assistance to British Intelligence in breaking the new German codes. One of those of talent Admiral Godfrey had in mind was a certain Lt Commander Ian Fleming, a naval intelligence officer and after the war, the creator of the James Bond character.

It is now clear that the Dieppe operation included a 'pinch raid' which was conceived by British Naval Intelligence and in which Lt. Commander Fleming played a leading role. Only those closely involved in planning the mission knew the full facts of it. With the Prime Minister only too aware of the U boat threat and his full support for the work of the Bletchley Park codebreakers, it can be assumed the operation had his complete blessing. The pinch raid depended on highly trained British Commandos going ashore from Dieppe's harbour, and storming the German Naval Headquarters a short distance away, in order to 'pinch' the code books which the codebreakers at Bletchley Park so desperately needed.

It is thought the entire Dieppe operation failed largely due to the fact that the element of surprise was lost when the initial attack went in too late and missed the cover of darkness. Consequently, the pinch never occurred.

By August and September 1942, U boats were again sinking allied shipping at an alarming rate. However, on the 30th October a pinch of German code books was achieved when they were retrieved from a sinking U boat after an attack by a British destroyer off the Egyptian coast. These gave the codebreakers all they needed to resume their activities and by January and February 1943, allied shipping losses had halved as a result.

Three men were involved in the retrieval of the documents and two went down with the sinking submarine. One was a Staffordshire man, Able Seaman Colin Grazier from Tamworth.

Both men were awarded the George Cross posthumously for their gallantry, the other, a canteen boy aged 16, and a civilian, was awarded the George Medal.

After the failure of the Dieppe operation, with the perception of no advantage gained and the great loss of life, particularly by the Canadians, many laid the blame on top army commanders for their apparent recklessness in planning the raid. But now with hindsight, some of the families of those lost see in the latest revelations that the operation did seek a more honourable goal. It also proved that a port on the north coast of France could not be successfully taken in order to aid the invasion of continental Europe.

THE PATHFINDERS OF BOMBER COMMAND

Formed on the 15th August 1942, at the direct request of the Air Ministry, the Pathfinders of Bomber Command was one of the elite group of squadrons of the RAF in the Second World War.

It was under the direct control of Air Chief Marshall Arthur Harris and, in 1943, became known as Bomber Command No 8 (Pathfinder Force Group).

Australian, Edward Christopher Bagot flew with this squadron as a navigator.

Only recruiting crews with a high navigational ability, its duty was to locate and guide the main bomber formations of the RAF to their targets in enemy held territory in Europe.

Prior to the formation of the Pathfinder Force, with most of the German industrial towns almost permanently covered in smoke haze, it was almost impossible to locate the towns, aside from the targets themselves, causing many bombs to be dropped miles from their designated targets. At night, with blackouts in force, this was even more difficult.

By dropping brilliant target indicators by night and using other advanced technology for the time, the Pathfinders were able to greatly increase the bombing accuracy of the RAF's aircraft from a 'hit and miss' force to one which could deliver anything from a single bomb to hundreds of tons of bombs relatively accurately onto a target anywhere in Western Europe.

Needless to say, most of these targets were very heavily defended and as the Pathfinders were in the vanguard of the RAF bomber attacks, they came in first for the enemy ground fire and night-fighter attacks and consequently suffered high casualties.

At it's peak, over 3,700 aircrew flew with the Pathfinders, flying over 51,000 sorties of the 360,000 total flown by all groups of the RAF during the war.

After the war, their Commander-in Chief Air Vice Marshall Don Bennett, himself an Australian, described the men of 8 Group as *'serious, meticulous, studious - and gallant. Their contribution to victory was unique'*

THE TRANSPORTATION OF CRIMINALS and the CONVICT SHIPS.

The policy of transporting criminals was first introduced in 1718 when convicts, pardoned from the sentence of death, were transported to the tobacco plantations in North America, the chief destination being Maryland. This system continued for 56 years until the American War of Independence. Experience of the policy had proved that many convicts went on to become useful members of local society after they had completed their sentences which had taught them new skills, particularly in agricultural practises, through the discipline instilled by their masters.
Africa was then considered an alternative destination for miscreants although soon dismissed, due to the unhealthy climate and hostility of some of the native peoples. Captain Cook's discovery of New South Wales in 1770 led to it being chosen as the next destination for Britain's outcasts, and the first convict ship sailed for Botany Bay on 13th May 1787.

During the first decade of the 19th century, the British public were turning against the regularity of capital punishment being meted out to criminals, not only because of their abhorrence of it, but because of the distress experienced by those who witnessed it. Executions were then a public spectacle and were designed as a deterrent to criminal activity.

At the instigation of Elizabeth Fry, the foremost pioneer of prison reform in England, Surgeon Superintendent Thomas Reid made two voyages on convict ships, the first being on the Neptune, the vessel on which John Ford travelled to Australia, and in 1822 he recorded his experiences in a journal.

His first duty was to draw up regulations for the prisoners during the journey and then to instigate a moral and religious regime. He took along with him bibles and prayer books for that purpose. He ensured the ship was kept clean and the prisoners' quarters kept warm. Of the twenty three convicts under 20 years of age, some as young as 13, he found only five of them were able to read and write, and so he set up a school under a convict school master in order to instruct them. By the end of the voyage, every boy could read and write.

The ship was well provisioned in food, medical requirements and clothing for the prisoners, so much so that few would have been accustomed to the new conditions they were experiencing. Thomas Reid even ensured the oxygen supply in the confined and cramped conditions of the lower decks of the ship was sufficient to prevent breathing difficulties.

All these measures were very well thought of by all the convicts to the point where they were moved to write a letter, both to the British Secretary of State and to Thomas Reid, for their appreciation of them. It was signed by every man on board.

After completing his, or her, sentence any convict proving themselves to have reformed sufficiently, and to have become useful members of the colony were given the opportunity to become settlers or, if they wished, could return to Europe provided they paid for their own passage. Later this was extended to include the opportunity for a reformed convict to apply in order for his wife and children to join him in his new country and in most instances, improved circumstances.

By 1853, Australia refused to take any more convicts as immigrants, although the policy did introduce many people who found themselves able to take advantage of the new opportunities afforded to them and who consequently helped to build new countries. John Ford with his entrepreneurial spirit was one of those.

As a result, it has been said that some colonial subjects of the then British Empire, and their descendants since, have been grateful to have been part of this chapter in British history. Never has the saying 'It's an ill wind that blows nobody any good', been more true.

CLEAN WATER PLEASE

Water from the reservoir at Blithfield flows first to the Seedy Mill pumping station, built in 1939, near Lichfield where it is treated and purified. It is then pumped to the storage or service reservoirs at Barr Beacon near Walsall, Gentleshaw near Cannock and Outwoods near Burton-upon-Trent. The water from the service reservoirs is then pumped through a 'grid' system of water mains to consumers over a large area of the south, mid and east Midlands, including Blithfield.

Prior to 1853, the story was very different.

In 1775, Walsall, Dudley, West Bromwich, Wednesbury, Cannock and Burton-upon-Trent were little more than villages about the size of Abbots Bromley is today. Only Wolverhampton and Birmingham were, what could be called today, a town.

The rapid industrialisation of these villages drew large numbers of people to them, from their hand to mouth existence of working the land to the new industries of coal mining, iron forging, metal working and a host of other trades. It would soon earn the area the name of the Black Country and ultimately, the Workshop of the World.

The movement of so many people into these settlements led to their expansion, with poorly built, cramped housing conditions and 'cottage industry' style industrial activities, which gradually overwhelmed the water supply. The relatively clean water from wells and springs which had before amply supplied the smaller populations, soon began to be contaminated by human and industrial waste. When this found its way into the water supply, diseases which were before relatively uncommon soon became a severe menace.

Cholera was one of these, and it was not until many had died of it that it was proved to be caused by contaminated water and so this situation had to be dealt with urgently.

In 1852 it was reported that:

...from want of water and being constantly surrounded by filth, the difficulty of cleanliness is so great that by degrees even clean persons loose heart, and give up in despair.

Also, the Inspector of the Central Board of Health reported in 1851 -

...The dwellings of the poor were unavoidably dirty, as they were generally small and badly constructed, without drainage of any sort. Epidemics and contagious diseases prevail at all times.

CHOLERA.

THE

DUDLEY BOARD OF HEALTH,

HEREBY GIVE NOTICE, THAT IN CONSEQUENCE OF THE

Church-yards at Dudley

Being so full, no one who has died of the CHOLERA will be permitted to be buried after *SUNDAY* next, (To-morrow) in either of the Burial Grounds of *St. Thomas's*, or *St. Edmund's*, in this Town.

All Persons who die from CHOLERA, must for the future be buried in the Church-yard at Netherton.

BOARD of HEALTH, DUDLEY,
September 1st, 1832.

W. MAURICE, PRINTER, HIGH STREET, DUDLEY

A consequence of the lack of clean water

Such was the need for water that it was obtained, and sold from mine workings, as was that rain water which had fallen on soot contaminated roofs.

In 1853, the newly formed South Staffordshire Water Company promoted a Water Bill in Parliament-

... *Whereas, the inhabitants of the City of Lichfield and of the Boroughs Parishes and places of Walsall, Wednesbury, Bilston, Darlaston, Sedgley, Tipton, West Bromwich, Rowley Regis, Dudley and Oldbury... are not sufficiently supplied with Water for domestic, manufacturing, trading and sanitary Purposes, it would be of great Advantage to the Inhabitants of such places if a more ample supply of pure and wholesome Water were provided...*

At that time these settlements covered an area of, roughly, 75 square miles and contained a population of a quarter of a million people.

After initially encountering a lack of public support for the proposals of the Act, the water company eventually began work to carry out their task. They directed water from Cannock Chase and Lichfield where there were abundant supplies of good quality water available, but were ten miles away from where it was urgently needed. Stowe and Minster Pools in Lichfield were dredged out of debris - including cannon balls and mortar shells from the Civil War and enlarged to become the water company's first reservoir. Tunnels were then driven through sandstone to convey water to a pumping station south of the city and then through a 22" cast iron pipe to a new storage reservoir at Walsall. By the late 1850's piped water from Lichfield was supplying clean water to the towns of the Black Country, the beating heart of the Industrial Revolution.

As with any scarce and valuable commodity, the clean water was prey to those who wished to steal it. In 1863, one notice warned:

A Notice to Water Stealer's.
Any person unlawfully Taking or USING WATER from a Tap
in communication with Pipes of
the Company is liable to a
PENALTY of FIVE POUNDS.[1]

Later, it appears consumers were beginning to revel in the new luxury for another notice appeared in 1873 as follows:

Water Wasting
A person was fined Ten Shillings[2] and costs for leaving a tap running.
The Company give notice that they purpose prosecuting any person
who may be detected wasting the water and they will give
5 shillings reward to anyone who will give evidence leading to
a conviction for wasting water.

Over the next decades, the water supply infrastructure was gradually extended and improved with the introduction of new pumping stations and steam engines to pump the water, and of course, new reservoirs.

By the middle of the 20th century demand for water by industry and domestic users had dramatically increased. With homes by now being equipped with indoor sanitary facilities and washing machines, water from one of the South Staffordshire Waterworks' flagship projects brought water from the new reservoir at Blithfield.

1 This fine would be the equivalent of nearly £600 today.
2 £50 and £25 respectively.

REFERENCES AND SOURCES

The 11th Century

Domesday Book Studies- Allecto Historical Editions 1987
West Stow Anglo Saxon Village
Chronicle of Britain and Ireland - ed. Henrietta Heald
Lower Booth Moated Site and Deserted Medieval Villages. - Historic England

The 12th Century

Notes on the Early History of Blithfield - Rev. D. S. Murray
Old Parish Boundaries of Staffordshire Volume 1: Pirehill - Tim Cockin
History of the Bagot Family - G Wrottesley (Collections for a History of Staffordshire Vol X1)
Domesday Book Studies- Allecto Historical Editions 1987
A Country House Saved - Nancy Lady Bagot

The 13th Century

Chronicle of Britain and Ireland - ed. Henrietta Heald
The People's Chronology - James Trager
Notes on the Early History of Blithfield - Rev. D. S. Murray
Queenship in the 13th Century - Margaret Howell
Queen Eleanor of Provence - Medieval Queens
The Medieval Stonemason - Carol Davidson Cragoe
The People's Chronology - James Trager

The 14th Century

The History of Parliament: The House of Commons vol 1386 - 1421. L. S Woodger
Chronicle of Britain and Ireland - ed. Henrietta Heald
Open Source Shakespeare - History of Richard II
History, Gazetteer, and Directory of Staffordshire - William White (1851)
General View of the Agriculture in the County of Stafford - William Pitt (Google Books)
The History of the Bagot Goats and Bagot's Park - Nancy, Lady Bagot

The 15th Century

The History of Parliament: The House of Commons vol 1386 - 1421.
ed. J S Roskell, L Clarke, C Rawcliffe
Chronicle of Britain and Ireland - ed. Henrietta Heald
History of the Bagot Family - G Wrottesley (Collections for a History of Staffordshire Vol X1)
Open Source Shakespeare - History of Henry V
The History of the Bagot Goats and Bagot's Park - Nancy, Lady Bagot
Keith Dowen Asst.Curator European Armour -The Royal Armouries
Photos Terence Cooper courtesy Peter Griffiths -The Lichfield Heritage Centre
Notes on the Early History of the Parish of Blithfield Rev. D S Murray.
History, Gazetteer, and Directory of Staffordshire - William White (1851)

The 16th Century

Notes on the Early History of the Parish of Blithfield - The Rev D.S. Murray.
Memorials of the Bagot Family (Google Digital Books) - William, 2nd Lord Bagot .
Chronicle of Britain and Ireland - ed Henrietta Heald
Collections for a History of Staffordshire Vol XI - G. Wrottesley
The Blithfield Sallet - C Blair - reprint from Archaeological
Journal Vol CXI July 1955 SRO - CB/08/ Blithfield
Chronicle of Britain and Ireland - ed Henrietta Heald
Bellfounding - Edward Jennings
V.C.H. History of Staffordshire Vol. II - Staffordshire Record Office
Glass Making in Bagot's Park Staffordshire in the 16th century - David W. Crossley via internet
Archaeomagnetic analysis of glassmaking sites at Bagot's Park in Staffordshire. -Article in Physics of the Earth and Planetary Interiors.

The 17th Century

Chronicle of Britain and Ireland - ed Henrietta Heald
The People's Chronology - James Trager

The History of Parliament on-line vol. 1604-1629 Ben Coates (SRO D4038/E/11/2)
Memorials of the Bagot Family (Google Digital Books) - William, 2nd Lord Bagot.
History of the Bagot Family - G Wrottesley (Collections for a History of Staffordshire Vol XI)
History, Gazetteer, and Directory of Staffordshire - William White (1851)
The Staffordshire Record Office
National Library of Wales - Dictionary of Welsh Biography
Notes on the Early History of the Parish of Blithfield - The Rev D.S. Murray
Collections for a History of Staffordshire- Staffordshire Glebe Terriers Part One Fourth Series Vol XXII.

The 18th Century

Memorials of the Bagot Family (Google Digital Books) - William, 2nd Lord Bagot (Google Books)
A Country House Saved - Nancy Lady Bagot
Overseers of the Poor SRO - D1386/5/2. Constables Accounts SRO D1386/5/3
Bagot Atlas 1724 SRO D3259/Add/1.
History, Gazetteer, and Directory of Staffordshire - William White (1851)

The 19th Century

The Staffordshire Record Office, Bagot family correspondence D5121/1/22/13-14
Chronicle of Britain and Ireland - ed. Henrietta Heald
British Warships in the Age of Sail - 1714-1792 -Rif Winfield.
Billy Ruffian - David Cordingly
Napoleon Bonaparte- England's Prisoner - Frank Giles
Ships of Trafalgar- The British, French and Spanish Fleets- Peter Goodwin
The Trafalgar Companion, A Guide to History's Most Famous Sea Battle and Life of Admiral Lord Nelson - Mark Adkin
Links With the Past - Mrs Charles Bagot.
(The Journals of Miss Mary Bagot) Travel Journal - Miss Mary Bagot - S.R.O. D3259/17
General View of the Agriculture of the County of Stafford - William Pitt (Google Books).
Letters to Sir William Bagot - Staffordshire Record Office.
Sir Charles Bagot SRO D4381/8
Dictionary of Canadian Biography Vol Vll 1836-1843- Jacques Monet
Quebec History Encyclopedia
The Canadian Encyclopedia
The Paget Family - The Gentleman's Magazine (Obituaries Vol 175 - 1843)
Ontario's Historic Plaques
The People's Chronology - James Trager
The Staffordshire Record Office - The Bagot Archive D3259/6/2
Chronicle of Britain and Ireland - ed. Henrietta Heald
The Great Depression of English Agriculture - T.W Fletcher - via Wikipedia
The Decline and Fall of the British Aristocracy - David Carradine -via Wikipedia
S.R.O. - The Bagot Archive D3259/6/1; D5121/2/12/1-9; D3259/14/16/1-5; D5121/2/11/1-3.
The Diaries of Louisa Lady Bagot 1815-1816 - S.R.O. D5121/3/9
Memorials of the Bagot Family (Google Digital Books) - William, 2nd Lord Bagot (Google Books).
A Country House Saved - Nancy Lady Bagot.
Dictionary of National Biography
The History of Admaston Village School 1857 - 2002 - Anne Webb
Admaston School - S.R.O. D1721/3/170.
History, Gazetteer, and Directory of Staffordshire - William White (1851).
The National Archive via Ancestry.com
Collections for a History of Staffordshire (The Staffordshire Record Society)
Dictionary of National Biography Vol 2

The 20th Century

A Popular History of the Great War Vol. l - ed. Sir J A Hammerton
The Commonwealth War Graves Commission - website
Record Details at Forces War Records -Military Genealogy Specialists
1911 Census - National Archive via Ancestry.com
6th Battalion The Buffs - War Diaries - National Archive via Ancestry.com

A Popular History of the Great War Vol. III - ed. Sir J A Hammerton
The Welsh Guards - history (website)
The National Archive
Whittaker's Peerage 1911
Welsh Guards War Diaries Sept. 1916, National Archive via Ancestry.com
Chronicle of Britain and Ireland - ed. Henrietta Heald
de Ruvigny's Roll vol 3 page 203, via Ancestry.com
Royal Flying Corps Regiment History War and Military Archives
1911 Census -National Archive, via Ancestry.com
Victoria, Australia Assisted and Unassisted Passenger Lists 1839-1923, National Archive via Ancestry.com
UK Outward Passenger Lists 1890-1960 - National Archive via Ancestry.com
England and Wales Free BMD Marriage Index 1837-1915, National archive via Ancestry.com
New Zealand WW1 Nominal Rolls via Ancestry.com
War Diary 4th Battalion 3rd New Zealand Rifle Brigade February 1917, via Archway -Archives New Zealand
2nd 6th Battalion Sherwood Foresters Notts and Derby Regiment War Diaries Feb 1917-Jul 1918 National archive via Ancestry.com
A Popular History of the Great War Vol. IV - ed. Sir J A Hammerton
The Kings Own Yorkshire Light Infantry 6th Battalion War Diaries- April 1917, National Archive via Ancestry.com
British Army WW1 Service Records 1914-1920 -National Archive via Ancestry.com
North Staffordshire Regiment 5th Battalion War Diaries- March 1918, -National Archive via Ancestry.com
A Popular History of the Great War Vol. V - ed. Sir J A Hammerton
16th Division Train War Diaries -National Archive via Ancestry.com
Army Service Corps Horse Transport Companies - The Long Long Trail -website
The 16th (Irish Division) The Long Long Trail - website
Trench Art - An Illustrated History - Jane Kimball
Station X - Michael Smith
The Dieppe Raid -Operation Jubilee - (and History T.V. ref David O'Keefe)
R.A.F. website- Bomber Command No 8 (Pathfinder Force Group)
Staffordshire Airfields in the Second World War - Marytn Chorlton -Countryside Books
The Pathfinders Bomber Commands Elite Squadrons -Martyn Chorlton -Countryside Books
Notes on the Early History of the Parish of Blithfield - Rev. D. S. Murray.
Uttoxeter Civil Defence Control Area - List of bombing and other principal incidents during the war- courtesy John Walton, Beamhurst Museum.
A Country House Saved - Nancy, Lady Bagot.
UK Prison Hulk Registers & Letter Books -1802-1849 National Archive, via Ancestry.com
Two Voyages to New South Wales and Van Diemen's Land - Thomas Reid (Google Books).
Links With The Past - Mrs Charles Bagot
Dictionary of National Biography Vols 1-20 -via Ancestry.com
South Staffordshire Waterworks Company plc -Archives - Chris Pattison.

The 21st Century

Notes on the Early History of the Parish of Blithfield - The Rev D.S. Murray
Domesday Book Studies- Allecto Historical Editions 1987
Chronicle of Britain and Ireland - ed. Henrietta Heald
Collections for a History of Staffordshire - (The Staffordshire Record Society 1996).
Sales Particulars of the Blithfield, Field and Leigh Estates
A Country House Saved - Nancy, Lady Bagot
Sales Catalogue - "Blithfield" Rugeley, Staffordshire
Sales particulars - The Blithfield Estate